EQUITY

EQUITY

IN THEORY AND PRACTICE

H. Peyton Young

A RUSSELL SAGE FOUNDATION BOOK

PRINCETON UNIVERSITY PRESS   PRINCETON, NEW JERSEY

Copyright © 1994 by Princeton University Press
Published by Princeton University Press, 41 William Street,
Princeton, New Jersey 08540
In the United Kingdom: Princeton University Press, Chichester,
West Sussex

Library of Congress Cataloging-in-Publication Data

Young, H. Peyton, 1945–
Equity : in theory and practice / H. Peyton Young.
p.   cm.
A Russell Sage Foundation book.
Includes bibliographical references and index.
ISBN 0-691-04319-1 (alk. paper)
1. Distributive justice.   2. Game theory.   I. Title.
HB72.Y68   1993
305—dc20   93-2273   CIP

This book has been composed in Times Roman

Princeton University Press books are printed
on acid-free paper, and meet the guidelines
for permanence and durability of the Committee
on Production Guidelines for Book Longevity
of the Council on Library Resources

Printed in the United States of America

10 9 8 7 6 5 4 3 2 1

For My Parents

Contents

Preface _____

Equity: simply a matter of the length of the judge's
ears.
   (*Elbert Hubbard*)

WHEN I TEACH this material to students, I warn them that the subject does not exist. Among all nonexistent subjects, in fact, equity occupies a distinguished position because it fails to exist in several different ways. The arguments against existence take three different forms. The first is that equity is merely a word that hypocritical people use to cloak self-interest. It has no intrinsic meaning and therefore fails to exist. The second argument is that, even if equity does exist in some notional sense, it is so hopelessly subjective that it cannot be analyzed scientifically. Thus it fails to exist in an *objective* sense. The third argument is that, even granting that equity might not be entirely subjective, there is no sensible theory about it, and certainly none that is compatible with modern welfare economics. In short, it fails to exist in an *academic* sense.

Set against these arguments is the fact that people who are not acquainted with them insist on using the term "equity" as if it did mean something. In everyday conversation we discuss with seeming abandon the equities and inequities of the tax structure, the health care system, the military draft, the price of telephone service, and how offices are allocated at work. For a term that does not exist this is a pretty good beginning. One is tempted to say that rumors of equity's nonexistence may have been somewhat exaggerated.

I hasten to add that equity, or at least a close relative, is very much alive and occupies a prominent place in moral philosophy. For philosophers, however, the central problem is to define what we mean by a just social order. Equity in this sense is concerned with the proper distribution of resources, rights, duties, opportunities, and obligations in society at large. This grand theme has animated political philosophers since antiquity, from Plato's and Aristotle's conceptions of the ideal state, to the social contract theories of Hobbes, Locke, and Rousseau, to the more modern theories of Rawls, Nozick, and Walzer. I shall refer to these as theories of *social justice*.

This book is not about equity in this sense. Rather, it is about the meaning of equity in concrete situations that we meet every day. Equity is, after all, an everyday concern. Families try to divide up the household chores equitably among their members. Businesses are sensitive to issues of equity in the salaries and perquisites that they offer to their employees. Public agencies worry about equity when they decide who has access to public housing; how much to charge for basic services such as water, electricity, and public transport; who gets a kidney for transplantation; and who gets into a nursery school (or a nursing home). Equity is a central concern in the most basic political decisions: the distribution of the tax burden, the duty to serve in the army, the apportionment of representation. All of these distributive problems can be and are solved without invoking theories of social justice. I am not saying that these theories are unimportant; they are of the utmost importance. What I am saying is that it is possible to analyze the meaning of equity in the small without resolving what social justice means in the large.

The aim of this book, then, is to examine how societies solve "everyday" distributive problems. Which patient gets the one available kidney for transplantation? Who is released from the army first? How much does the municipality charge for connecting a new house to the water supply? How many seats in Congress does one state receive compared to another? On what theory is one person taxed at a 33 percent rate, another at 15 percent, and a third not at all? What is a fair method for dividing an estate among heirs when they have different preferences for the property it contains? These are the kinds of questions that we shall examine in this book.

Equity is a complex idea that resists simple formulations. It is strongly shaped by cultural values, by precedent, and by the specific types of goods and burdens being distributed. To understand what equity means in a given situation we must therefore look at the contextual details. The book is built around seven illustrative cases: the demobilization of soldiers from the U.S. Army at the end of World War II; the allocation of kidneys among transplant patients; the apportionment of representation among political parties and states; the adjudication of conflicting property claims; the allocation of costs and benefits among participants in joint enterprises; the distribution of the tax burden; and the division of inheritances. This list is by no means exhaustive, nor is the treatment of any one topic complete. Indeed, I am well aware that I have stretched myself quite thinly over a number of different literatures, and probably have not done justice to any one of them. The goal, however, is not to give a definitive treatment of taxation, or political representation, or games of fair division. Rather, my aim is to call attention to common themes that cut across different areas of application, and to show that these pieces fit together into a larger picture. This has forced me to be selective in the treatment of various topics. I apologize to those who feel that the selections should have been made differently.

My interest in fair allocation grew out of a long and fruitful collaboration with my colleague Michel L. Balinski on apportioning seats in the United States House of Representatives. On the face of it the problem is simple. The Constitution stipulates that representation be allocated among the states in proportion to their populations, subject to the requirement that every state receive at least one seat. The apparent solution is to compute the exact proportional share that each state deserves, and round the results. On closer inspection, however, this "solution" does not work because the rounded numbers typically do not add up to the required total. If we try to circumvent the problem by using some "pseudo-rounding" technique, we quickly run into a host of perplexing paradoxes and conundrums. The practical importance and theoretical challenge of this problem has engaged the attention of both statesmen and mathematicians for over two hundred years.

Many other problems of applied equity follow a similar pattern. What seems simple at first turns out to be riddled with puzzles and contradictions. Inevitably, we must turn to logical analysis to sort them out. The study of equity turns out, therefore, to have close ties with the axiomatic method in mathematics. From simple and intuitively plausible propositions about the meaning of equity, one draws general and sometimes surprising conclusions about the form that an equitable rule must take.

The axiomatic method has two weaknesses however. The first is that, while each axiom seems reasonable by itself, when piled on top of one another they almost inevitably lead to "impossibility" theorems. This confirms the skeptic's predisposition to believe that the problem had no solution anyway. The proper conclusion, however, is that not all desirable conditions can be satisfied simultaneously. Some choice must be made. A second difficulty with the axiomatic method is that it can easily become disengaged from the problem that it was intended to solve. The invention of axioms and conditions is a fascinating business. The danger is that the exercise can take on a life of its own and lead to results that are mathematically elegant, but that have little or no relation to the realities of the underlying situation. To guard against this tendency I have tried to mix formal definitions and theorems with informal arguments and examples based on real data. The narrative therefore moves back and forth between observation and analysis, between theory and application, in an attempt to bring order to a complex subject without sacrificing too much realism.

The text is intended to be a "primer" and does not presuppose any mathematical background, though a taste for logical argument and some familiarity with economic concepts would certainly help. Technical definitions and arguments are relegated to footnotes and the appendix. The appendix does not cover all mathematical aspects of the subject, but focuses on a particular set of axioms and their consequences that are central to the argument. The text can be read independently of this material. Although there is a definite progression of ideas in the sequencing of the chapters, each can be read on its own for those who prefer to pick and choose among topics. Bibliographical notes are provided at the end for readers who want to go into greater depth.

Acknowledgments

AMONG my many intellectual debts, I owe particular thanks to Kenneth Arrow, Michel Balinski, Howard Raiffa, Thomas Schelling, and Amartya Sen for their encouragement and inspiration. I have also greatly profited from discussions with Jon Elster as we pursued parallel paths in our study of "local" justice. Others who have offered insightful criticism and from whom I have learned much include Marcus Berliant, Steven Brams, Vincent Crawford, Dean Foster, Aanund Hylland, Herve Moulin, Barry O'Neill, Peter Ordeshook, John Roemer, and William Thomson. I am grateful to Karen Baehler, Marek Kaminsky, Sang-Young Sonn, and Amanda Wolf for a careful and thoughtful reading of the manuscript. Special thanks go to my wife, Fernanda, for her support and patience over the last few years as this project took shape. Finally, I would like to acknowledge generous financial support from the Russell Sage Foundation and the hospitality of the Brookings Institution and the International Institute for Applied Systems Analysis where this work was completed.

EQUITY

1

Overview

Fair: equitably, honestly, impartially, justly; according to rule.
  (*Oxford English Dictionary*)

1. The Division of Common Property

Every society has rules for sharing goods and burdens among its members. In
primitive hunting tribes, for example, territory is usually held in common, and
members of the community divide the kill according to their position in the
social structure and their role in the hunt. These sharing rules, which in some
cases are elaborately defined,[1] express a notion of *equity* in the division of
jointly produced goods. By "equitable" I do not necessarily mean ethical or
moral, but that which a given society considers to be *appropriate* to the need,
status, and contribution of its various members. Appropriateness is shaped in
part by principle and in part by precedent. It expresses what is reasonable and
customary in a given distributive situation. To deviate from a rule that is
founded on both reason and precedent would violate the stakeholders' legitimate expectations, and this would be inequitable.

As economies become more complex, however, notions of common property
and just shares gradually evolve into a system of private ownership. Resources
that had formerly been held in common are divided up among individuals, and a
complex legal edifice for protecting property rights and regulating their transfer
springs into being. It is a common misconception, however, that this process of
dividing common property eventually runs its course, and that in advanced
economies virtually all property rights, or at least all important ones, have been
privatized. A moment's reflection will reveal that this is not the case. Property
rights are constantly being created, destroyed, revised, and reassigned by soci-

[1] "Among the Birhors [a tribal group in east-central India] after a monkey hunt, once a chief has
roasted a little of the meat and offered it to the spirits of the chase, the entrails, tails, and feet of the
monkeys are divided equally among the men and women who served as beaters. Each man who
provided a net also gets a hind leg. The two flankers each receive a hind leg as dividend, and the
chief gets the neck and half of the back meat of each animal killed, in addition to his hunter's share.
If some meat is left after this distribution, it is divided into as many portions as there are eligible
persons, plus an extra share for the chief" (Coon, 1971). Coon cites other examples of sharing rules
based on contribution and status.

ety, and every time this happens a problem of distribution is encountered. In fact these situations often arise through the operation of the market itself.

One source of new property, for example, is technical innovation. Resources that were once outside the general system of ownership may acquire great value due to technological advances, and the community must then decide how to allot the rights to their use. An example is the spectrum of broadcasting frequencies for radio and satellite communications. Their allocation is governed by Article 33 of the 1965 International Telecommunications Convention, which stipulates that, because "radio frequencies and the geostationary orbit are limited natural resources . . . they must be used efficiently and economically so that countries . . . may have *equitable access* to both . . . according to their needs and the technical facilities at their disposal." The meaning of equitable access is not spelled out, but has evolved over the years through periodic negotiations among the parties.[2]

Another example of "new" common property created by technical innovation is the deep ocean bed, which is strewn with nodules rich in nickel, cobalt, manganese, and other valuable minerals. The commercial mining of these nodules first became a realistic prospect in the 1970s, and the allocation of the mining rights was one of the principal topics addressed by the Law of the Sea Conference convened by the United Nations in 1973. The conference participants fell into two groups: industrialized countries such as the United States, West Germany, and Japan, that had the know-how and capital to mine the minerals, and the less developed countries (LDCs) that did not.[3] The conference adopted the general principle, which had been enunciated earlier by the General Assembly, that the seabed is part of the common heritage of mankind—a "global commons" in which all countries have a stake. Nodule exploitation was to be undertaken on behalf of the international community. The Conference went on to propose the formation of two new agencies to supervise deep ocean mining: an International Seabed Authority that would license all mining activities, and an international mining entity known as the "Enterprise" to mine the seabed on behalf of the LDCs.

To protect against the possibility that commercial mining interests in the industrialized countries would steal a march on the Enterprise and lock up most of the desirable sites, the Law of the Sea Treaty adopted a variant of an allocation method sometimes used by children to share a piece of cake: one divides and the other chooses. In the context of the Treaty, the "cake" is the ocean bottom. Every time that a mining company applies to the Seabed Authority for permission to mine at a given location, it is required to develop two parallel sites from which the Enterprise can choose one. By this device the

---

[2] International Telecommunications Convention, 1973, article 33 [italics added]. See also Stern (1982).

[3] The following account is based on Sebenius (1984).

Enterprise is guaranteed right of access to at least one-half of all developed sites, indeed, in their estimation they get the better half.

A second force behind the creation of new property is economic expansion. Traditionally this occurred by the conquest and settlement of new territory, which in feudal societies was distributed by the patronage of princes. In modern society a more complicated problem arises when economic expansion puts pressure on common resources that cannot be physically divided. Increasing air pollution, for example, has led some governments to restrict the quantities of noxious gases that may be released into the atmosphere. By so doing they establish limited rights to the use of the atmosphere and divide these rights among competing claimants. This may be done in a variety of ways. One is to place *uniform limits* on all polluters in a given category, for example, to restrict the amount of sulfur dioxide that each electric power plant can emit in a twenty-four-hour period. A second approach is to allot each polluter a quota of emissions permits, and allow them to trade among themselves. The latter solution is more efficient than the former (at least in theory), but it requires finding an acceptable basis for distributing the permits initially.

A concrete example is a market in sulfur-dioxide emissions permits that was recently established among electric power utilities in the United States. Beginning in 1992, each electric power plant will receive a quota of permits that is proportional to its emissions over a three-year base period. The permits may be traded within certain geographical regions. This allocation is subject, however, to a maximum rate beyond which a plant does not qualify for any more permits. The idea is that past usage defines each plant's relative entitlement up to a point, but a ceiling is imposed that effectively penalizes dirty plants. One could say that this solution is equitable in the sense that it imposes a similar burden of reduction on all plants relative to their status quo position provided that their status quo position is justifiable.

Third, new common property results from the formation of new enterprises. When two firms engage in a joint venture, for example, they must decide how to split the profits from their partnership. Doctors who share an office must divide the cost of equipment, secretarial help, and rent. Similarly, international organizations like NATO and the U.N. who provide various goods and services jointly must decide how to divide the costs among their members.

Finally, many kinds of common property are not privatized even in market economies, but are allocated by society on a contingent basis. The right to vote, the duty to serve in the army, educational opportunities, and health care are rarely left to the workings of the market, but are allocated to specific individuals according to notions of merit or desert, and cannot be transferred to others.

In spite of the fact that distributive issues permeate both economic and political life, they have not been studied very systematically by economists or political scientists. There are exceptions, of course, but I think it is fair to say that distributive justice has not been a central topic in political economy since the decline of classical utilitarianism in the early part of this century.[4] In part the neglect is due to the lack of a coherent analytical framework for studying distributive issues that is compatible with the modern ordinalist approach to analyzing economic welfare. In part it is due to the way in which economic theory happens to have developed. The standard model of economic exchange posits that all resources and property rights—including ownership of firms— are fully delineated and vested in individuals. The focus is on the process by which resources are allocated to their most efficient uses through the utility-maximizing choices of individuals. Thus, right at the outset, the issue of how common property should be divided *ex ante* is side-stepped. Somehow property *has been* divided, and one goes on from there to analyze how markets allocate resources efficiently. The division of common property introduces a complicating element into this story that most economists have chosen to ignore.

The fact is, however, that common property is continually being created by the market system itself through economic expansion, the advancement of technology, and the formation of cooperative enterprises. And many of the most important goods and burdens in society are allocated by political institutions rather than by the market. So it is fallacious to assume that the allocation of common property is a once-and-for-all affair; it is an ongoing process.

2. Micro vs. Macro Justice

At this point a caveat is in order. As I said in the preface, we shall not be concerned here with distributive justice in the large, that is, with the question of what constitutes a just social order. Rather, we are interested in distributive justice in the small, that is, how institutions divide specific types of benefits and burdens. Social justice is a crucial issue, of course, because it is ultimately concerned with the legitimacy of different forms of government. For various reasons, however, theories of justice in the large have little to say about what it means in the small. They do not tell us how to solve concrete, everyday distributive problems such as how to adjudicate a property dispute, who should get into medical school, or how much to charge for a subway ride.

The reason for this failure is that issues of local justice tend to be compartmentalized. Society makes no effort to coordinate distributive decisions across different domains, nor would it make sense to try. Kidney agencies do not give precedence to patients who failed to get into a university; a person's tax bill is not reduced because his party received less than its quota of seats in the last election; a soldier does not qualify for extra leave because the government located a waste dump near his home. There is no mechanism comparable to the

---

[4] See particularly Baumol (1986), Moulin (1988), and Elster (1992).

invisible hand of the market for coordinating distributive decisions at the micro level into just outcomes at the macro level. To the extent that gross inequities exist because of the cumulative effects of local decisions, they can be rectified at the societal level by redistributive policies, not by trying to coordinate the decisions of local allocative institutions.

The upshot of this compartmentalization is that each type of fair division problem is treated on its own merits based on the norms and precedents that have evolved to deal with that particular class of situations. Property claims are dealt with according to precedents in property law, taxes according to traditions in public finance, kidneys according to standards in the medical profession. The relevant standards differ appreciably from one domain to another and from one culture to another. While generalizations are difficult, however, they are not impossible: similar concepts keep reasserting themselves in diverse applications. This fact allows us to develop a common language, and a set of principles, that apply to a wide variety of distributive problems.

3. The Terms of Discussion

An *allocation problem* arises whenever a bundle of resources, rights, burdens, or costs is temporarily held in common by a group of individuals and must be allotted to them individually. An *allocation* or *distribution* is an assignment of the objects to specific individuals. Allocation is not the same thing as exchange. An allocation is a decision about who gets a good or who bears a burden, and is usually decided by a group or by an institution acting on behalf of the group. Exchange involves many voluntary, decentralized transactions, and can only occur after the goods and burdens have been allocated. Allocation comes first, exchange afterward.

Allocations often involve burdens instead of goods, but we shall usually speak in terms of goods. Moreover, this convention involves no loss of generality, because exemption from a burden is a good. Admittedly, there are situations in which it is natural to focus on the negative rather than the positive side of the ledger, such as taxation, military duty, and layoffs. Furthermore, perceptions of equity may sometimes be affected by this distinction. It undoubtedly makes a difference, for example, whether we frame the job allocation issue as: Who should be fired? or Who should be hired? For purely expository purposes, however, there is no harm in talking about goods rather than burdens.

Goods come in many forms. They may be homogeneous and divisible, like money or water. They may be inhomogeneous and divisible, like land, broadcasting bandwidths, or fishing grounds. They may be homogeneous and indivisible, like seats in a legislature or exemptions from military duty. Or they may be heterogeneous and indivisible, like kidneys for transplantation, places in selective colleges, and jobs.

The supply of the good may be either fixed or variable. The number of seats in the United States House of Representatives, for example, is fixed by statute at 435. The number of kidneys available for transplantation varies from one day to the next. It is important to recognize that the quantity of the good may be affected by the procedure for distributing it. The structure of the income tax code certainly affects the amount that individuals earn and the degree to which they report it, hence it determines the total amount of taxes raised. The perceived fairness of the kidney allocation formula may affect the propensity of donors to give.

More generally, an allocation is usually the result of three different types of decisions.[5] One decision concerns the total amount of the good to be distributed. Determining the number of seats in the House or the amount to be levied by taxation are examples of such *supply decisions*. The second type of decision concerns the formula or principle by which the good is allotted among the eligible parties. The formula for distributing legislative seats and the personal income tax schedule are examples of such *distributive decisions*. The first and second types of decisions are normally made by institutions. The third type of decision is made by individuals in response to these institutional choices. A taxpayer's choice about how much to earn given the tax rate schedule is an example of a *reactive decision*. The combination of all three levels of decision-making yields an *effective* allocation.

The major focus of this study will be on decisions of the second type, that is, on rules of distribution and the principles invoked to justify such rules. In general an *allocation rule* is a method, process, or formula that allocates any given *supply* of goods among any potential *group* of claimants according to the salient *characteristics* of those claimants. An apportionment rule, for example, determines how many seats each party gets in a legislature as a function of the party vote totals and the total number of seats. A rule of taxation specifies the amount of tax owed by each household as a function of the household's ability to pay and the amount of tax that must be raised. A kidney distribution rule determines who gets the next kidney as a function of each patient's medical condition, how long he or she has been waiting, the suitability of the kidney for the patient, and other factors.

The allocation rules that we see in practice usually exhibit one of three broad conceptions of equity. *Parity* means that the claimants are treated equally, either because they actually are equal or because there is no clear way to distinguish among them. *Proportionality* acknowledges differences among the claimants and divides the good in proportion to these differences. *Priority* asserts that the person with the greatest claim to the good gets it. Parity, proportionality, and

---

[5] This taxonomy (though not the terminology) draws on Calabresi and Bobbit (1978) and Elster (1992).

priority also figure prominently in the major theories of distributive justice, as we shall see in the next section.

While these conceptions of equity describe the general *structure* of a rule, however, its *content* derives from specific normative principles. Consider the problem of deciding who has priority to get the next available kidney. On philosophical grounds one could argue that the person who is worst off has highest priority, which suggests giving it to the patient who is in greatest danger or pain. Alternatively, one could argue that the kidney should go where it is likely to do the most good, for example, to the one most likely to survive. Yet a third option is to appeal to a social norm, like first come first served, that derives its legitimacy from precedent. This suggests giving it to the one who has been waiting longest.

These *normative* principles may be contrasted with the ways that distributive decisions are made in practice. Who actually does get the kidney? Who does the company lay off when times are bad? Who gets custody of the child in a divorce? These *empirical rules* of equity, as revealed by the choices that institutions make, are usually more complex and nuanced than any single normative principle. Instead they often represent a balance or compromise between competing principles.

4. Normative Theories of Justice: Aristotle, Bentham, and Rawls

There are three general theories of justice that figure prominently in discussions about equity. The oldest and most prominent is Aristotle's *equity principle,* which states that goods should be divided in proportion to each claimant's contribution. Plausible as this idea may be, it has two substantial limitations. First, we must have some way to measure the contribution of each claimant on a cardinal scale. Sometimes such a measure is natural, for example, the amount of time each worker put into a joint effort. In other situations the measure of contribution is not so clear. In a divorce proceeding, for example, how does one ascertain the relative contribution that husband and wife made to their joint estate or to rearing their children? Second, for proportionality to be workable, the goods must be divisible. When they are not, one could make them divisible by distributing chances at receiving the good, but then proportionality loses some of its plausibility. For example, if *A* has fought twice as long in the army as *B* and only one of them can be discharged, should *A* get *twice* as many chances at being discharged as *B?* Or is it fairer simply to discharge *A* first because he fought longer than *B?*

A second theory of justice is classical utilitarianism, which asserts that goods should be distributed so as to maximize the total welfare of the claimants (the *greatest good for the greatest number*). For this notion to make sense, utility must be understood as a measure of psychic satisfaction or well-being that can be measured on a cardinal scale and added across individuals. This doctrine, which was the dominant one in nineteenth-century welfare economics, has fallen into disrepute for several reasons. First, no method is provided for comparing levels of satisfaction among different individuals. Modern utility theory defines an individual's utility solely in terms of his preferences for different states of the world: state x has higher utility than state y if and only if x is strictly preferred to y. In this revealed preference approach to utility, the units in which utility is measured are quite arbitrary, so it is meaningless to add and subtract them across individuals. Second, even if we could devise some method for comparing individual utilities, it is not clear that the utilitarian *principle* is ethically sound, since it might require imposing great harm on a few in order to confer a small benefit on the many.

A third approach to social justice that meets these objections to some extent is due to John Rawls (1971). It is impossible to do justice in this short space to Rawls's theory, which is intricately constructed and contains many subtle and important qualifications. However, the central distributive principle may be simply stated: the least well-off group in society should be made as well off as possible. This is known as the *maximin or difference* principle. Contrary to first appearances it is not a welfarist conception of justice, because "well-off" does not refer here to a person's subjective level of satisfaction. Rather, it refers to the *means* or *instruments* by which satisfaction or happiness can be achieved. Economic income is one such means; others include opportunity, power, and self-respect. Rawls calls these *primary goods*.

If we restrict our attention just to one primary good, such as income, the principle says that income should be distributed so that the person with the least income has as much income as possible. This does not necessarily imply that everyone has equal income, however, because redistributing income from rich to poor may reduce or eliminate the incentive for the rich to become rich, thereby impoverishing everyone. Rather, the principle refers to the effective distribution of income after economic incentives are taken into account. Thus Rawls's principle avoids two of the problems inherent in classical utilitarianism. First, it is based, at least in part, on observable characteristics of individuals (such as income) rather than on interpersonal comparisons of welfare. Second, it avoids the ethical problem of benefiting the many at the expense of the few.

On the other hand, Rawls's theory is not without its drawbacks. In the first place, income is not the only currency in which justice is evaluated: other primary goods (e.g., self-respect) are involved that do not lend themselves readily to objective comparisons. Moreover, even if we could make such comparisons, it is not clear how we should *weight* different primary goods. Second, and most important, it is not clear that the maximin principle satisfies our intuitions about justice. Is it just to impose serious inconveniences on almost everyone in society in order to raise the opportunities, the income, or the self-respect of the least fortunate by a miniscule amount?

5. No Envy

The conceptual difficulties posed by the utilitarian and Rawlsian principles have led some economists to adopt an entirely different approach to distributive justice. Here we shall briefly sketch the central idea, which will be taken up again in chapter 9. A distribution is said to be *envy-free* if no one prefers another's portion to his own. This concept does not require interpersonal comparisons of utility, because each person evaluates every other person's share in terms of his *own* utility function.

Envy-freeness is an admirable—indeed an enviable—idea. It was first proposed in a very strong form by Tinbergen (1953), who argued that an equitable society is one in which no person wants to *change places* with another. "By places we mean their whole situation: especially their occupations and incomes, but also personal conditions such as health, size and health of their families, levels of education, abilities, etc."[6] Attractive as this concept may be in theory, it is impossible to achieve if people envy the personal characteristics of others, which is probably the most common object of envy. For example, A might envy B because B is tall. To eliminate A's envy requires that A be made wealthier than B. On the other hand, B might be indifferent between being tall and short. Hence if A is compensated, B would be envious. So there may be no reasonable way of eliminating envy in Tinbergen's sense.

A more pragmatic formulation was subsequently suggested by Foley (1967). We do not require that society *in general* be envy-free; we only require that no person prefer another's portion *of a particular allocation of goods*. If an estate is being distributed among heirs, for example, the "no envy" criterion says that no heir should prefer another's portion of the property to his own. They might envy each other because of other goods that they own, or because of their different abilities and circumstances of life, but not because someone else received a more desirable portion.

This idea makes sense provided that the parties have equal claims on the goods, and the goods are divisible. An example would be an inheritance in which the heirs are bequeathed equal shares. Of course, if the estate contains only one homogeneous good, such as money, an allocation is envy-free if and only if it is divided equally. Hence there are no novel implications in this case. The principle takes on greater interest when the property consists of different kinds of goods. Suppose, for example, that A and B are equal heirs to an estate that contains $200,000 in cash and 300 acres of land (all of which is of similar quality). Suppose further that A values the land at $1000 an acre and B values it at $500 an acre. If A gets all of the land and B all of the money, each prefers his

---

[6] Tinbergen (1953), pp. 55–56. The translation is given in Thomson (1990c), who provides an excellent survey of the literature on envy-freeness and related concepts. See also Thomson and Varian (1985) and Baumol (1986).

own portion to the other's, so the allocation is envy-free. Moreover, it is efficient because they have no desire to trade.

Typically, in fact, there are many allocations that are both envy-free and efficient. In the above example, there is no envy if A gets 250 acres and no cash, while B gets all the cash plus 50 acres of land. There is also no envy if A gets all the land plus \$25,000, while B gets \$175,000 but no land. These and all distributions in between are both envy-free and efficient, but it is not clear that all of them are equally fair.

One way to resolve this problem of indeterminacy is to resort to an allocation *process* that is perceived to be fair by both parties. Consider the traditional method of divide and choose. By the toss of a fair coin one of them is designated to be divider (say A). Since B gets to select the portion she prefers, she will certainly not envy A's portion. However, A can also protect himself from envy by creating two portions that he values equally. Then no matter which portion B selects, A will not strictly prefer it to the one left over for himself. Note, however, that the divider can manipulate the outcome if he knows the chooser's preferences. For example, A could split the estate into the following two portions: one containing \$175,001 and no land, the other containing all the land plus the rest of the money. B slightly prefers the first portion to the second, while A greatly prefers the second portion to the first. The resulting allocation is envy-free and efficient, but is it fair? This suggests looking for equity principles that discriminate more finely among envy-free allocations, a topic that we explore in chapter 9.

6. Distributive Judgments and Interpersonal Comparisons

The appeal of no envy is that it does not require making interpersonal comparisons of utility, so it has an operational meaning within the framework of modern utility theory. The weakness of the concept is that it only applies when the parties have equal claims on the good, which is often not the case. Indeed, most fair division problems revolve around the question of how *differences* in claims—due to disparities in merit, desert, contribution, need, and so forth—should be taken into account, in which case the no envy principle is more or less irrelevant.

To take a concrete example, consider the problem of allocating one kidney between two patients. Suppose that patient A is in her thirties and has no other major health problems, while B is in his sixties and is diabetic. On the other hand, B has been waiting for two years and cannot survive much longer on dialysis, while A has been in the queue for less than two months and can wait longer. Under these circumstances who should receive the transplant? Obviously, whoever does not get the kidney will envy the other in the sense that he or she prefers the other's portion. (Note, however, that A may well prefer to be A

without a kidney than to be *B* with one.) From society's point of view, envy is not the most relevant issue here. What matters is that medical resources be put to effective use, and that suffering be alleviated. These principles sometimes conflict: the former argues for giving the kidney to *A*, while the latter suggests giving it to *B*. While these choices are not simple, a decision that is objectively based on such values may well be regarded as fair by the losing party, even though in a narrow sense the loser has reason to envy the winner.

The problem with no envy is that it dispenses with interpersonal utility comparisons by not making interpersonal comparisons of any kind. The fact is, however, that distributive decisions almost always involve comparisons and value judgments. It is pointless to assume them away; we need instead to ask *on what basis* they are made. When a doctor or a social agency decides to give a kidney to patient *A* rather than to patient *B*, a value judgment is being made and people are being compared. The decision is not about who wants it most, but about who needs it most or who will benefit most. These judgments are not made by consulting the parties' utility functions, but by looking at objective measures such as expected longevity and time in the queue. Any theory of equity with explanatory power is going to have to come to terms with the fact that we make comparative judgments of this sort all the time. Moreover, there is nothing in *utility theory* that says that such comparisons cannot be made; the theory is simply silent on *how* they are made.

7. Why Classical Formulas Fail

The book is constructed around a stock of examples that illustrate why equity cannot be reduced to simple, all-embracing solutions such as the difference principle, the greatest good principle, or the proportionality principle. To illustrate why these ideas do not get us very far, consider the situation in which a single indivisible object is to be allotted among the members of a group, all of whom lay claim to it to different degrees. For example, which parent gets custody of the child in a divorce? Which soldier gets the privilege of being discharged from the army first? Which patient with renal disease gets the one available kidney? What site should be chosen for a hazardous waste dump? Who inherits the summer house?

One might think that the way out of these difficulties is to transform the indivisible good into a divisible one. In a moment we shall argue that this does not resolve the equity problem, but first let us consider how it could be done. There are three standard methods for transforming an indivisible good into a divisible one: randomization, rotation, and conversion. Under *randomization* each claimant has a probability of getting the good; under *rotation* the claimants take turns at using the good; under *conversion* they exchange the indivisible good for a divisible one and split the proceeds.

The relative suitability of these methods depends on the circumstances. A kidney might be allocated by lottery, for example, but it cannot be shared effectively. By contrast, the heirs to a summer house would probably prefer to share it than take equal chances at getting exclusive use of it, and they might prefer selling it to sharing it if they cannot get along. Rotation is customary in resolving child custody disputes, while lotteries and sale would be considered quite unusual.

Yet another way of handling indivisibilities is to *compensate* those who do not get the good, or, in the case of a burden, to compensate those who do. For example, one might auction off the good among the claimants: the highest bidder gets it and pays appropriate compensation to the losers. Similarly a burden, such as a waste dump, may be auctioned by having each party offer to take on the burden in return for compensation. The one who demands the least compensation accepts the burden and the others divide the cost.

Each of these mechanisms—randomization, rotation, conversion, and compensation—changes the original allocation problem into a new one that involves divisible goods. But none of them goes to the heart of the distributive issue, which is: how much is each claimant entitled to? Does everyone who avoids getting the waste dump pay an equal portion of the cost? Does everyone who has to live with it receive equal compensation? Does patient A deserve twice as many chances at getting the kidney as patient B because she has been waiting twice as long? Should the mother get five days of custody per week and the father only two? On what theory or principle are these shares determined? This is the nub of the distributive problem, and it is not resolved by introducing divisible goods.

8. The Priority Principle

The evidence suggests, moreover, that indivisible allocations are often handled by confronting the indivisibility directly instead of trying to circumvent it. He who has the greatest claim gets the good; the others do not. We shall call this the *priority principle*. The basis of priority may be quite simple, such as seniority in avoiding job layoffs. It may follow from economic considerations, for example, choose the waste dump site that is least costly. More often priority is based on a mixture of criteria. What is the best site given both cost and safety consider-ations? Which patient should get the kidney given differences in their chances of survival, time in the queue, and immediate need? (All of these factors enter into the national formula for allocating kidneys in the United States.) Priority in these situations is not one-dimensional, it involves trade-offs among various principles.

This pattern holds true for a wide variety of indivisible goods. There are lists for getting into day care centers, for being admitted to universities, for being hired, for being laid off, for receiving public housing, for getting into a nursing home. Each such list expresses a concept of who is most deserving, who is next-most deserving, and so forth, given the claimants' circumstances and the good being distributed. Each captures a notion of equity, but it is not equity in the Aristotelian sense of proportionality. It is equity based on *priority*. Priority is an ordinal rather than a cardinal principle because it does not say *how much more* deserving one claimant is compared to another; it simply says that one claimant *is* more deserving than another.

How then is priority determined in a concrete case? In some situations priority is largely a matter of judgment. Deciding which soldier is most deserving of early discharge, which parent wins custody, or who gets the kidney are issues on which reasonable people may differ. In this case fairness reduces to a procedural question of how to strike an *equitable balance* between diverse points of view. This brings us to a classical problem in group decision making, namely, how to design a process that fairly aggregates individual opinions into a collective decision. This project is not without its perils, because collective decisions are inherently more problematic than individual ones due to the "paradox of voting." Nevertheless there do exist equitable ways of aggregating individual opinions into a consensus, as we shall argue in chapter 2.

In other situations, priority is less a matter of judgment and more a matter of logic. An example is the apportionment of representation among political states or parties (chapter 3). Here the equitable ideal is clear—one person, one vote. But in practice the ideal cannot be met due to the lumpy character of the goods. Seats cannot be subdivided. The issue then becomes how to achieve equity *as near as may be*.

9. The Consistency Principle

A fruitful approach to this problem is to begin by asking what solution is most equitable when there are just *two* claimants. This case is usually simple to grasp intuitively. Once a standard of equity has been established for two-claimant situations, we may then solve a many-claimant problem according to the following principle: *allocate the good so that every two claimants divide the amount allotted to them as they would if they were the only two claimants*. This *consistency principle* turns out to be one of the most powerful unifying ideas in the theory of fair allocation.

To illustrate the concept in a concrete case, consider the apportionment of legislative seats among states. Here the *ideal* is one person, one vote. Each state's allotment should be exactly proportional to its population. Unfortunately the ideal cannot be met because the seats come in whole units. To solve this problem, we begin by asking what apportionment comes closest to meeting the ideal when there are just two states. The natural answer is to give each state the whole number *closest* to its exact share. In other words, we round the shares to the nearest whole number.

For example, suppose there are ten seats to divide between two states with populations 142,000 and 858,000, respectively. The share of the first state is 1.42 and the share of the second is 8.58. The natural solution is to give 1 seat to the first and 9 seats to the second. This satisfies the ideal of one person, one vote as near as may be. When there are more than two states we follow the same principle, that is, we distribute the seats so that every pair of states shares the number of seats allotted to them as near as may be. It is a remarkable fact that such a distribution always exists. Moreover, it is computed by constructing a priority list that determines which state gets the first seat, which state gets the second seat, and so forth until all the seats have been distributed. This is an instance of a very general result, which states roughly that *any allocative rule that satisfies the consistency principle also satisfies the priority principle and vice versa*.

These results are not mere theoretical curiosities. The rule described above, for example, was used to apportion the United States House of Representatives for much of the nineteenth and early twentieth centuries, and it is now one of the standard methods for apportioning legislatures in other countries. Thus we see how a few well-chosen principles can be used to deduce practical solutions to difficult allocative problems. We also see why classical formulas like pure proportionality do not take us as far as we need to go.

10. When Proportionality Fails for Divisible Goods

It might be objected, however, that the above examples are special because the bone of contention is indivisible. Surely when the good is *divisible* and the claimants can be compared by some numerical measure of *entitlement,* classical principles like proportionality work very well. In chapters 4, 5, and 6 we argue, however, that even in this case, proportionality is not necessarily the most appropriate solution.

Suppose, for example, that A and B are heirs to an estate that contains a field. One document says that A gets the whole field, while another document says that B gets the eastern half of the field. The documents are inconsistent, but equally valid. How should the inconsistency be resolved? An equitable solution is to give the western half of the field to A (since it is undisputed) and to divide the disputed eastern half equally between them. Thus A would get three-fourths of the field and B one-fourth.

Now consider a slightly different situation: A is willed all of the field and B is willed half of the field, but the document does not say *which* half. Under the preceding principle A would get three-fourths of the field and B one-fourth. But the proportional principle would award two-thirds of the field to A and one-third to B, because A was willed twice as much land as B. This seems no more equitable than the first approach, which is a well-known principle in the Tal-mudic law of contracts (see chapter 4). This does not prove that proportionality is inequitable, but it does show that proportionality is not the *only* equitable solution.

A second difficulty with proportionality (and many other rules) is its failure to take economic incentives into account. Consider, for example, two commu-nities who plan to share the cost of a common waste disposal site. The total development cost is one million dollars. If they fail to agree, town A will develop its own site for $700,000 and town B will develop a separate site for $400,000. Thus there are economies from cooperation. Suppose for the sake of argument that A generates three times as much waste as B. (A's site does not cost three times as much because of economies of scale.) The Aristotelian solution would be to charge in proportion to their contributions: A would pay $750,000 and B would pay $250,000. A is not likely to agree to this proposal, however, because it would be cheaper to go it alone. Thus proportional division is not satisfactory because it fails to take into account the parties' opportunity costs. Equal division fails for the same reason. This issue is taken up in chapter 5, where we show how to define equity in the presence of incentive constraints.

Perhaps the most serious problem with proportionality, however, is that it does not always accord with our *intuitions* about equity. A prominent example is income taxation. Many developed countries tax higher incomes at a higher rate than lower incomes, and have done so almost since the inception of income taxation. This *progressivity principle* is by no means unique to taxation, but is seen in many other kinds of assessments. When hard times force firms to cut wages, for example, it is not unusual for the cuts to be progressive, with higher-paid employees suffering a greater percentage reduction than lower-paid ones. In both cases the rationale is clear: those who are better off can absorb the loss more easily. Of course, taxation is a more complex problem than a one-time assessment, because the tax schedule casts a shadow on the future that affects the propensity of taxpayers to work and invest. Hence distributive goals must be considered in relation to their incentive effects. It turns out, however, that some types of progressive schedules are no worse in this respect than flat-rate taxes; indeed they may even lead to fewer distortions, as we argue in chapter 6.

Each of these cases illustrates why proportionality (as well as the other classical principles) do not always yield satisfactory answers, even when the goods are perfectly divisible. If we want to explain what equity means in practice, we must look for more subtle and nuanced kinds of solutions.

11. Games of Fair Division

In chapters 7 and 8, we turn our attention to situations where the allocative decision is not entrusted to an institution, but is negotiated by the claimants directly. Suppose, for example, that a group of countries are negotiating their respective shares in a producers' cartel. The purpose is to limit production and drive up the price so each country naturally wants to claim as large a share of the output as possible. The bargaining chip that each holds is the threat to pull out of the agreement and drive down the price by increasing production unilaterally.

At first blush it would seem that equity considerations play little or no role in such bargains. What determines the outcome is the power relation among the claimants: the skill and patience with which they bargain and the credibility of their alternatives. While these factors are important, however, they rarely determine the outcome. Indeed, if everyone simply demands the maximum amount for himself, there is a good chance that the process will end in stalemate. The key to resolving a distributive bargain is not to make self-serving demands, but to make a proposal that the *others* find plausible and justifiable.[7] This is precisely where equity arguments come in: they *coordinate* the expectations of the bargainers by establishing a plausible basis for the agreement (see chap. 7). Equity principles are the *instruments* that people use to resolve distributive bargains.

Of course there are some situations in which the claimants may find it difficult, if not impossible, to agree in principle. Suppose, for example, that several heirs are bequeathed shares of an estate that consists of various types of divisible goods. Since the shares themselves are not in dispute, each claimant could simply take his share of each of the goods and go home. But this solution is almost certainly inefficient if they value the goods differently. Is there some basis on which they could reach agreement on a distribution that is both fair and efficient? The answer to this question is not immediately apparent. Indeed, since they almost certainly do not know each other's utility functions, they cannot even determine what the efficient outcomes are.

The solution is to design a *procedure* for dividing the goods that the claimants believe to be fair. By a "procedure" we mean a game with prescribed rules and moves that results in a specific division. A classical example is the game in which one player divides the property into two piles and the other gets first choice. How do we know that this game is fair? One answer is that it leads to fair outcomes when played by rational players. For example, the divide and choose game yields a division that is envy-free, so we could argue that it is fair. A second answer is that no advantage accrues from playing one role instead of another. This is analogous to saying that the playing field is *level:* the players can expect to do as well no matter which end of the field they have to play on. In this sense divide and choose is *not* fair because it confers an advantage on the divider. This inequity can be eliminated by changing the game in various ways, as we show in chapter 8. One variation is to allow the role of divider and chooser to alternate between the two players, with the chooser in one round becoming divider in the next round if he does not like the divider's current offer.

---

[7] Schelling (1960).

A second approach is to let both parties bid to be divider. Each bid is a fraction between 0 and 1 that represents the bidder's commitment to give up that fraction of all the goods if the other side does not like his proposed division.

These and other modifications of divide and choose make the playing field more or less level. However, they also lead to substantially different outcomes when played by rational, knowledgeable agents. To evaluate which of these processes is fairest, we must have some way to evaluate the fairness of the outcomes they produce. This raises a difficulty, because the equilibrium outcomes of these games are framed in terms of their *utility* to the claimants, which is almost never accessible information. Indeed, the players will not even be able to *reach* these outcomes unless their utility functions are common knowledge, which is almost never the case. Thus, while some games of fair division yield outcomes that are fair in theory, there is no guarantee that these outcomes will result in practice.

12. Equity and Efficiency

This leads us to a natural question. Is there any way to design an allocation procedure that leads to outcomes which are *visibly* fair and efficient, and does not require that the claimants know each other's utility functions? In chapter 9 we suggest an answer to this question. Suppose that the claimants have well-defined shares in the common property (not necessarily equal shares), and different preferences for the goods it contains. A *competitive allocation* is one for which there exists a set of *prices,* such that every claimant likes his portion best among all the portions that he can afford to buy given the value of his share at these prices. Such an allocation can be discovered through a marketlike mechanism that does not require the claimants to know anything about each other's utilities. Moreover, the resulting allocation can be justified on grounds of equity. *It is the only efficient and consistent way of reallocating the property that leaves everyone at least as well off as he was initially.*

This result provides both a theoretical and practical answer to the question of how to allocate divisible goods both fairly and efficiently without making inordinate demands on the players' information. It also sounds a theme that runs throughout the book. In problems of *local* justice, equity and efficiency often complement each other. Principles of equity are the *instruments* by which societies resolve distributive problems when efficiency by itself yields indeterminate results.

2

Equity and Priority

The person of honour is in equity to go in first.
(*Rules of Civility [1673]*)

1. Methods for Distributing Indivisible Goods

Consider the problem of allocating an indivisible good when the rule is at most one unit to a customer and there is not enough to go around. For example, which patients should receive organs for transplantation? Which soldiers in the Army should be allowed to go home first? Who gets the corner office? Which occupant of the lifeboat gets eaten when the food runs out? In each of these situations the issue is who should get and who should go without, taking into account such factors as need, contribution, and the welfare of the group as a whole. The diversity of such problems is apparent from the various methods for resolving them.

Forced Equality

When equal treatment is the paramount consideration, the good may be given to no one. For example, works of art that are deteriorating because of exposure to many visitors (e.g., the Lascaux caves in France or Leonardo's painting of the Last Supper) cannot be visited by the general public even though a few could be allowed to view them without causing further damage. Rather than admit some members of the general public and exclude others, it is more convenient to deny access to the general public altogether. Similarly, everyone may be forced to bear a burden even though not everyone has to. Some countries have compulsory military service for all eighteen-year-olds, for example, even though they do not need this many people to serve in the army. In both cases the principle is absolute equality. No differences in entitlement are recognized; everyone must receive the same amount. When the good or burden is indivisible, meeting this ideal can be quite wasteful.

Lotteries

One way to avoid the inefficiency of forced equality is to give everyone an equal *chance* at getting the good or bearing the burden. Then everyone is treated equally before the fact, though not afterward. During the latter part of the Vietnam War, for example, the U.S. military called up young men according to their birth dates, which were prioritized by a random draw. Franchises for local-area cellular telephone service are currently allotted by chance among a pool of "qualified" applicants. Firms may assign offices to employees by lot, a similar method is sometimes used to allocate indivisible items among the heirs to an estate. Lotteries usually involve equal chances, but there is no reason why some claimants should not be given more chances than others. For example, if one heir is left two-thirds of the estate and the other one-third, then the former could be given twice as many lottery tickets for each item as the latter. In the Netherlands, positions in medical schools are allocated by lottery among qualified students, with more chances given to those with higher grades.[1]

Rotation

In some circumstances it is more appealing to divide an indivisible good by taking turns. Communes, for example, sometimes inscribe household chores on an inner wheel and the members' names on an outer wheel, then turn the wheel each day to determine who is assigned to which chore. The heirs to a valuable painting may choose to hold the property rights jointly and take turns hanging the painting in their homes. Children are often time-shared between divorced parents. Unlike lotteries, there is no tension here between *ex ante* and *ex post* fairness. On the other hand, the sharing process can substantially change the character of the good itself. Half custody of a child is not the same thing as half a child.

Compensation

Another device for resolving indivisibilities is to compensate those who do not get the good (or, in the case of a burden, to compensate those who do). The heir who gets the summer house, for example, could pay his siblings their share of its assessed value. The town that is selected for the hazardous waste dump can be compensated by the towns that are not selected. While this idea is attractive in theory, it is often unclear what the appropriate amount of compensation is. If *A* deserves a kidney more than *B* (say because *A*'s case is more urgent), should *B* be compensated for having to wait, and if so, by how much? One might be tempted to say that it is the price that *B* would be willing to pay to buy the kidney from *A*, but this is not correct. (If *B* is unable to buy it, this does not establish that *B* should not be compensated.) At issue is the amount that *B* should be compensated so that the two are treated fairly *ex ante*. One approach would be

---

[1] Willem Hofstee (1983).

to compensate B just enough so that neither prefers what the other receives (i.e., the allocation is envy-free). The weakness of this concept is that it is based solely on the claimants' strength of preference for the good, and fails to take into account differences in desert.

Queuing

A more standard approach to allocating indivisibles is to give them out to those who are first in line. Examples include lining up for free tickets to a public concert or to enroll one's child in a special school. Queuing is akin to a lottery, since it is partly a matter of chance who gets in line first. But not wholly: one can be first by spending the most time in line. In this sense queuing is like an auction: those who bid the most time get the good. (Furthermore, it could be argued that it is a fair auction since everyone is naturally endowed with equal amounts of time. This is not to say that time is worth the same amount to everyone, but then neither is money.) The difficulty, of course, is that queuing is wasteful. A more efficient approach is to have claimants *subscribe* for the good. This is a common device for doling out places in public housing, nursing homes, and schools, as well as allocating other scarce goods such as organs for transplantation.

Priority Lists

A more general form of the waiting list is the priority list, in which claimants are ranked according to some measure of need, desert, contribution, seniority, or (more typically) a combination of factors. Admission to public housing, for example, typically depends on financial need, family size, and length of time on a waiting list. Priority to receive an organ for transplantation depends on the urgency of the case, the likelihood of success, and so forth. In the private sector, unions have criteria for determining who gets laid off first, and companies have formulas for assigning office space and other perquisites to managers. Each such priority list reflects an equity judgment about who deserves the good most.

Priority lists are probably the most widely used of any of the above methods for allocating indivisible goods. They are simple in concept, they have the advantage of allocating the good itself rather than something else (like a time-shared good), and they make the basis for the allocation explicit. This is an important consideration for public agencies and other institutions (including firms) who need to be able to justify their actions and to protect themselves from charges of playing favorites. For the same reason, priority lists are an important source of information for students of equity, for they tell us what distributing agencies think the relevant criteria are.

In this chapter we shall examine two cases in which the priority lists were created quite systematically: (i) the point system employed by the United States Army to demobilize soldiers at the end of World War II, and (ii) the priority system used in the United States to allocate kidneys among renal patients. In studying these cases we shall be interested in two questions: How was priority determined? And how do the revealed priority criteria compare with theories of distributive justice? We shall find that classical rules—Aristotle's equity principle, Bentham's greatest happiness principle, Rawls's difference principle—simply do not explain what we observe in these and similar cases. Aristotle's principle does not even apply: what does proportionality mean when a claimant can receive either one unit or nothing? Maximizing total welfare, or maximizing the position of the least well-off, do not mean much either when we cannot measure how well off the claimants are.

Instead, we shall discover that priority is a complex and nuanced idea in which various considerations are balanced against one another: present need, past contribution, potential benefit, time spent waiting, and so forth. While the answers are not simple, however, the format of the answer—a priority list—is both simple and significant. As we shall see in later chapters, some notion of priority undergirds almost all satisfactory methods of fair distribution.

2. The Demobilization of U.S. Soldiers at the End of World War II[2]

Toward the end of World War II, it became possible to release several million American soldiers from active service in Europe, though millions more had to be retained in order to continue the war against Japan. The U.S. Army command was therefore faced with the touchy question of which soldiers to release first. There were two competing schools of thought on this subject. One group argued for retaining combat veterans and discharging those who had seen little service, on the grounds that this policy would maximize the effectiveness of the remaining forces. The contrary view was that retaining the men who had served the longest, and discharging those who had sacrificed the least, would cause such disaffection in the ranks that it would seriously undermine morale. In other words, it would *not* have the effect of maximizing the effectiveness of the remaining forces. Nor would it be politically palatable to constituents whose sons were serving in the Army.

To help resolve the question of who should be released first, it was proposed that the opinions of the men themselves be sounded out. Beginning in 1943, the Army surveyed thousands of soldiers to identify the factors they considered most important in the decision about whom to let out first. Troops based in the U.S. named the following four factors: length of time in the Army, age, amount

---

[2] This account is based on Stouffer et al. (1949), chap. 11.

of overseas service, and number of dependents. They were then asked to compare the relative importance of these factors using the method of paired comparisons. A portion of the questionnaire read as follows:

a) After the war when the Army starts releasing soldiers back to civilian life, which of these two groups of men do you think should be released *first*? (Check *only one*)

_____ Men with dependents

or

_____ Men over 30 years of age

b) Which of *these* two groups of men should be released *first*? (Check *only one*)

_____ Men who have been in the Army longest

or

_____ Men with dependents

c) Which of *these* two groups of men should be released *first*? (Check *only one*)

_____ Men over 30 years of age

or

_____ Men who have served overseas

d) Which of *these* two groups of men should be released *first*? (Check *only one*)

_____ Men who have served overseas

or

_____ Men who have been in the Army longest

e) Which of *these* two groups of men should be released *first*? (Check *only one*)

_____ Men over 30 years of age

or

_____ Men who have been in the Army longest

f) Which of *these* two groups of men do you think should be released *first*? (Check *only one*)

_____ Men with dependents

or

_____ Men who have served overseas

About 90 percent of the individual responses to this questionnaire were *internally consistent:* they contained no intransitivities such as preferring length of time in the Army to dependents, dependents to overseas service, and overseas service to length of time in the Army.

Table 2.1 shows the frequency with which each criterion was listed first, second, third, and last among those who gave transitive responses. Evidently O was considered to be the most important factor by a solid majority of respondents. We may also conclude that D was considered more important than both L and A by a majority. This is obvious in the case of A, which was ranked last by 62 percent. D was ranked first or second by 64 percent, but L was ranked first by

TABLE 2.1
Priority of Demobilization Choices among Men Stationed in the Central Pacific Area in March, 1944 (5,115 responses)

	Percentage of Transitive Responses in Which the Factor Was Ranked:			
	First	*Second*	*Third*	*Fourth*
Overseas Service (*O*)	54	39	6	1
Dependents (*D*)	38	26	25	11
Longevity in Army (*L*)	5	26	43	26
Age (*A*)	3	9	26	62

only 5 percent, so D must have been ranked ahead of L by at least 59 percent. We may therefore say that the ordering $O > D > L > A$ represents a "consensus" on the relative importance that should be assigned to the four factors. (A more precise definition of "consensus" will be given in section 6.)

The survey conducted by the Army also permitted soldiers to write in additional criteria that they considered to be important. These write-in candidates revealed a factor that had been omitted in the design of the first questionnaire (which had been based solely on a sample of servicemen in the U.S.). This additional factor was "exposure to combat." Most overseas men felt that priority should be given to those who had seen combat over those who had not. The importance of this factor in the thinking of overseas soldiers as compared with a separate survey of those stationed at home is evident from table 2.2.

These data reveal that the soldiers' expressed preferences were positively correlated with their own situations, which is hardly surprising. What is surprising is that self-serving responses were not more widespread. The data show, for example, that between 23 and 36 percent of those who had *not* seen combat nevertheless rated combat as the most important factor for discharge. What is the explanation for this? One reason, perhaps, is that soldiers developed a degree of sympathy for their comrades—especially for men in their own units—which led them to identify with others' situations. Another possible explanation is that they recognized that their own situations might change over time. Those currently stationed in the U.S. might see combat duty later, for

TABLE 2.2
Percentage in Each Group Saying That Men Who Had Seen the Most Combat Should Be Let Out First

Overseas Combat Men	55%
Overseas Noncombat Men	36
United States Men	23

example, and they might prefer the prospect of doing combat duty knowing that it would give them a greater prospect of being let out early. Perhaps the most important reason, however, is that biasing one's answer would have little effect: out of thousands of responses any single one is not likely to change the results very much.

The goal of the Army questionnaires was to determine not only the priority that the soldiers assigned to the various criteria, but the "importance weights" that should be assigned to these criteria. The latter cannot be determined from the data in table 2.1, because the soldiers were not asked to express the *trade-offs* that they would make between the various criteria. This was the goal of a follow-up survey conducted by the Army in August 1944. In this questionnaire, the soldiers were asked to compare situations involving various combinations of factors. A sample question was the following:

Here are three men of the same age, all overseas the same length of time—check the one you would want to have let out first.

> (a) _____ A single man, through two campaigns of combat
> (b) _____ A married man, with no children, through one campaign of combat
> (c) _____ A married man with 2 children, not in combat.

Based on the results of these surveys, the Army command adopted a point system for rating the importance of the various factors as follows. (Note that in the final version the age factor was dropped entirely). Soldiers with 85 points or more were demobilized first.

Length of time in the Army	1 point per month
Length of time overseas	1 point per month
Combat	5 points per campaign star or combat decoration
Dependents	12 points per child under 18, up to three

One might wonder why a more natural criterion of combat duty was not used, such as length of time in combat. The explanation is that reliable records were unavailable for the length of time that each soldier actually had spent in combat. Furthermore, there was the difficulty of defining the term "in combat" unambiguously. The substitute measure adopted (number of campaign stars) was not entirely satisfactory either, since many noncombatants were awarded these stars also. It also discriminated in favor of the Air Force, which was in the habit of awarding numerous decorations to its fliers. In spite of these faults, the campaign-stars criterion had the virtue of being simple, well documented, and defensible, which are desirable features of any bureaucratically administered formula.

Did the point system adopted by the Army have the intended effect, that is, was it regarded as fair by the men? To investigate this question, the Army conducted a follow-up survey in June 1945, to see if there were differences in opinions between those who had been demobilized early and those who had not. As was to be expected, the men in the former category rated the point system more favorably—82 percent rated it as good or fairly good. Nevertheless, men in the latter category were also predominantly favorable—65 percent of them rated it as "good" or "fairly good."

The point system also had another important benefit. Immediately after it was announced, the Army command was deluged with calls and letters from members of Congress requesting special treatment for this or that category of men. To these requests the Army responded that they were merely following the stated preferences of the soldiers themselves, and that to modify the system after the fact would only generate resentment. This argument provided a solid defense against attempts to manipulate the system.

The rationale behind the point system, and the reasons for its general acceptance, are perhaps best summarized by the official announcement made to the public in September 1944:

> The simplest plan of demobilization would have been to return . . . surplus units to this country and discharge their personnel intact. Such a method, however, would operate with great unfairness to many individuals who have had long and arduous service but are not assigned to one of the units declared surplus.
>
> If only units in Europe were considered, this basis of expediency would work unfairly to units long in the Pacific or at outpost bases in the American theater. It would operate unfairly to men who have seen extended combat in Europe and the Pacific and have been returned to this country for reassignment. It would release men only recently assigned as replacements to units long in combat and would discriminate against veterans of many campaigns in units not selected to return.
>
> Consequently, it was determined that the fairest method of selection would be through the selection of men as individuals rather than by units, with the selection governed by thoroughly impartial standards.
>
> For the standards, the War Department went to the soldiers themselves. Experts were sent into the field to obtain a cross section of the sentiments of enlisted men. Thousands of soldiers, both in this country and overseas, were interviewed to learn their views on the kind of selective process they believed should determine the men to be returned to civilian life. Opinions expressed by soldiers themselves became the accepted principle of the plan. (Stouffer et al., 1949, p. 525.)

3. The Point System for Allocating Kidneys in the United States

In recent years, kidney transplantation has evolved from an experimental, high-risk medical technique to a routine treatment for kidney failure. Currently over nine thousand kidney transplants are performed each year in the United States,

and over 90 percent of these are deemed to be long-term successes. Nevertheless, demand greatly exceeds supply. There are about 14,000 patients on the
waiting list for kidneys, and over 90,000 patients on long-term dialysis.

In recognition of the growing difficulty of matching supply and demand,
Congress passed the National Organ Transplant Act in 1984. This legislation
called for "a national system, through the use of computers and in accordance
with established medical criteria, to match organs and individuals included in
the recipient list." This Act and its subsequent amendments led to the establish-
ment of the Organ Transplantation and Procurement Network, which is oper-
ated by the United Network for Organ Sharing (UNOS). UNOS policy is that
"organs offered for transplantation are viewed as national resources, and thus
the allocation of those organs must be based on fair and equitable policies. . . .
The point system for kidney allocation was developed to accomplish major
objectives intrinsic in a fair system: to alleviate human suffering; to prolong
life; to provide a nondiscriminatory, fair and equitable system for organ allocation; to develop technology and foster research necessary for advancement and
improvement of the quality of life of transplant recipients; to maximize organ
usage and to decrease organ wastage; and to be accountable to the public that is
assuming ever-increasing societal and economic responsibilities for life-long
care required by transplant patients."[3]

In this section we shall examine the allocation system adopted by UNOS to
fulfill these objectives. Like the Army's demobilization formula, the kidney
formula is based on a priority list in which rank-order is determined by assigning point values to various pertinent factors. These factors and their weights
were determined after extensive discussions by committees consisting of medical experts, ethicists, representatives of patient groups, and members of the
general public. In 1987, for example, a public opinion survey was conducted to
determine the criteria that the public considers to be relevant to the allocation
decision. Eighty-one percent of the respondents (based on a sample size of
2,051) felt that medical need, not social or economic factors, should be the
basis for the decision. This survey and the opinions of transplant professionals
led to the adoption of three broad criteria of entitlement:

1. efficacy—the likelihood that the transplant will be a success;
2. need—the lack of alternatives such as dialysis;
3. disadvantage—patients who are difficult to match should be given a handicap.

The point system originally adopted by UNOS was based on a formula that had
already been in use in the Pittsburgh area for several years.[4] Renal patients are

---

[3] UNOS Final Statement of Policy, p. 13.

[4] The formula appears to have been prompted by a "scandal" in which the Pittsburgh Press
alleged that the transplant center at Presbyterian-University Hospital was passing over local
patients—including some who had been waiting for years to receive a kidney—in favor of wealthy
foreigners who, in return, made large donations to the hospital. (Pittsburgh Press May 12, 1985 and
Nov. 3, 4, 5, 1985.)

placed on the waiting list when they are certified by their doctors to be eligible. Waiting lists are maintained for each local transplant center as well as at the regional and national levels. A patient may be entered on all of them simultaneously. Patients are sorted according to the types of kidneys for which they are medically eligible. The donor kidney must be of the correct blood type[5] and the correct tissue type, that is, the recipient must not have cytotoxic antibody formations against the kidney. Further, the kidney should be about the right size. Juvenile kidneys are not very well suited for transplantation in adults and vice versa.[6]

The goal of efficacy suggests that kidneys should be allocated where they will yield the maximum benefit. One measure of efficacy is the expected gain in useful years of life. As this criterion is rather difficult to pin down, however, indicators of the probability of success are used. Studies have shown, for example, that the more antigens that are matched between donor and recipient the higher the likelihood of success. The original UNOS formula awarded two points for each of the six possible antigen matches between donor and patient. In addition, a bonus of up to six points was awarded if the logistics of getting the kidney to the patient were favorable.[7]

The second consideration is medical urgency. Typically this situation arises when a patient cannot remain on dialysis because all of the available dialysis sites have been used up. In this case the patient receives a bonus of ten points.

The third consideration is to try to avoid lengthy waits for a kidney. Some renal patients are inherently disadvantaged because they are highly sensitized, that is, they have antibodies against a high proportion of the rest of the population, and hence against most prospective donors. Such patients are given a handicap to compensate them for biological "bad luck." They are awarded 1 point for each 10 percent of the general population against which they have antibodies. Thus, if a patient is sensitized against 80 percent of the population, he would receive 8 points. In addition, a patient earns points the longer he has been waiting (whether or not he is highly sensitized). Again this amounts to compensation for bad luck—not biological bad luck but circumstantial bad luck that a suitable kidney did not become available. The UNOS formula gave a patient *ten points minus ten times the fraction of patients who have been waiting longer.* For example, if there were five patients who were eligible for a given kidney then the patient who had been waiting longest got a waiting score of 10,

---

[5] There are four blood types: A, B, AB, and O. A type O kidney can be accepted by a patient of a different blood type, but a patient of type O will reject a kidney that is *not* of type O. This means that O-type patients are inherently disadvantaged unless O-type kidneys are reserved for them. By contrast, a type AB patient can receive a kidney of any blood type, so these patients are inherently advantaged. For this reason it is UNOS policy to match blood types between donor and recipient. Note that this is not dictated by efficiency considerations, but rather by equity.

[6] The rule is that kidneys from juveniles aged ten or less are given to patients aged fifteen or less unless there are no such patients when the kidney becomes available.

[7] The logistics criterion has since been rendered relatively unimportant because of improved techniques for preserving kidneys.

TABLE 2.3
Characteristics of Five Patients in a Given Blood Group for Determining Priority

Patient	Months	Antigens Matched	Sensitization (%)	Logistics	Urgency
A	5	2	10	0	0
B	4.5	2	20	0	0
C	4	0	0	5	0
D	2	3	60	0	0
E	1	6	90	0	0

the next got a score of $10(1 - 1/5) = 8$, and so forth. If there were n patients, the kth person in line would get a score of $10(n - k + 1)/n$. Together the handicap for high sensitization and points earned for waiting time assured that highly sensitized patients would eventually move toward the top of the list.[8]

We shall illustrate the formula with a small example. Suppose that five patients are on the list. Two kidneys from a single donor become available that could be matched with any one of them. In other words, blood type, antibody profile, and age are compatible between the donor and all five patients. Let the patients have the characteristics shown in table 2.3. Their point values are shown in table 2.4.

This implies that the two available kidneys should go to patients E and D in that order. This formula has a paradoxical feature, however. Suppose that the two kidneys do not become available at the same time. (This might happen because one of them is diverted to another transplant center, for example.) The first kidney clearly goes to E, since E has highest priority. Now consider the individuals remaining after E has gone home. The point values for waiting time change, because they depend on the *number* of people in the queue as well as on their *relative position*. The waiting time scores are now: A 10; B 7.5; C 5; D 2.5. This implies the following total scores: A 15; B 13.5; C 10; D 14.5. Therefore, if another kidney of the same type comes along, then A would receive it ahead of D! This solution seems nonsensical. Why should the priority of two patients, for the same type of kidney, *switch* depending on who else is in line? If a priority system means anything, then surely it tells us which of two claimants has priority over the other, irrespective of who else is a claimant.

This "priority paradox" poses less of a problem in a modified version that UNOS adopted in 1989. The revised formula differs from the earlier one in four ways. First, it substantially reduces the importance of waiting time by awarding 1 point (instead of 10 points) to the person waiting longest, and fractional points to those further down the waiting list. Thus waiting time does not count for much, and the priority paradox occurs less frequently. Second, the new formula

---

[8] In the revised version of the formula, high sensitization and waiting time receive less weight than before.

TABLE 2.4
Point Values for Five Patients Before and After Patient E Receives a Kidney

| | Months Waiting | | | | | Total | |
Patient	Before E Deleted	After E Deleted	Antigens	Sensitization	Log & Urg	Before	After
A	10	10	4	1	0	15	15
B	8	7.5	4	2	0	14	13.5
C	6	5	0	0	5	11	10
D	4	2.5	6	6	0	16	14.5
E	2	——	12	9	0	23	——

reduces the maximum handicap given to highly sensitized patients from 10 points to 3 points, though local centers have some discretion in defining what "highly sensitized" means. Third, both logistics and medical urgency are eliminated from the formula. (Doctors may submit special requests in exceptional cases however.) Fourth, points for antigen matches no longer follows a simple linear scheme in which two points are awarded for each match. Rather, the number of points varies according to the specific combination of antigens that are matched (more precisely that are not mismatched). The rationale is to award more points for antigen matches that increase expected graft survival time.[9] The effect of these changes is to give more weight to the efficient use of the resource—as measured by expected graft survival time—and somewhat less weight to urgency, time in line, and the bad luck of being unable to accept a large proportion of donated kidneys.

4. General Principles

Let's step back from specific cases now and consider the allocation problem in a more general setting. Suppose that a number of indivisible units of some good (kidneys, army discharges, etc.) are to be allocated among a group of claimants, the rule being at most one to a customer. We do not assume that the claimants should be treated equally. On the contrary, in most situations some claimants will have a stronger *a priori* claim on the good than others do. The relative strength of a person's claim rests on various observable characteristics of that person—need, contribution, time spent waiting, and so forth.

> CLAIMANT TYPE. The *type* of a claimant is a complete description of the claimant for purposes of the allocation, and determines the extent of a claimant's entitlement to the good.

[9] A six-antigen match trumps most other considerations. If such a match is found on the national list, the kidney must go to that patient (assuming it is suitable in other respects) even though it has to be flown across the country.

A "type" usually involves a description of the candidate in several different dimensions or attributes. In the Army demobilization case, a soldier's type was determined by four numbers: the number of months in the Army, the number of months spent overseas, the number of campaign stars, and the number of dependents. In the original UNOS kidney formula, the patients were rated in six dimensions: antigen profile, sensitization, blood type, urgency, the logistical difficulty in getting the kidney to the patient, and time spent waiting.

A *distributive problem* consists of a group of claimants and a number of units to distribute, where there are not enough (or just barely enough) units to go around. A *solution* allocates the available units among the claimants so that every claimant gets at most one unit. This is called a *zero-one allocation*. A *zero-one allocation criterion* (or *method*) is a formula or process that determines at least one zero-one allocation for every possible distributive problem.

We now propose two basic principles of equity that any such criterion should satisfy. The first is that it be *impartial:* no distinctions should be made among the claimants except insofar as they differ in type. In particular, claimants of the *same* type should be treated equally. This means, for example, that, if there is one unit of the indivisible good to distribute between two claimants of the same type, then an impartial criterion does not give a determinate answer—the good can be awarded to either claimant with equal justice. (In practice one could flip a fair coin to determine the outcome.)

IMPARTIALITY. An allocation criterion is *impartial* if the solutions depend only on the claimants' types and the total quantity to be allocated.[10]

The second principle asserts that distinctions according to type should be made in a consistent manner. To explain this idea, consider two claimants that may be of different types, say τ and τ'. Suppose that there is exactly one unit of the good to share between them. Three outcomes are possible (i) the method awards the good only to τ; (ii) it awards the good only to τ'; (iii) there is a tie and both allocations are declared to be equally valid. In the first case τ is favored over τ', in the second case τ' is favored over τ, and in the third case neither is favored *a priori*. We say that the criterion is *pairwise consistent* if this decision between τ and τ' would always be made in the same way *independently of the other claimants present and how much they receive.*

CONSISTENCY. A zero-one allocation criterion is *pairwise consistent* if, whenever two types τ and τ' share one unit, then they always share it in the same way—either τ gets it exclusively, or τ' gets it exclusively, or there is a tie between them. The decision does not depend on what other claimants are present or how much they get.

[10] Let $\tau = (\tau_1, \tau_2, \ldots, \tau_n)$ be a list of claimants by type and let a_0 be the number of units of the good to be distributed. A *solution* to the problem (τ, a_0) is a $0 - 1$ vector $\boldsymbol{a} = (a_1, a_2, \ldots, a_n)$ such that $\Sigma a_i = a_0$. A *criterion* $F(\tau, a_0)$ associates one or more solutions to every problem (τ, a_0). F is *impartial* if it is symmetric in the variables τ_i. In other words, for every permutation π of the indices $1, 2, \ldots, n$, $\boldsymbol{a} \in F(\tau, a_0)$ if and only if $(a_{\pi(1)}, a_{\pi(2)}, \ldots, a_{\pi(n)}) \in F((\tau_{\pi(1)}, \tau_{\pi(2)}, \ldots, \tau_{\pi(n)}), a_0)$.

Not every criterion is consistent. In fact, the original UNOS formula for allocating kidneys violates this principle. In table 2.4, patient D has priority over A when patient E is present, but A has priority over D when E is not present. Such inconsistencies seem unreasonable. Moreover, they are easily avoided. In the UNOS formula, for example, the difficulty arose because the point value for waiting time depended on the total number of people in the queue. This could easily be rectified by assigning a small point value to each additional month (or day or hour) that the patient has been waiting. The patient's priority would then depend only on data inherent to that patient, not on data about the other patients.[11] The key is to define each patient's type solely in terms of information about that claimant, and then order the types according to some notion of priority.

STANDARD OF COMPARISON. A *standard of comparison* is a list of all types, ordered from highest to lowest priority. Distinct types may have equal priority, in which case we say they are *on a par.*[12]

PRIORITY METHOD. The *priority method* based on a given standard distributes the available units to the claimants who have highest priority.

If the good runs out part-way through some priority class, then any members of this class are equally eligible to get the good. Suppose, for example, that there are four types of claimants—A, B, C, D—and that A has highest priority, B and C are tied for next-highest priority, and D has lowest priority. If there are only two units to distribute, the priority criterion would given them *either* to A and B, *or* to A and C. The tie could be resolved by a chance device, such as tossing a fair coin.

The Army's demobilization rule is an example of a priority method, where priority is determined by the total number of points earned by each type of soldier, and all soldiers with the same point score fall into the same priority class. The kidney formula is more complicated, although it too is based on a point system. The key difference is that, unlike discharges, kidneys are not all alike. To be eligible for a specific kidney, a renal patient must have a compatible blood type and lack antibodies against the kidney, for otherwise it will be rejected. Moreover, the expected survival time depends on the quality of the antigen match between the donor and the patient. In effect, the UNOS formula establishes a *set* of priority lists, one for each kidney. Each patient stands higher on a given list the more suitable the kidney is for that patient, and the less suitable it is for others.

[11] If one wishes to limit the total number of points that a patient can earn by waiting (which seems to have been the rationale for the original UNOS system), one can assign a diminishing point value to each additional month that the patient has been on the waiting list. For example, if m is the number of months in the queue, one could assign 1 point for the first month, .9 point for the second, $(.9)^2$ for the third, $(.9)^3$ for the fourth, and so on. Then no one would ever earn more than 10 points for waiting.

[12] In other words, a standard of comparison is a weak ordering of the types.

It is clear that every priority method (based on a fixed priority standard) is pairwise consistent. Indeed, whenever two claimants share one unit, then it goes to the person who has higher priority among those two claimants. The decision is therefore independent of the other claimants present. (The other claimants may affect the number of units the two claimants have to share, but it does not determine *how* they share them.) It turns out that priority methods are the *only* allocation methods that satisfy the two basic principles of equity.

A zero-one allocation criterion is impartial and pairwise consistent if and only if it is a priority method.

As we shall see in subsequent chapters, these two properties are central to almost all reasonable methods of equitable allocation, whether the goods are divisible or indivisible.

5. Point Systems

The Army's discharge formula is an example of a priority method, but it is a rather special one known as a *point system*. Each soldier is awarded a certain number of points in each of four different attributes, and his overall priority is determined by the total number of points earned. Similarly, a patient's priority for getting a kidney is based on a point system. Not every priority method is a point system however. To see why a point system is not always appropriate, consider two soldiers, A and B. A has been in the Army for three years, has no family, and has not been posted overseas. B has been in the Army for eighteen months, has one child, and has also not been posted overseas. According to the Army's discharge formula, A has 36 points and B has 30 points, so A has priority over B.

Now suppose that both of them are reassigned overseas for one year and that they see extensive combat duty. Afterward both are eligible for discharge. Under the Army's point system, A would still have priority over B because both receive the same number of additional points for length of service and overseas combat. It could be argued, however, that the overseas combat duty worked a greater hardship on the man with the family, and that B might now have priority over A. In other words, there might be *complementary effects* between overseas combat duty and dependents that are not captured by a point system.

A point system is only justified when there are no complementarities between the various attributes. To make this idea more precise, suppose that each type of claimant is evaluated in m attributes or dimensions. Consider any two types t and t' that are the same in all but two attributes. Say they differ in attributes 1 and 2 and are equal in attributes 3 to m. Now consider two other individuals s and s' that are just like t and t' in the first two attributes, that are like each other in all other attributes, but that are not necessarily like t and t' in these other attributes. We say that the priority relation is *separable in attributes* 1 and 2 if the priority between t and t' is the same as the priority between s and s'. If the priority relation is separable in every pair of attributes, it is said to be *separable*. This is a necessary and sufficient condition for a priority to be representable by a point system.

If the claimant types are evaluated in a finite number of attributes, and there are a finite number of distinct types, then a priority method can be represented by a point system if and only if the priority relation is separable.

Within each dimension, a point system may assign points in a linear or nonlinear fashion. In the Army's discharge formula, for example, each additional campaign star was worth 5 points, and each additional month overseas was worth 1 point. This is a linear scoring scheme. The first month of overseas service is valued at the same rate as the fortieth month; the first campaign star counts for as much as the tenth. But this is not always reasonable. At some point one can imagine that decreasing returns set in, and the value of each additional campaign star trails off the more of them one has earned. In fact this is the case for scoring dependents: no credit is given for more than three children. The original kidney formula awarded two points for each antigen matched, but the revised version of the formula is not linear because each specific combination of antigens has its own point value.

Whether or not a priority method is representable by a point system (linear or otherwise) depends on the specific structure of the underlying priority relation. From a pragmatic standpoint, however, there is an argument for choosing a simple format since it is easier to explain and to implement. This suggests that, unless the priority relation is clearly *not* separable, a point system may be a good approximation and command greater acceptance than a method that is based on overly fine distinctions.

6. Participatory Equity

The perceived fairness of a priority formula rests, of course, on the legitimacy of the process by which it is determined. The cases discussed above suggest two alternative approaches to this problem. The one followed by the Army was to survey the opinions of the affected parties. The one followed by the kidney agency was to seek opinions from representatives of various concerned groups—medical experts, hospital administrators, ethicists, donor groups, patient groups—instead of asking the patients directly. In both cases, differences of opinion (sometimes substantial) must be reconciled in order to arrive at a prioritization that represents something like a social "consensus." This is the *opinion aggregation* or *social choice problem,* and it is not a simple one. Indeed, it has a venerable history going back to the French Enlightenment, where it was first studied in the context of designing fair voting procedures.

Suppose that each voter in a group ranks the available candidates according to their perceived desirability or competence. How should the voters' diverse opinions be aggregated into a consensus ordering of the candidates? Two of the major thinkers about this problem were contemporaries in eighteenth-century France. Jean Charles de Borda was a mathematician and experimental physicist who was noted for his design of advanced navigational instruments, and helped design the metric system. Marie Jean Antoine Nicolas Caritat, Marquis of Condorcet, was a prominent mathematician and social philosopher who was politically active during the French Revolution. They represented rival factions in the French Academy of Sciences: Borda was allied with the experimental physicists, whereas Condorcet was a leading spokesman for the purist faction dominated by the mathematicians and philosophers. They were among the first to recognize the importance of the social choice problem and to propose solutions to it. Their proposals are quite practical, and they also play a central role in the modern theory of social choice. We shall briefly outline their methods as they apply to the present problem, namely, determining a single priority list from a collection of individual opinions about who should have priority over whom.

Fix a specific class of allocation problems, such as kidney transplants or army demobilization, and let T be the set of types that are relevant to the good being distributed. In this discussion we shall assume that T is finite. Imagine that a group of individuals is asked to rank the types according to some notion of priority. That is, each individual gives his opinion as to the most appropriate ordering. In some cases the opinions will be highly correlated and there is no particular difficulty in identifying the consensus ordering. (This is the case in table 2.1 for example). In other situations there is no clear consensus, and one must try to balance the various opinions fairly.

Consider the following example. A committee is asked to evaluate three hypothetical patients A, B, C for a kidney transplant. Let us suppose that the relevant attributes are: (i) efficacy (expected years of life remaining if the operation is performed); (ii) urgency (expected years of life remaining if the operation is not performed); and (iii) time spent waiting (in years). The attributes of the three hypothetical patients are shown below (in years):

	Efficacy	Urgency	Time Waiting
A	10	2	1.5
B	5	1	0.5
C	20	5	3

We can well imagine that there will be differences of opinion about which of these situations takes precedence over the others. Suppose, for example, that the committee consists of sixty individuals who rank the three situations as follows:

TABLE 2.5
Opinions of Sixty Respondents about the
Relative Priority of Three Patients

Number of Committee Members with the Given Opinion				
13	*10*	*6*	*13*	*18*
A	A	B	B	C
C	B	A	C	B
B	C	C	A	A

In 1770 Borda proposed a method for finding the ordering that most fairly balances conflicting opinions.[13] The idea is to assign a score to each alternative based on how high the alternative stands in the voters' lists. Consider the ranking of some individual voter, and assign a score of 0 to the last-ranked alternative, a score of 1 to the next-to-last alternative, and a score of 2 to the top-ranked alternative. Then sum each alternative's score over all voters. Thus in the above example the Borda score of A is $13 \times 2 + 10 \times 2 + 6 \times 1 + 13 \times 0 + 18 \times 0 = 52$. Similarly, the score of B is 66 and the score of C is 62. Therefore the Borda ranking is: B first, C second, A third. The general rule is as follows.

BORDA'S RULE. Given a list of voter opinions about the ranking of the alternative types, the *Borda score* of each alternative is the total number of types that are ranked below it, summed over all individual opinions. *Borda's rule* orders the alternatives according to their Borda scores.

Another way of computing the Borda ordering is as follows. Let $T = \{t_1, t_2, \ldots, t_m\}$ be the set of types to be ranked. For each pair of alternative types t_i and t_j let v_{ij} be the number of voters who rank t_i strictly above t_j. The set of all such pairwise vote tallies can be summarized in an m-by-m matrix V called the *vote matrix*. It can be shown that the Borda score of t_i is just the ith *row sum* of the vote matrix. Table 2.6 shows the vote matrix associated with the opinions in table 2.5.

When many alternatives must be compared, it is onerous to require each respondent to rank all of them. In this case one might ask each voter to make just a few pairwise comparisons (i.e., to say which of two types has higher priority

---

[13] The paper was read before the Academy in 1770 but not published until 1784.

TABLE 2.6
Vote Matrix Corresponding to the
Opinions in Table 2.5

	A	B	C	Row Sum
A	0	23	29	52
B	37	0	29	66
C	31	31	0	62

over the other in selected situations) and then to consolidate the answers into a vote matrix such as the one above. The Borda method can then be applied by tallying the row sums. Having voters compare only selected pairs has a further advantage: by designing the questionnaire so that each voter compares types unlike himself, one can reduce the tendency of voters to bias their answers in favor of their own situation.[14]

Borda's method is both simple and natural, but it has a serious drawback, as his rival Condorcet was quick to point out. In the above example Borda's method ranks C second to B even though C *obtains a strict majority over* B. In fact, C obtains a strict majority (31 votes) over both B and A. Therefore, Condorcet asserted, C should be ranked first.

MAJORITY ALTERNATIVE. A *majority alternative* is an alternative that would receive a strict majority of the votes when compared pairwise with every other
alternative.

The above example shows that Borda's method need not rank the majority alternative first. To remedy this defect, Condorcet suggested an alternative method that always does place the majority alternative in the top spot provided that such an alternative exists. The idea is *to choose the ranking(s) that are supported by the maximum number of pairwise votes.* To explain this idea concretely, consider the preceding example. The Borda ranking $B\,C\,A$ contains three propositions: B has priority over C, C has priority over A, and B has priority over A. Moreover, each of these propositions is supported by some of the voters. For example, the proposition "B has priority over C" is supported by 29 voters. Similarly, the proposition "C has priority over A" is supported by 31 voters, and the proposition "B has priority over A" is supported by 37 voters. Hence the total number of votes that support the three paired comparisons in

---

[14] This does not mean that the incentive to misrepresent opinions is completely eliminated. Under almost any voting rule there are some situations in which it pays a voter to misreport his true opinion. In other words, a voter can sometimes obtain a preferred outcome (i.e., a preferred consensus ranking) by misrepresenting his opinions about certain pairs of alternatives (Gibbard, 1973; Satterthwaite, 1975). For a voter to take advantage of this opportunity, however, he must know the others' preferences. This is unlikely when there are many voters or many alternatives.

$B \, C \, A$ is $29 + 31 + 37 = 97$. This is called the *Condorcet score* of the ranking $B \, C \, A$.

Let us now consider a different ordering, say $C \, B \, A$. This contains the three assertions: C has priority over B, B has priority over A, and C has priority over A. The first assertion is supported by 31 votes, the second by 37 votes, and the third by 31 votes. Thus the Condorcet score of this ranking is 99, so Condorcet would say that it better reflects the opinions of the group than the ranking $B \, C \, A$.

CONDORCET'S CRITERION. Given a set of types and a ranking of these types by each member of a group, a *Condorcet ranking* is one in which the pairwise assertions of priority as supported by the maximum number of individuals in the group. [15]

The Condorcet ranking must always place the majority alternative first if there is such an alternative. The reason is that, if the majority alternative were not in first place, then by switching it to first place we could increase the Condorcet score. For example, the Borda ranking in the above example was $B \, C \, A$, which puts the Condorcet alternative (C) second. By switching the position of B and C, we increase the total Condorcet score, because more people support the proposition "C has priority over B" than the converse proposition "B has priority over C."

Condorcet was the first to point out, however, that there are situations in which no majority alternative exists. Consider the example in table 2.7. There are thirteen voters with the following opinions on the alternatives A, B, C:

TABLE 2.7
A Cyclic Majority: A Defeats B,
B Defeats C, C Defeats A

6	5	2
A	B	C
B	C	A
C	A	B

A majority of voters ranks A over B (8), a majority ranks B over C (11), and a majority ranks C over A (7). Hence there exists no majority alternative. This phenomenon is known as the *paradox of voting*.

[15] Condorcet's rule can be computed directly from the vote matrix as follows. Let T be the set of types to be ranked, and let $v = (v_{ij})$ be the vote matrix, where v_{ij} is the number of voters who rank the ith type above the jth type. For each *strict* ordering P of T, the *Condorcet score* of P is the sum of all entries v_{ij} such that τ_i is ranked above τ_j in P. A *Condorcet ranking* is one that has maximum Condorcet score. In some examples the maximum is achieved on several distinct rankings, in which case a tie-breaking rule may be used.

Examples like this show that there is no obvious way to extend simple majority rule to situations with more than two alternatives. No matter how we rank the alternatives *A, B,* and *C,* one of them will have a strict majority over some other alternative that is ranked higher. This observation is at the heart of a key result in voting theory known as Arrow's Impossibility Theorem, which states that there is no method for aggregating individual rankings into a single consensus ordering that meets the following three conditions. *Unanimity:* if all voters rank some alternative *A* above another alternative *B,* then *A* is ranked above *B* in the consensus. *Nondictatorship:* the consensus ranking is not dictated by the same individual in all situations. *Independence of irrelevant alternatives:* the relative rank of each pair of alternatives in the consensus order depends only on the individual opinions regarding that pair.[16]

This result has sometimes been interpreted to mean that there exists no satisfactory method for aggregating individual opinions into a consensus ordering. In our view this conclusion is too pessimistic. What Arrows' result shows is that no aggregation rule satisfies all conceivable conditions. More particularly, it shows that no reasonable rule satisfies independence of irrelevant alternatives (IIA). This suggests that IIA may be too strong a condition. It turns out, in fact, that Condorcet's criterion satisfies a slightly less demanding version of IIA. Let us say that two alternatives are *adjacent* in the consensus ordering if one is ranked just above the other. Notice that, in a Condorcet ranking, two adjacent alternatives are always ranked in the natural way, namely, the higher-ranked one has a majority over (or ties) the lower ranked one. (If this were false, then by switching the positions of the two alternatives we would obtain a ranking with higher Condorcet score.) In other words, Condorcet's criterion satisfies IIA for every two adjacent alternatives; indeed it is just simple majority rule for every two such alternatives. It can be shown that, subject to several regularity conditions, Condorcet's criterion is the *only* aggregation procedure that satisfies IIA in this weaker sense.[17]

7. Summary

In theory there are many ways of allocating an indivisible good fairly among competing claimants, including lotteries, rotation, and compensation schemes. In practice, however, society often allocates a scarce indivisible good by appealing to some notion of *priority* among the claimants. Moreover, there is justification for this approach in that priority methods are the only ones that allocate the good both impartially and consistently over different situations.

---

[16] See the appendix, Theorem 5, for a more precise statement of these conditions and Arrow's theorem.

[17] See the appendix, Theorem 6. We also show that this weaker form of IIA is just a disguised form of the pairwise consistency condition.

The criteria on which priority is based vary greatly from one case to another. A common feature of these schemes, however, is that priority involves a *multi-dimensional* assessment of each claimant's situation. Indeed, we may even speculate that multidimensionality is an essential part of the perceived fairness of such schemes. They also show why various classical definitions of equity— such as Aristotle's proportionality principle, Bentham's greatest good principle, or Rawls's difference principle—are inadequate to describe how society really solves distributive problems. Proportionality does not get us very far when there is at most one unit to a customer: you either get the good or you don't. And even though the good could in theory be made divisible (say by lottery) and then allocated proportionally, this does not seem to be the preferred solution in most instances.

The utilitarian greatest good principle and Rawls's difference principle do not describe how society makes these choices either. Discharge from the Army was not based on who *wanted* to get out most, or who could *benefit* most from getting out. Rather, it was viewed partly as an earned entitlement, and partly as an entitlement arising from the needs of others (the soldier's dependents).

Admittedly, some of the classical principles are partly visible in these priority schemes. The kidney formula, for example, awards points for a good match between donor and patient. This can be interpreted as a form of the utilitarian principle: scarce organs should be put to their most beneficial use. Note, however, that the goal is not to maximize utility (in the sense of individual satisfaction) but to maximize life expectancy and avoid waste. Nor is this the only criterion that enters into the kidney formula. In taking urgency into account, we see a shadow of the Rawlsian principle: the kidney should go where it is needed most. Awarding points for high sensitization has a similar flavor, since it gives a handicap to those who, through no fault of their own, are disadvantaged.

These examples suggest that equity is not as single-minded as the classic prescriptions suggest. Equity is a complex, nuanced, multifaceted idea that can be described as a *balancing* of competing considerations. Just where the balance is stuck is, of course, a matter on which reasonable people may differ. Hence it is important to incorporate diverse views into the design of the allocation formula. The methods of Borda and Condorcet represent two practical approaches to this aggregation problem, though neither is above criticism. Indeed, Arrow's Impossibility Theorem shows that there is no completely satisfactory method for aggregating individual opinions into a social consensus. This is not to suggest, however, that no aggregation scheme should be used. Rather, we would argue that opinion surveys of affected groups have a legitimate place in determining priorities, and that an aggregation scheme may be necessary to balance diverse responses in an objective way.

3 _____

Equity as Near as May Be

> That which cannot be done perfectly must be done
> in a manner as near perfection as may be.
> (*Daniel Webster*)

1. The Apportionment of Indivisible Goods

We now shift our focus to situations where the equitable *ideal* is not in doubt, but it cannot be achieved because the goods are indivisible. A classical case is the apportionment of representation among political constituencies. In the United States, for example, seats in the House of Representatives are apportioned among the states according to a mathematical formula that depends on the states' populations. In countries that use proportional representation systems, the goal is to allocate seats among the various political parties in proportion to their vote totals. In both cases the *ideal* is one person, one vote: every person should have an equal share of representation, and every representative should be answerable to the same number of people.[1] The ideal can almost never be met in practice, however, because of the indivisible nature of representatives. Some states will almost certainly get more than their fair share, and others less, due to the "rounding" problem. The question then becomes: what is meant by "equity as near as may be" when perfect equity cannot be achieved?

This surprisingly difficult problem has concerned statesmen, political analysts, and mathematicians for over two hundred years. The reason is the central importance that apportionment plays in representative government. The difference of just one seat can be crucial in tipping the balance of power in a legislature. Hence the design of apportionment formulas is of abiding interest to politicians. Similar problems arise in many other settings, however. Teachers are assigned to courses in proportion to the number of students who register for them. Medical personnel are assigned to army units in proportion to the number of soldiers in each unit. Computers and support staff are allocated to divisions in a firm according to measures of need or demand.

_____

[1] Proportionality is often qualified by special provisions for small states and parties. Geographical states are usually guaranteed a minimum number of representatives no matter how small their populations. In the United States, for example, every state must receive at least one representative, while in France every department must receive at least two. The opposite holds true for parties: typically a party receives no representation unless it exceeds a minimum *percentage* of the votes cast.

In general, an *apportionment problem* arises whenever a set of similar, indivisible objects must be distributed among a group of claimants in proportion to their claims. Since the historical and theoretical debate on apportionment has been motivated mainly by the distribution of legislative seats, we shall frame the discussion in these terms.

2. Apportionment in the United States

In the United States, the distribution of representation has been an actively debated topic ever since the Constitutional Convention in 1787. The main issue for the Convention, however, was not the choice of formula but the *basis* of representation. What constitutes a state's claim to be represented: the number of its inhabitants? the number of eligible voters? the size of its economic product? the fact that it is a state?

The solution embodied in the Constitution is, in effect, a compromise between these criteria. First, every state has a right to equal representation in the Senate irrespective of its size, and, in the House, every state is entitled to at least one representative. Second, the basis of representation in the House is, essentially, the number of inhabitants rather than the number of citizens or the number of eligible voters. Third, a concession was made to the argument—advanced mainly by the southern delegations—that property also qualifies for representation. This compromise was embodied in the old "three-fifths rule," whereby slaves were counted at the rate of three-fifths of free persons. (This unhappy clause was nullified by the Fourteenth Amendment in 1868.) Even today, the basis of apportionment remains slightly different from a simple head count of the residents. In 1970 and again in 1990, the million or so members of the Armed Forces serving overseas were imputed to their "home" states for purposes of apportionment.

The Constitution did not give an explicit formula for apportioning the House. Article I, Section 2 states only that

> Representatives and direct Taxes shall be apportioned among the several States which may be included within this Union, according to their respective Numbers, which shall be determined by adding to the whole Number of free Persons, including those bound to Service for a Term of Years, and excluding Indians not taxed, three fifths of all other Persons. . . . The Number of Representatives shall not exceed one for every thirty thousand, but each State shall have at least one Representative.

The problem of translating this statement into a concrete method has engaged American statesmen ever since the first census was taken in 1792. Alexander Hamilton, Secretary of the Treasury, and Thomas Jefferson, then Secretary of State, immediately weighed in with alternative formulas, backed up by suitably ingenious arguments. Later, in the 1830s, Daniel Webster and John Quincy

Adams contributed new proposals. Today, the methods of Hamilton, Jefferson, and Webster are among the most widely used methods for apportioning legislatures around the world. By contrast, the method currently employed to apportion the U.S. House is somewhat of an oddity. In this chapter we shall examine how these methods evolved historically, and argue that exactly one of them meets the ideal of one person, one vote, "as near as may be."

3. Statement of the Problem

An apportionment *problem* involves a group of states with given populations, and a whole number a of seats to distribute among them. The population of state i will be denoted by p_i. An *apportionment* assigns a whole number of seats a_i to each state i, the sum of the allotments being a_0. An *apportionment method* is a criterion that determines one or more apportionments for every apportionment situation.

The idea is that every state receive its exact proportional share of seats, known as its *quota*.

> QUOTA. The *quota* of a state is the fraction that the state's population represents of the total population, multiplied by the total number of seats.[2]

Typically the quotas will not be whole numbers. The problem, then, is to find a solution in whole numbers that is as *nearly proportional* to the populations as possible. In keeping with this interpretation, we shall make three further assumptions that hold throughout the subsequent discussion. First, the apportionment method is *impartial*—the only information about a state that matters is its population. Second, if a perfect apportionment is possible—that is, if the quotas are all whole numbers—then it should be the unique solution. Third, the apportionment should depend only on the relative sizes of the states' populations. If, for example, all the populations grow by the same percentage, then the apportionment should not be affected. These assumptions will be assumed to hold without further notice throughout this chapter.

The inherent difficulties in apportionment can be illustrated via the following example. Consider three states with the populations shown in Table 3.1, and suppose that they must divide 21 seats.

It seems evident that A should receive at least 14 seats, B at least 2, and C at least 4. The question is: Which state should receive the twenty-first seat? The issue is not of minor importance. For example, the decision as to whether state B should receive 2 or 3 seats makes a difference of 50 percent in the per capita representation of the residents of that state.

---

[2] Thus if the populations of n states are $p_1, p_2, \ldots, p_n$ and there are a_0 seats to be distributed, the *quota* of state i is $q_i = a_0 p_i / (\Sigma p_j)$.

TABLE 3.1
A Three-State Apportionment Problem
with 21 Seats

State	Population	Quota
A	7,270,000	14.24
B	1,230,000	2.41
C	2,220,000	4.35
Total	10,720,000	21.00

In the next several sections we shall describe the major methods that have been devised to solve this type of problem. By and large, these methods were proposed in response to specific situations by politicians who were familiar with the practical issues involved. When these methods were put into practice, however, certain unexpected defects and "paradoxes" sometimes became apparent that had to be remedied. This led to the construction of new methods, some of which, in turn, exhibited new defects. Through this process of trial and error, several fairness principles have emerged over the years that seem compelling in the context of apportionment. Although no method satisfies all of these principles, we shall show that one method comes close.

4. The Methods of Hamilton and Jefferson

Perhaps the simplest and most obvious answer to the problem presented in table 3.1 is to award the "extra" seat to the state having the highest fractional remainder. This idea was first proposed by Alexander Hamilton, Secretary of the Treasury, after the results of the first census were tallied in 1791. More precisely, Hamilton's proposal was as follows.

HAMILTON'S METHOD. *First give to each state the integer part of its quota. If any seats remain to be apportioned, give one each to the states with highest fractional remainders.*

In the first example of table 3.1 this yields the apportionment: 14 for A, 3 for B, and 4 for C.

Jefferson, who was Hamilton's principal rival in the cabinet, proposed an entirely different scheme.

JEFFERSON'S METHOD. *Choose a common divisor representing the target number of persons per congressional district. Divide it into each of the state populations to obtain quotients, and give each state the whole number in its quotient. If the total number of seats allotted by this process is too large in-*

crease the divisor, if the total is too small decrease the divisor, until a value is found that apportions the correct number of seats.[3]

Consider the example of table 3.1. A natural first choice for the common divisor d is the total population divided by the total number of seats, namely, 510,476. This yields the quotients 14.24 for A, 2.41 for B, and 4.35 for C—which are, in this case, the same as the quotas. After dropping the fractional remainders we obtain the allotment: 14 seats for A, 2 for B, and 4 for C. This only sums to 20 seats, however, and we are supposed to allocate 21. Therefore a smaller common divisor must be selected. If we take $d = 484,000$, then the quotients are 15.02 for A, 2.54 for B, and 4.59 for C. After dropping the fractions this yields the allotment: 15 for A, 2 for B, and 4 for C, which sums to 21. Hence it is the Jefferson apportionment.[4] Jefferson's method gave one more seat to Jefferson's (and Washington's) home state of Virginia. Indeed it gave Virginia 19 seats when its quota was only 18.31!

Jefferson's method can yield even more bizzare results than this. Suppose that, in the above example, 22 seats are to be divided among the three states. It may be checked that the Jefferson solution gives 16 seats to A, 2 seats to B, and 4 seats to C.[5] Yet, with 22 seats, the quotas are 14.92 for A, 2.52 for B, and 4.56 for C. In other words, Jefferson gives state A *more than one whole seat in excess of its quota*. This raises doubts about the fairness of Jefferson's method that we shall examine in the next section.

5. The Bias of Jefferson's Method

Jefferson's method was used to apportion the House of Representatives from the 1790s through the 1830s. Increasingly, however, it became clear that the method systematically favors large states. Consider, for example, the pattern of apportionments to New York as compared to Delaware during this period (see table 3.2).

In every one of the apportionments from 1790 to 1830, Delaware had a quota greater than 1.5, yet in four out of the five cases it received only one seat.

---

[3] In other words, if p_i is state i's population and d is the common divisor we compute the quotient p_i/d and give state i $[p_i/d]$ seats, where [ ] denotes integer part of. If $\Sigma a_i > a_0$ increase the value of d; if $\Sigma a_i < a_0$ decrease the value of d. It is a simple exercise to show that there always exists a value of d such that $\Sigma[p_i/d] = a_0$, where $[p_i/d]$ is the integer part of p_i/d. There is typically an interval of d-values such that $\Sigma[p_i/d] = a_0$, but they must all yield the *same* apportionment. Suppose, indeed, that d and d' are two different values such that $\Sigma[p_i/d'] = \Sigma[p_i/d] = a_0$. Suppose further that $d' > d$. Then for every i, $[p_i/d'] \leq [p_i/d]$. However, by assumption $\Sigma[p_i/d'] = \Sigma[p_i/d]$. It follows that $[p_i/d'] = [p_i/d]$ for every i, so the apportionment is the same in both cases.

[4] It may be checked that any common divisor between 454,376 and 484,666 yields the same apportionment.

[5] Any divisor between 444,001 and 454,375 yields this result.

TABLE 3.2
Jefferson Solutions for New York and Delaware, 1790–1830

Year	1790	1800	1810	1820	1830	Total
New York's Quota	9.629	16.661	26.199	32.503	38.593	123.585
New York's Allotment	10	17	27	34	40	128
Delaware's Quota	1.613	1.782	1.952	1.685	1.517	8.549
Delaware's Allotment	1	1	2	1	1	6

Meanwhile, New York received 34 seats when its quota was 32.40, and 40 when its quota was 38.59. Is this fair?

These data lead us to suspect that Jefferson's method is biased toward large states. Intuitively, the reason is the following. By dropping the fractional part of the ratio p_i/d, a large state gives up only a small part of its entitlement, whereas a small state may give up a major part. For example, if one state's ratio is 40.5 and another's is 1.5, then dropping the fraction—as Jefferson's method requires—results in a 1.2 percent loss for the large state but a 33 percent loss for the small one. In general, dropping the fractional part means that the per capita representation of a small state tends to be marked down by a larger percentage than the per capita representation of a large state. So larger states are likely to be favored by Jefferson's method, and smaller states disfavored. While this argument suggests the direction of the bias, however, it does not tell us much about its magnitude. The *amount* of bias can be defined as the difference between a state's allotment and its quota, averaged over many apportionments.

BIAS. An apportionment method is *unbiased* if, over many apportionments, the difference between each state's average allotment and its average quota is approximately zero.

If a method is unbiased, then, on average, every state should receive its quota of seats. As a theoretical tool this definition needs to be supplemented by an assumption about the likelihood of different apportionment situations. Various models can be imagined: for example, one could assume that the populations are uniformly distributed within certain limits.[6] The definition can also be applied to empirical data. Given a series of apportionments over a number of years, select a specific state and compute the average difference between the state's quota and the number of seats it actually received. Over a large sample of problems, the difference should be close to zero if the apportionment method is unbiased.

Consider, for example, how New York would have fared if Hamilton's method had been used over the twenty-one censuses in U.S. history. Its average

[6] Balinski and Young (1982, pp. 118–28) discuss various ways of defining bias and of modeling population distributions probabilistically.

quota would have been 34.703, and the average number of seats allotted would have been 34.666.[7] In other words, during this period New Yorkers would have received, on average, 99.8 percent of their quota of representation under Hamilton's method. The difference is negligible. Under Jefferson's method, by contrast, New York would have received on average about 35.952 seats or about 3.5 percent more than their due. This discrepancy is not negligible, and confirms our earlier argument that Jefferson's method is biased toward large states.[8]

6. The Methods of Daniel Webster and John Quincy Adams

The concern over the built-in bias in Jefferson's method came to a head after the 1830 census. The issue was particularly important to New England, which was steadily declining in political importance (and number of seats) due to the rapid growth of New York State and the addition of states west of the Appalachians. John Quincy Adams, who was at that time serving as a Representative from Massachusetts, wrote to his colleague in the Senate, Daniel Webster, advocating a new apportionment method that would benefit New England. Adams's proposal was simple: Follow the general outlines of Jefferson's method, but instead of dropping the fractional part of each ratio p_i/d, round it up to the next largest integer. In other words, if any ratio p_i/d is not a whole number, award an extra seat for the fraction.

> J. Q. ADAMS'S METHOD. *Choose a common divisor representing the target number of persons per congressional district. Divide it into each of the state populations to obtain quotients, and round the fractional part of each state's quotient up to the next whole number. If the total number of seats allotted by this process is too large increase the divisor, if the total is too small decrease the divisor, until a value is found that apportions the correct number of seats.*

The political logic of this proposal is quite clear: it turns the tables on Jefferson by giving a marked advantage to the small states. In particular, Adams expected

---

[7] Apportionments by various methods are given for each of the nineteen censuses (1790–1970) in Balinski and Young (1982). Apportionments for the 1980 census are given in Balinski and Young (1985), and for 1990 in Huckabee (1991).

[8] We ignore here the constitutional requirements of at least one seat per state. When minimum requirements are imposed, the quota is not quite the right measure of a state's fair share. The problem is that when every state with a very small quota is given one or more seats, there may not be enough seats left over to give the other states their quotas, even in an average sense. The quotas may be modified to take account of minimum requirements as follows. Given requirements m_1, $m_2, \ldots, m_n$ for each of n states, and an apportionment problem (p, a_0), define the *modified quota* of state i as follows: $q_i = \max\{cp_i, m_i\}$ where the factor c is uniquely determined such that $\Sigma q_i = a_0$. Bias can be measured by computing the expected or average difference between the state's modified quota and the number of seats it is allotted. Using this measure, the bias of Jefferson's method toward the large states over U.S. history is even more pronounced.

that it would give a political shot in the arm to New England. Webster judged it more prudent, however, to propose a solution that was less blatantly self-serving. This led him to formulate the following variant of Jefferson's method.

> WEBSTER'S METHOD. *Choose a common divisor representing the target number of persons per congressional district. Divide it into each of the state populations to obtain quotients, and round each quotient to the nearest whole number. If the total number of seats allotted by this process is too large increase the divisor, if the total is too small decrease the divisor, until a value is found that apportions the correct number of seats.*

Webster's proposal remedies the bias toward the larger states that is inherent in Jefferson's method, but does not go too far by trying to shift the balance toward the other extreme. In spite of his eloquent arguments, however, Webster did not prevail in the 1830s debate. Nevertheless, discontent with Jefferson's method continued to grow, and following the 1840 census it was displaced by Webster's method. Unfortunately, the victory was short-lived. In 1850, a supposedly new method was proposed by Representative Samuel F. Vinton of Ohio, which in fact was nothing but a thinly disguised version of Hamilton's method. By a quirk of political fate, "Vinton's Method of 1850" was voted into law, and remained on the books until after the turn of the century.

7. The Standard Two-State Solution and Its Generalization

Before proceeding with our account of the history, it is helpful to step back for a moment and ask a simple question. What is the most natural solution to the apportionment problem when there are just *two* states? Consider the following example. State A has a population of 8,200,000, state B has a population of 1,800,000, and they are to divide 10 seats. According to Jefferson's method, the solution is that A gets 9 seats and B receives 1 seat (use the divisor 910,000). Surely this is unsatisfactory, however. The natural solution is to round A's quota of 8.2 *down* to 8 and to round B's quota of 1.8 *up* to 2. Both Webster's and Hamilton's methods give this answer.

More generally, for *every* two-state problem the methods of Webster and Hamilton give the same answer. The reason is that when there are just two states, there will be exactly one state with a remainder of .5 or more and another with a remainder of .5 or less.[9] Hence ordinary rounding works. Thus Webster's method is identical with Hamilton's, and the solution is to give each state the whole number of seats that is closest to its quota. This solution warrants a name.

___

[9] If both states have a remainder of exactly .5, then either state may be rounded up (and the other rounded down). Hence there are two solutions in this case.

STANDARD TWO-STATE SOLUTION. The *standard two-state solution* gives to each state the number of seats that is closest to its quota.

The methods of Hamilton and Webster can be understood as two different ways of extending this idea to more than two states. Webster's method is, however, the more satisfactory of the two approaches. To see why, consider again the example in table 3.1. Hamilton's solution gives *A* 14 seats, *B* 3 seats, and *C* 4 seats. Consider states *A* and *B*, which together receive 17 seats. Suppose that *A* and *B* had to divide 17 seats by themselves without any reference to *C*. *A*'s quota of 17 seats is 14.54, and *B*'s is 2.46. Therefore, according to the standard solution (which is the same as the Hamilton solution), *A* should receive 15 seats and *B* should receive 2 seats. But this is *inconsistent* with Hamilton's solution for the three-state problem, which gives *A* 14 seats and *B* 3 seats. The Hamilton solution *appears* to generalize the standard two-state rule, but it does not do so in a consistent manner.

CONSISTENCY WITH THE STANDARD TWO-STATE SOLUTION. *An apportionment method is (pairwise) consistent with the standard two-state solution if every two states divide the number of seats allotted to them according to the standard solution.*

Webster's method is the unique apportionment method that is consistent with the standard two-state solution.[10]

8. The Alabama Paradox

During the nineteenth century the number of members in the House was increased every decade to accommodate new states and a growing population—a process that revealed yet another flaw in Hamilton's method. Following the 1880 census, the chief clerk of the Census Office, C. W. Seaton, computed apportionments using Hamilton's method for all House sizes between 275 and 350. In a letter to Congress he stated that: "While making these calculations I met with the so-called 'Alabama' paradox where Alabama was allotted 8 Representatives out of a total of 299, receiving but 7 when the total became 300. Such a result as this is to me conclusive proof that the process employed in obtaining it is defective."[11]

[10] This result is proved in the appendix, Theorem 10.

[11] Seaton's letter is reprinted in the Congressional Record, 47th Congress, 1st Session, 1881, 12:704–5. A similar anomaly involving Rhode Island had been pointed out after the 1870 census by Representative Ulysses Mercur of Pennsylvania, but it prompted little interest at the time. (Congressional Globe, 42nd Congress, 2nd Session, p. 60.)

ALABAMA PARADOX. A method suffers from the *Alabama paradox* if there is a situation in which the total number of seats increases, all populations remain fixed, and some state receives strictly fewer seats than before.[12]

This phenomenon can be illustrated by the example in table 3.1. If there are 22 seats to be apportioned instead of 21, then the quotas are: 14.92 for *A*, 2.52 for *B*, and 4.56 for *C*. Therefore the Hamilton apportionment is 15 for *A*, 2 for *B*, and 5 for *C*. Comparing this with the Hamilton solution for 21 seats, we see that *B* has lost a seat in going to a larger House! The reason is that the quota of *B* increases less rapidly in *absolute* terms than the quotas of *A* and *C*. *B*'s remainder was largest when 21 seats were to be distributed, and the smallest when 22 seats are available. Hence it does not get an extra seat even though there are more to go around.

The Alabama paradox is peculiar to Hamilton's method. For example, it cannot occur under either Webster's or Jefferson's method, or indeed under any method that employs a common divisor. The reason is quite simple: If the number of seats is increased by one, then the common divisor d must be decreased enough to push up the ratio p_i/d of some state sufficiently high that it gets one more seat. Since this lower common divisor is applied to *all* of the states, none of them can lose a seat in this process. Therefore any such method avoids the Alabama paradox.

Congress was understandably disturbed by these findings, but no measures were taken to revise the apportionment statute for some years to come. Instead, the size of the House was enlarged sufficiently so that the effects of the Alabama paradox would not be felt. After the census of 1900, however, the difficulties with Hamilton's method became so acute that they could no longer be side-stepped. In 1901, for example, a report was submitted to the Congress giving Hamilton apportionments for all House sizes between 350 and 400. Maine kept bobbing up and down between 3 and 4 seats, as shown in Table 3.3. On discovering this, Representative Littlefield of Maine vented his righteous indignation against the chairman of the Select Committee on the Census: "In Maine comes and out Maine goes . . .God help the State of Maine when mathematics reach for her and undertake to strike her down." To which the chairman responded, "If Dame Rumor is to be credited, the seat of [Littlefield] is the one in danger . . . if the gentleman's statement be true that Maine is to be crippled by this loss, then I can see much force in the prayer he uttered here when he said "God help the State of Maine."[13] After this episode, Hamilton's method was effectively abandoned, though the statute itself remained on the books for

---

[12] If there are ties, avoiding the Alabama paradox means that there exists *some* apportionment of the larger-sized house that gives no state fewer seats than it received in the smaller-sized house.

[13] Congressional Record, 56th Congress, 2nd session, 1901, 34 (House), pp. 591–93 and pp. 729–30.

TABLE 3.3
Effect of Hamilton's Method on Maine: 1900

House Size	350–382	383–385	386	387–388	389–390	391–400
Maine's Allotment	3	4	3	4	3	4

another decade. The House was enlarged to 386 members, a number with the property that no state lost a seat. In 1911, the apportionment statute was changed and once again Webster's method became the law of the land. But not for long. That same year an entirely new proposal surfaced that has evolved into the method used today.

9. The Method of Joseph Hill

In 1911, Joseph A. Hill, chief statistician in the Census Bureau, wrote a letter to the chairman of the House Committee on the Census describing an entirely new approach to the apportionment question. Hill began with the proposition that the *per capita* representation in each of the states should be made as nearly uniform as possible. Here "*per capita* representation" means the number of a state's representatives divided by the number of its inhabitants. The question is: what does it mean for these numbers to be "as nearly uniform as possible"?

Consider, for example, the Webster solution to the problem in table 3.1. State *A* receives 15 seats and state *B* receives 2 seats. Thus the per capita representation in *A* is 2.063 per million and in *B* it is 1.626 per million. Clearly, then, state *B* is less well represented than *A*, and the absolute difference in representation is .437 per million. Now suppose that we take away one of *A*'s seats and give it to *B*. Then *B*'s per capita representation becomes 2.439 and *A*'s becomes 1.926, a difference of .513. Accordingly, the transfer is not justified if we measure the discrepancy by looking at the absolute difference in per capita representation. But, said Hill, we should look at the *relative* difference rather than the absolute difference between the two numbers. In the first case *A* has 26.9 percent more representation per capita than *B;* in the second case *B* has 26.6 percent more representation per capita than *A*. Therefore the transfer is justified because it lessens the *relative* discrepancy in per capita representation between the two states.

> HILL'S METHOD. *Allocate the seats among the states so that no transfer of a seat between any two states reduces the percentage difference in per capita representation between them.*

It is by no means clear, however, that such an allocation exists when there are more than two states. The reason is that, in transferring a seat from *A* to *B* in order to reduce the amount of inequality between those two states, there is no guarantee that the inequality between some other two states—say B and C—will not increase. This problem was answered in 1921 by a professor of mathematics at Harvard, Edward V. Huntington. He demonstrated that a solution satisfying Hill's criterion always does exist; moreover, there is a simple and elegant method for computing it. To describe Huntington's solution, we need to introduce the following concept.

GEOMETRIC MEAN. The *geometric mean* of two numbers is the square root of their product.

HUNTINGTON'S RULE FOR COMPUTING HILL'S METHOD. *Choose a common divisor representing the target number of persons per congressional district and divide it into each of the state populations to obtain quotients. Round the quotient down if it is less than the geometric mean of the two nearest whole numbers; otherwise round it up. If the total number of seats allotted by this process is too large increase the divisor, if the total is too small decrease the divisor, until a value is found that apportions the correct number of seats.* [14]

To illustrate how Huntington's rounding procedure works in practice, consider table 3.1 again. Choose $d = 500,000$ as a trial common divisor. The ratios p_i/d are 14.540 for A, 2.460 for B, and 4.440 for C. The geometric mean of 14 and 15 is $\sqrt{14 \times 15} = 14.491$, which is less than 14.540, hence A must be rounded up. Similarly, B must be rounded up because $\sqrt{2 \times 3} = 2.449 <$ 2.460. But rounding both A and B up would apportion too many seats. Therefore the common divisor must be increased. If one takes $d = 502,000$, then the ratios are 14.482 for A, 2.450 for B, and 4.422 for C. Thus only B's ratio exceeds the geometric mean, and the Huntington apportionment is 14 for A, 3 for B, and 4 for C.

It is easy to see that this algorithm is monotonic in the house size, because it employs a common divisor. Hence Hill's method avoids the Alabama paradox.

Huntington christened his technique for computing a Hill apportionment the "method of equal proportions" and thereafter viewed the method as his own invention. He also devoted the next twenty years to promoting it, both in congressional testimony and scientific journals, as *the* most suitable method of apportionment. Moreover, his quest was ultimately successful. On November 15, 1941, President Franklin D. Roosevelt signed into law a bill establishing

[14] The proof that this algorithm yields a Hill apportionment runs as follows. Let $a_1, \ldots, a_n$ be the apportionment that results from rounding the ratios p_i/d in the manner described. Then for every i we have $\sqrt{a_i(a_i - 1)} \le p_i/d \le \sqrt{a_i(a_i + 1)}$. This is equivalent to $a_i(a_i - 1)/p_i^2 \le 1/d^2 \le a_i(a_i + 1)/p_i^2$. Since this holds for every i, it follows that for every i and j, $a_i(a_i - 1)/p_i^2 \le a_j(a_j + 1)/p_j^2$. Now suppose, by way of contradiction, that this apportionment fails Hill's pairwise comparison test. Then there exists a pair of states i, j such that state i is better represented than state j, and a transfer of one seat from i to j would lessen the relative inequality between them. This means that $[(a_j + 1)/p_j)]/[(a_i - 1)/p_i] < (a_i/p_i)/(a_j/p_j)$. But this implies that $a_i(a_i - 1)/p_i^2 > a_j(a_j + 1)/p_j^2$, which contradicts the earlier inequality.

Hill's formula as the statute method for apportioning the U.S. House of Representatives. It has been used ever since. Once again Webster's method was displaced in favor of a supposed improvement.

Two events conspired to deliver Huntington this victory. One was political: in 1941 it happened that the methods of Webster and Hill differed in the assignment of exactly one seat. Hill's method gave one more to Arkansas, and one less to Michigan, than did Webster's method. In that era, Arkansas was a solidly Democratic state, while Michigan had Republican leanings. In switching from Webster's method to Hill's, the Democrats saw a sure way to pick up one more seat. The vote reflected this: all House Democrats (except those from Michigan) voted for the change, while all Republicans voted against.

The second reason for Huntington's triumph was that he had the backing of the lions of the mathematical community, including John von Neumann, Luther P. Eisenhardt, Marston Morse, and others who supported his method over Webster's in a series of reports to the National Academy of Sciences. Their argument was essentially the following. First, the only methods that should be considered are those that avoid the Alabama paradox. Second, of those methods that avoid the paradox, the method of equal proportions (Hill's method) is the only one that is "mathematically neutral" in its treatment of small and large states. But is this correct?

10. Bias

As we stated earlier, a method is *unbiased* if every state can expect to receive its quota of seats on average over many apportionment situations. To test whether Hill's method is unbiased in its treatment of small and large states, consider each of the twenty censuses from 1790 to 1980. First eliminate from consideration all states whose quota is less than .5. These states are favored (by any method) because of the constitutional provision that every state must receive at least one seat. After these states have been removed, rank the states according to population. The largest one-third of the states will be called "large," the next one-third "medium," and the bottom one-third "small." (If the number of states is not divisible by three, the extras are put into the "medium" category). Next, compute the apportionment by Hill's method for each census year. Let a_S be the number of seats that the small states would have received under Hill's method in any given census. Compute the difference between a_S and the total quota q_S of the states in S. The average of these differences measures the extent to which Hill's method would have favored (or disfavored) the small states in a given period.

Over the twenty-one censuses from 1790 to 1990, the results are as follows. The average quota for the class of small states (as a group) was 25.74, and on average they would have received 26.72 seats under Hill's method or about 3.1

percent more than their due.[15] By contrast, Webster's method would have given the small states on average about 25.76 seats, which is almost exactly on target.

This empirical finding is backed up by theoretical analysis. It is possible to estimate the theoretical probability that the small states will be favored in any given apportionment, and the extent of the favoritism. If the populations of the fifty states are distributed approximately as they are now, the small states can expect to receive about 3 percent more than their quotas. By contrast, Webster's method is almost exactly neutral.

Given these results, it seems odd that several prestigious committees of the National Academy of Sciences reached the conclusion that Hill's method is even-handed in its treatment of small and large states. Obviously they could not have looked at the data, and indeed they did not.[16] Rather, they reasoned their way toward a solution. The argument was quite ingenious, and had originally been formulated by Huntington in his 1921 paper:

> Between any two states there will practically always be a certain inequality which gives one of the states a slight advantage over the other. A transfer of one representative from the more favored state to the less favored state will ordinarily reverse the sign of this inequality, so that the more favored state now becomes the less favored, and vice versa. Whether such a transfer should be made or not depends on whether the amount of inequality between the two states after the transfer is less or greater than it was before. . . . The fundamental question therefore at once presents itself, as to how the "amount of inequality" between two states is to be measured.[17]

Huntington examined each of the ways in which the difference in representation between two states can be written (i.e., the *absolute* difference in the number of persons per representative, the *relative* difference in the number of persons per representative, the absolute difference in the number of representatives per person, and so forth). Each such measure of "inequality" between two states can be translated into a method for apportioning seats, namely, distribute the seats so that the amount of inequality between every two states is minimized. Under such a distribution, transferring a seat from one state to another

---

[15] These results are based on the solutions given in Balinski and Young (1982, 1985) and Huckabee (1991).

[16] That task was undertaken by Huntington's rival, Walter F. Willcox, who was one of the country's foremost applied statisticians. As early as 1915 Willcox had enunciated his position in his presidential address to the American Economic Association: "The use of [Hill's method] has recently been advocated. To use it, however, would . . . result in defeating the main object of the Constitution, which is to hold the scales even between the small and the large states. For the use of [it] inevitably favors the small state . . . the method of major fractions [Webster's] is the correct and constitutional method of apportionment" (Willcox, 1916). Willcox reached this conclusion in the old-fashioned (and in those days rather tedious) way of computing solutions to many sample problems. Huntington and Willcox debated the question of bias in the pages of *Science* for over a decade and a half. See the bibliographic notes to this chapter.

[17] E. V. Huntington (1921).

would not be desirable because it would *increase* (or at least not decrease) the amount of inequality between them. Here Huntington was implicitly using the pairwise consistency principle: distribute the seats among the states so that every two states share their allotted number of seats as they would if they were the only two states.

It is not at all obvious that such a distribution exists, and one of Huntington's major contributions was to show that only *some* out of the sixteen possible ways of measuring inequality could be *consistently* extended to any number of states. Furthermore, different ways of expressing inequality sometimes lead to the same method. Huntington showed that in total there are only five apportionment methods that are consistent with some pairwise measure of inequality. Interestingly, *every one* of them had turned up in prior debates on the problem. Four of the five methods have already been discussed: Jefferson, Adams, Webster, and Hill. The fifth had been proposed in an 1832 letter to Daniel Webster by one of his former teachers at Dartmouth, Professor James Dean.[18]

Table 3.4 shows the five methods and the most natural measures of inequality that they minimize. Note that Webster's method minimizes the absolute difference between the number of representatives per person for every pair of states, whereas Dean's method minimizes the absolute difference between the average district sizes for every pair of states. Hill's method minimizes the relative difference in district sizes (as well as the relative difference in number of representatives per person) for every pair of states.

The mathematicians appointed to study the problem by the National Academy of Sciences rested their case for Hill's method on two main points. First, they noted that Hill's method minimizes both the relative difference between district sizes and the relative difference between number of representatives per person. Hence one does not have to choose between these two criteria if one accepts the relative difference as the correct measure of difference. (It leaves open the question, however, of why the relative difference should be preferred to the absolute difference.) Second, they pointed out that the five methods can be ranked according to their tendency to favor small versus large states. Moving from left to right in table 3.4, it can be shown that the methods increasingly favor the large states relative to the small states. Thus Adams is most favorable to the small, and Jefferson's is most favorable to the large.[19] The method of Hill

---

[18] Dean's proposal was to minimize the absolute difference between the numbers of persons per representative $p_i / a_i - p_j / a_j$ for every pair of state. This solution can be implemented by choosing a common divisor d and then rounding the ratios p_i / d at the *harmonic mean* of the two whole numbers closest to p_i / d. (The harmonic mean of two numbers a and b is $2ab/(a + b)$.)

[19] Take any two methods in the list, say Webster and Hill, and apply these methods to the same apportionment problem. If the solutions differ, then Hill's method necessarily transfers seats *from* larger states *to* smaller states as compared with Webster's method. In other words, Hill's method *always* favors the smaller states relative to Webster's method. We express this relation by writing Hill > Webster. It may be shown that the five "modern" methods are ordered as follows: Adams > Dean > Hill > Webster > Jefferson. See Balinski and Young (1982, pp. 118–19).

TABLE 3.4
Inequality Measures for Five Pairwise Consistent Methods

Method:	Adams	Dean	Hill	Webster	Jefferson
Inequality Measure:	$a_i - a_j(p_i/p_j)$	$p_j/a_j - p_i/a_i$	$\dfrac{a_i/p_i}{a_j/p_j} - 1$	$a_i/p_i - a_j/p_j$	$a_i(p_j/p_i) - a_j$

Note: State i has population p_i and a_i seats, while state j has population p_j and a_j seats. It is assumed here that i is better off than j in the sense that $a_i/p_i > a_j/p_j$.

is mathematically neutral, said the NAS committee, because it is the "middle" of the five methods. It is certainly fortunate for this reasoning that the number of methods under consideration was odd!

The flaws in this reasoning are all too obvious. It establishes that Hill's method favors the small states less than two methods (Dean and Adams) and favors them more than two other methods (Jefferson and Webster). It does not show that Hill's method is unbiased in any absolute sense. Indeed, as we have already seen, Hill's method is measurably biased toward small states.

11. Consistency and Priority

CONSISTENCY. An apportionment method is *pairwise consistent* if, whenever two states share a given number of seats, they always share them in the same way independently of the other states present.

Each of the five methods in table 3.4 is pairwise consistent, because each minimizes a pairwise measure of inequality. We shall now show that each is based on some notion of *priority* for getting one more seat, that is, on a standard of comparison.

To illustrate, suppose two states have populations p_1 and p_2 and that they are allotted a_1 and a_2 seats, respectively. If one more seat becomes available, to which state should it be given? We might argue as follows: since state 1 currently has p_1/a_1 persons per district, whereas state 2 has p_2/a_2 persons per district, it seems reasonable to give the seat to the state that is currently worst off. In other words, we give the next seat to state 1 if $p_1/a_1 > p_2/a_2$ and to state 2 if $p_2/a_2 > p_1/a_1$. (If $p_1/a_1 = p_2/a_2$ the next seat could go to either state.) This establishes a standard of comparison among the states in which we hand out seats one at a time, always giving the next seat to the state with largest current district size. It turns out that this is the same as Adams's method.[20]

[20] Let $p_1, p_2, \ldots, p_n$ be the populations of n states and let d be a common divisor that yields an Adams apportionment of a_0 seats. Then $p_i/d \le a_i \le p_i/d + 1$ for each i, from which it follows that $p_i/a_i \le d \le p_i/(a_i - 1)$. This is equivalent to saying that $p_i/a_i \le p_j/(a_j - 1)$ for every i and j which is equivalent to using the priority index p_i/a_i to determine who gets the next seat.

TABLE 3.5
Priority Standard Based on Current Average District Size (Adams's Method)

State	Population	Seats							
		0	*1*	*2*	*3*	*4*	*5*	*6*	*7*
A	4,800	∞^1	$4,800^4$	$2,400^5$	$1,600^6$	1,200	960	800	686
B	1,500	∞^2	$1,500^7$	750	500	375	300	250	214
C	700	∞^3	700	350	233	175	140	117	100

Consider the following example. Seven seats are to be allocated among three states with the populations shown in table 3.5. To apply Adams's method, divide each state's population by 0 seats, 1 seat, 2 seats, . . . , 7 seats to obtain the priority numbers shown.

Now dole out the seats one at a time, always giving the next seat to the state with highest priority. Thus we begin by giving each state one seat, since the first three priority numbers are infinite. The next highest priority number is 4,800, so *A* gets the fourth seat. After this, the next two highest numbers are 2,400 and 1,600 so *A* also receives the fifth and sixth seats. Finally, *B* gets the seventh seat (with priority number 1,500) and the final allocation is: 4 for *A*, 2 for *B*, and 1 for *C*.

Another way of comparing states is to ask which would have the most people per representative *after* receiving one more seat. In other words, we give the next seat to the state for which the ratio $p/(a + 1)$ is highest. For the three-state problem in table 3.5, it may be checked that this yields the allocation: 6 for *A*, 1 for *B*, and 0 for *C*. It turns out that this is identical to Jefferson's method.

STANDARD OF COMPARISON. A *standard of comparison* is an ordered list of all pairs (p, a) where p is a state's population and a is the number of seats it could be allotted. Any pair (p, a) has strict priority over the pair $(p, a + 1)$, that is, priority decreases the more seats a state has.[21]

The standards of comparison for the five classical methods are shown in table 3.6.

Given a standard of comparison, consider a tentative allocation of seats among a group of states. Let a_i be the number of seats assigned to state i, and let p_i be its population. We shall say that state i is *more deserving* than state j if i stands higher in the priority list, that is, if (p_i, a_i) has strict priority over (p_j, a_j). It is natural to consider transferring a seat from the less deserving state j to the more deserving state i. We shall say that this transfer is *justified* provided that j is strictly less deserving *after* the transfer than i was *before* the transfer.

---

[21] In other words, a standard of comparison is a weak ordering of all pairs (p, a) such that p is a positive integer, a is a nonnegative integer, and (p, a) has strict priority over $(p, a + 1)$.

TABLE 3.6
Priority Standards for the Five Classical Divisor Methods

Method:	Adams	Dean	Hill	Webster	Jefferson
Priority Standard:	p/a	$p/\left(\dfrac{a(a + 1)}{a + 1/2}\right)$	$p/\sqrt{a(a + 1)}$	$p/(a + 1/2)$	$p/(a + 1)$

EQUITY. An allocation is *equitable* relative to a standard of comparison if no transfer is justified.

An equitable allocation can be found by the following simple algorithm. Suppose that there are a_o seats to give out among a group of n states. Consider all of the pairs (p_i, a), where p_i is the population of state i and a is an integer between 0 and a_o. Arrange these pairs in a list from highest to lowest priority. Give the *first* seat to the state that stands highest in this list, the *second* seat to the state that stands next-highest in the list, and so forth until all a_o seats have been distributed. This process yields an equitable allocation, because at each stage the next seat is given to the state that is most deserving. Hence no transfer is justified. This process is called a *priority method,* and generalizes the idea of priority method defined in chapter 2. (If there are minimum requirements, e.g., one seat per state, begin by giving each state its minimum requirement and thereafter give each successive seat to the state that has highest priority.) When the standard of comparison has the general form shown in table 3.6 (i.e., the state's population p is divided by some number between a and $a + 1$), the method is called a *divisor method.*

We say that an apportionment method is *impartial* if the solutions depend only on the populations of the states and on the total number of seats to be allotted. It is *balanced* if two states with equal populations never differ by more than one seat. The following result shows that, as in the zero-one case, priority methods are essentially the only ones that satisfy the two fundamental principles of impartiality and consistency.

> An apportionment method is equitable relative to a fixed standard of comparison if and only if it is balanced, impartial and pairwise consistent. Moreover, every such method avoids the Alabama paradox.[22]

The proof of the second statement is simple. If a method is impartial and pairwise consistent, we know it is based on a priority standard. So, if one more seat becomes available, it will go to the state with highest priority. Hence no state loses a seat when there are more to go around. The two principles therefore

[22] See the appendix, Theorem 7. The proof is essentially the same as in Balinski and Young (1982, pp. 141–46).

have important (and desirable) consequences for other aspects of an allocation rule.

12. Staying within the Quota

We may summarize the argument to this point as follows. For a two-state apportionment problem, the natural solution is to round the quotas to the nearest whole numbers. Both Hamilton and Webster agree in this case, whereas Jefferson and Adams give unjustifiable results. Furthermore, both Hamilton and Webster are unbiased, whereas all of the other historical methods either favor large or small states as a class. When we consider more than two states, we find that Webster's method generalizes the standard two-state solution in a more natural way than Hamilton does. Specifically, Webster's method is pairwise consistent, and it is the *unique* method that is consistent with the standard two-state solution. Second, Webster's method avoids the Alabama paradox, whereas Hamilton's method does not. On both of these counts Webster's method is superior to Hamilton's. Nevertheless, Hamilton's method has a feature that Webster's method lacks.

> STAYING WITHIN QUOTA. An apportionment method *stays within quota* if no
> state gets more than its quota rounded up nor less than its quota rounded down.

Hamilton's method stays within quota by definition. However, Webster's method sometimes violates quota. Consider the Webster solutions shown in table 3.7. State A gets only 4 seats, when its quota is 5.013.

TABLE 3.7
A Webster Solution for Four States that Violates Quota

State	Population	Quota	Ratio (d=170)	Webster Solution
A	752	5.013	4.424	4
B	101	0.673	0.594	1
C	99	0.660	0.582	1
D	98	0.653	0.576	1
Total	1,050	7.000	6.176	7

13. The Population Paradox

The preceding example shows that if staying within the quota is deemed an essential property of a fair solution, then Webster's method must be abandoned. Staying within the quota comes at a high price, however, because it introduces other paradoxes. Consider the example in table 3.8.

TABLE 3.8

A Webster Solution for Four States That Does Not
Violate Quota (Based on the Divisor 193)

State	Population	Quota	Webster
A	753	3.984	4
B	377	1.995	2
C	96	0.508	0
D	97	0.513	1
Total	1,323	7.000	7

This is a variant of the example in table 3.7. (We may think of table 3.8 as the result of a new census, for example.) The states and the number of seats to be divided are the same as before, but the populations have shifted: States *A* and *B* have gained residents, while states *C* and *D* have lost residents. Suppose that we insist that the solutions to *both* problems stay within the quota. Let us also require that a larger state not get fewer seats than a smaller state. In the example of table 3.7 there are just two apportionments that satisfy these criteria: (5, 1, 1, 0) and (6, 1, 0, 0) to *A*, *B*, *C*, *D*, respectively. In the example of table 3.8 there are three such apportionments: (4, 2, 0, 1), (4, 1, 1, 1), and (3, 2, 1, 1). No matter which pair of solutions is chosen, state *D* gains a seat and state *A* loses seats. But this is nonsensical. *D* has *lost* residents while *A* has *gained* residents. Why, then, should *A give up* a seat to *D*?

POPULATION PARADOX. A method exhibits the *population paradox* if a state that loses population gains a seat at the expense of a state that gains population.

The preceding examples show that every method that stays within quota exhibits the population paradox.[23]

Recall that a divisor method is one that is based on a standard of form $p/d(a)$ where $d(a)$ is a number between a and $a + 1$ for every integer a. Let us now observe that no divisor method suffers from the population paradox. The argument is simple. Suppose in fact that the population of state *i* goes up, while the population of state *j* goes down. (The populations of the other states may also shift.) Then the priority of all pairs of form (p_i, a) must increase relative to the priority of all pairs of form (p_j, b). Hence it cannot happen that state *i* gets *fewer* seats than before while state *j* gets *more* seats than before.

It is considerably less obvious (but true) that the only credible apportionment methods that avoid the population paradox are divisor methods. To state this result precisely we need to introduce two further ideas. We shall say that an apportionment method is *homogeneous* if the solutions depend only on the

---

[23] Balinski and Young (1982, pp. 79–80).

relative sizes of the state populations and the number of seats to be distributed. A method is *exact* if, whenever all the quotas are whole numbers, each state gets its quota. Both of these conditions make good sense given that the seats are supposed to be distributed in proportion to the populations. We may then state the following.

> *Among all apportionment methods that are impartial, pairwise consistent, homogeneous, and exact, the divisor methods are the only ones that avoid the population paradox.*[24]

A particular consequence of this result and the preceding one is that *every divisor method sometimes violates quota*. More generally it says that no apportionment method satisfies all of the fairness principles that appeal to our intuition. This result is disturbing; indeed to the skeptic it may suggest that the problem has no solution at all. This conclusion is unwarranted. It does pose a practical choice, however. Since not all principles can be satisfied at once, we must decide which method satisfies all of the fairness principles that appeal to our intuition. This result is disturbing; indeed to the skeptic it may suggest that the problem has no solution at all. This conclusion is unwarranted. It does pose a practical choice, however. Since not all principles can be satisfied at once, we must decide which are most important. This boils down to a choice between the population paradox and violating quota. Here two remarks are in order. First, the examples in tables 3.7 and 3.8 might serve to convince the reader that satisfying quota is not really as reasonable as it appears at first. The basic problem is that satisfying quota imposes a much tighter constraint on the large states than it does on the small states relative to the size of the states' populations. Hence, as the populations of the states shift relative to one another—which they inevitably will do—there may not be enough room to adjust the allotments of the large states relative to the small states in a reasonable way.

On the whole, therefore, we would argue that violating quota is probably the lesser evil. This means we must choose a divisor method. We would argue further that Webster's is the most reasonable among the divisor methods . There are three reasons for this. First, it is the only method that yields sensible results when there are just two states. Second, it is essentially the only divisor method that is unbiased in its treatment of small and large states.[25] Third, it can be shown that, when the number of states is large, the probability that Webster's method actually does violate quota is exceedingly small. For example, computer simulations show that, in apportioning 435 seats among the fifty

---

[24] One may replace the condition "avoid the population paradox" with the weaker stipulation that a smaller state never gets more seats than a larger state. See the appendix, Theorem 8.

[25] See Balinski and Young (1982, pp. 118–28).

states, the probability that Webster's method would violate quota is less than one in a thousand.[26]

14. Summary

In this chapter we have shown that no apportionment method satisfies all conceivable interpretations of equity "as near as may be." Nevertheless, there are very few methods that can be deemed to be even minimally acceptable. Lack of bias seems to be a necessary requirement within the framework of one person, one vote.[27] If, in addition, one wants to stay within the quota, then Hamilton's method is the obvious solution. But this is susceptible to the population and Alabama paradoxes; moreover, it violates the fundamental consistency principle. All of these difficulties can be avoided by using a divisor method. And among the divisor methods, the only demonstrably unbiased choice is Webster's. Although Webster's method can violate quota in theory, the probability that this will occur in practice is negligible. As a a practical matter, then, Webster's method satisfies all of the relevant principles.

Thus, unlike the situations discussed in the preceding chapter, one method seems uniquely suitable for solving the problem. The key difference between this case and situations discussed in preceding chapters is that here the equity standard—one person, one vote—is not a matter of opinion, it is laid down by the Constitution. The only issue is how close one can come to it. By applying three elementary principles—impartiality, consistency, and unbiased treatment of large and small—one is led by a process of logical deduction to the conclusion that Webster's method is the most appropriate way to solve the problem.

[26] Balinski and Young (1982, p. 81).

[27] There are some contexts in which a slightly biased method may be appropriate. In proportional representation systems, for example, there is a danger of political instability caused by a proliferation of small parties. One may therefore wish to build in a deliberate bias toward larger parties in PR systems. Jefferson's method is a natural choice in this context, and in fact it is one of the most commonly used PR methods. For a specific justification of Jefferson's method in this setting see Balinski and Young (1982, pp. 87–93).

4

Equity, Equality, Proportionality

> It is when equals have or are assigned unequal
> shares, or people who are not equal, equal shares,
> that quarrels and complaints break out.
>   (*Aristotle*)

1. Aristotle's Equity Principle

Proportionality is deeply rooted in law and custom as a norm of distributive justice. When a firm goes bankrupt, all unsecured creditors in the same precedence class are repaid in proportion to the amounts that they are owed. If the heirs to an estate are willed more than the estate is worth, the probate court would usually divide it in proportion to the various bequests. Should someone be injured by a group and it is not clear who did it, the accused parties may be assessed in proportion to the likelihood that they were responsible.[1] When the industrialized countries signed an accord in 1987 to reduce the amount of ozone-damaging chemicals that they release into the atmosphere, they agreed to cut their emissions in proportion to their current emissions over a period of years.[2]

In situations like these, the parties are held liable for (or entitled to) different amounts because they differ in some respect—contribution, bequest, blame—that can be measured on a cardinal scale. The *proportionality principle* asserts that their shares should be in proportion to their differences. The prominence of this idea in western culture undoubtedly owes much to Aristotle, who anointed it as a universal principle of distributive justice: "A just act necessarily involves at least four terms: two persons for whom it is in fact just, and two shares in which its justice is exhibited. And there will be the same equality between the shares as between the persons, because the shares will be in the same ratio to

---

[1] For example, the New York State Court of Appeals recently held that companies that manufactured the drug DES (taken to reduce nausea during pregnancy) can be held liable for injuries caused to the fetus even when it cannot be demonstrated which firm actually manufactured the DES that the mother took. The Court ruled that damages should be allocated *in proportion to* each firm's share of the national DES market, which is taken to measure the risk they created for the public at large (1989, New York Lexis, 389).

[2] Montreal Protocol on Substances that Deplete the Ozone Layer, 1987.

one another as the persons. . . . What is just in this sense, then, is what is proportional, and what is unjust is what violates the proportion."[3]

For proportionality to be workable, the good must be divisible, and the extent of each claimant's entitlement (or liability) must be expressible in a common metric. These two conditions are quite restrictive. In the kidney and demobilization cases, for example, neither holds: the goods are not divisible and there is no single measure that determines how much more of the good one claimant gets as compared to another. Point systems for allocating these resources determine who has priority over whom, not the ratio of one person's claim to another. Yet when the two conditions *are* met, proportionality seems eminently reasonable—so much so that it is hard to imagine any other solution. In this chapter we shall show that, even in this case, proportionality is not as compelling as it seems at first blush.

To gain perspective, it is helpful to look at cultures in which proportionality is not such a prominent norm. A case in point is the Talmudic law of contracts.[4] Consider the following problem, which was posed nearly two thousand years ago in a "mishna" from the Babylonian Talmud.[5]

Two hold a garment; one claims it all, the other claims half. What is an equitable division of the garment?

According to Aristotle's equity principle, the first claimant should receive $2/3$ and the second claimant $1/3$. The solution proposed in the Talmud is different: $3/4$ to the first claimant and $1/4$ to the second. The logic of this division was subsequently explained in an eleventh-century commentary by Rabbi Shlomo Titzhaki, known as "Rashi": The first claimant concedes nothing to the second claimant, while the second, in claiming only half of the garment, implicitly concedes the "other half" to the first. Hence the first claimant is entitled to *at least* half of the garment. Accordingly, only half of the garment is actually at issue, and it should be divided *equally* between the two claimants. Hence the allocation $3/4$, $1/4$.[6]

---

[3] *Ethics,* book V, pp. 177–79.

[4] The following discussion of Talmudic solutions relies on Aumann and Maschler (1985). See also O'Neill (1982).

[5] Baba Metzia 2a. The Babylonian Talmud is the collection of Jewish religious and legal decisions set down during the first five centuries A.D. It consists of two parts: the Mishna, which are short statements of the law (called "mishnas") that were transmitted by oral tradition; and the Gemara, which consists of commentaries on the Mishna by rabbis of a later period.

[6] Other instances of this same principle are mentioned in the Talmud. For example, if one person claims the whole and the other claims one-third, then the answer is $5/6$ for the first and $1/6$ for the second [Tosefta to the first chapter of Baba Metzia].

2. Claims Problems

The contested garment is an example of a *claims problem:* Several individuals have claims on a common asset, and the claims exceed the amount available. We assume that the asset is perfectly divisible, and that the claims are expressed in the same units as the asset. A *solution* to a claims problem is a division of the total amount *a* among the various claimants, subject to the restriction that no one receives more than his claim and no one receives less than zero.

We shall distinguish two situations: (i) the claims are against specific *portions* of the common asset; (ii) the claims are against a *pool* of common assets.

Case (i). Each individual has a claim or liability against a specific portion of the asset.

Suppose that a field is claimed by two heirs. One document says that *A* gets the whole field, while a second document says that *B* gets the eastern one-half of the field. The documents are equally valid. How should the field be divided? The answer is straightforward. The western one-half of the field is claimed only by *A,* whereas the eastern one-half is claimed by both *A* and *B.* So it is reasonable to award the western one-half exclusively to *A,* and to divide the eastern one-half equally between *A* and *B.* Thus *A* gets ³/₄ of the field and *B* gets ¹/₄, which is the same as the contested garment solution.

Case (ii). Each individual has a claim to some quantity of a common asset, but the claims are not against specific portions of the asset.

Here two further cases must be distinguished: voluntary and involuntary claims. Involuntary claims involve no choice or effort on the part of the claimant; they arise from gift, deed, or inheritance. An example would be a will that reads "Mr. *X* bequeaths $50,000 to *A* and $75,000 to *B*" but there is only $100,000 in Mr. *X*'s estate. Voluntary claims, by contrast, result from a deliberate act, say an investment of time, money, or effort. An example would be a business venture to which *A* and *B* contribute different amounts of capital. Suppose, for instance, that *A* contributes $50,000 and *B* contributes $75,000, and the enterprise is later liquidated for $100,000. How should this amount be divided among the two investors?

Formally these two situations are the same, but this does not mean that they should be adjudicated according to the same principle. When claims and resources are created by voluntary actions, one must examine how a rule of equity affects those actions *ex ante.* The choice of a bankruptcy rule, for example, will affect how much investors are willing to put at risk. Here equity cannot be evaluated in the abstract; one must look at its consequences for individual behavior, that is, on its *incentive* effects. This issue is taken up in section 10, where we show that it lends support to the proportional rule under some circumstances. For the moment, however, we shall focus on situations where the claims are involuntary and ask what equity means when incentives are not an issue.

3. The Contested Garment Rule

Let's return to the problem of inconsistent legacies. Two heirs have been willed sums of money that exceed the total value of the estate. Say that the first heir was left $200,000, the second was left $300,000, and there is only $300,000 available. What is an equitable allocation of the $300,000?

The standard solution in modern probate law would be to abate the bequest in proportion to the claims.[7] Thus the first claimant would receive $120,000 and the second $180,000. This is not the only reasonable solution however. Consider the following argument, which parallels the reasoning behind the contested garment solution. Neither heir should receive more than he was bequeathed. In particular, the first should receive no more than $200,000. By implication the second has an exclusive claim on the $100,000 that is left over after the first has been paid in full. By contrast, the first heir has no exclusive claim, because nothing is left over after the second has been paid in full. The *contested portion* is the excess over and above the uncontested portions, in this case $200,000. Let the rule be that the contested portion is split equally among the claimants. The first heir would therefore receive $100,000 (half of the contested $200,000), while the second would receive half of the contested amount ($100,000) plus the uncontested amount ($100,000) for a total of $200,000. The general rule is as follows.

> CONTESTED GARMENT RULE. Let two individuals have positive claims against a common asset, where the sum of the claims exceeds (or equals) the total amount available. Each claimant's *uncontested portion* is the amount left over after the *other* claimant has either been paid in full or has been paid all that is available (whichever is less). The *contested garment rule* gives each claimant his uncontested portion plus one-half of the excess over and above the sum of the uncontested portions.[8]

It is interesting to study how the contested garment (CG) rule changes when the claims remain fixed and the size of the estate varies. To be specific, let the claims be 200 and 300. When the total amount a_0 is very small, say 10, the CG

---

[7] Atkinson, *Handbook of the Law of Wills*, 1953, p. 757.

[8] Let the claims be denoted by c_1 and $c_2 > 0$, and let the total amount be a_0, where $0 \leq a_0 \leq c_1 + c_2$. The uncontested portion for claimant 1 is $m_1 = (a_0 - c_2)_+$, namely the larger of $a_0 - c_2$ and zero. Similarly, the uncontested portion for claimant 2 is $m_2 = (a_0 - c_1)_+$. The contested garment solution is $a_1 = m_1 + s/2$ and $a_2 = m_2 + s/2$ where $s = a_0 - m_1 - m_2$.

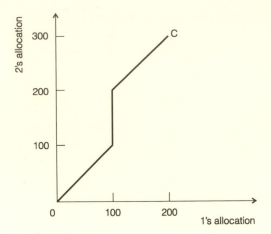

Fig. 1. Contested Garment solutions when 1's claim is 200, 2's claim is 300, and the total amount is between 0 and 500.

solution is to divide it 5 and 5. Indeed equal division holds over the whole range $0 \le a_0 \le 200$. If a_0 is relatively large, say 490, the solution is 195, 295, which means that the loss is split equally. This "equal loss" prescription holds for all values of a_0 between 300 and 500. For values of a_0 between 200 and 300, the solution is to give 100 to claimant 1 (which represents 50% of his claim) and to give claimant 2 the rest. The solutions for every amount a_0 between 0 and 500 are illustrated in figure 1.

In general, the contested garment rule awards the claimants equal amounts when a_0 is smaller than the smallest claim, awards the claimants equal losses when a_0 is larger than the largest claim, and gives the smallest claimant exactly half of his claim for all other values of a_0. In some ways this solution makes more sense than proportional allocation. For example, if a_0 is smaller than the smallest claim, one could argue that the *amount* of the claims is irrelevant. Since none of them can be met, the claims should be set aside and everyone should share equally. The opposite holds true when the shortfall is very small. Suppose that the estate *would* have been enough to satisfy all of the claims except for a small fee that must be paid to the probate court. It would not be absurd to divide this fee equally among the heirs. The idea is that the claimants tend to focus on their gains when the amounts to be distributed are small, whereas they tend to focus on their losses when the amounts to be distributed are large. Under the contested garment rule the psychological watershed occurs at the halfway mark. If a claimant receives less than half of his claim, the claim is moot and he is happy to get something, whereas if he receives more than half, the claim looms large and he is unhappy about the shortfall. Equity requires that all parties be on the same side of the watershed, and that they perceive themselves to be treated equally.

The contested garment criterion can also be justified by procedural arguments. Imagine that the parties run to the court to file their claims. The first to arrive is paid the full amount of his claim (or whatever is available if his claim cannot be fully satisfied), and the second gets whatever is left over. This process is like a "run" on the bank. Of course, there is nothing particularly fair about it, since those who run the fastest have the advantage. It would be fairer simply to flip a fair coin to determine who goes first and who goes second. Even better, they could compute the expected payment that each would receive if they *were* to flip a fair coin. This is a fair *arbitration* of the run-on-the-bank procedure. The reader may verify that this leads to precisely the contested garment solution.

4. The Shapley Value

We turn now to the question of how to extend the contested garment criterion to more than two claimants. One approach would be to convert a case (ii) situation into a case (i) situation by applying the claims to different portions of the asset. Divide the asset into *n* parts, one for each claimant, so that the parts overlap as little as possible. Then divide each part equally among those who claim it. Unfortunately, the outcome is indeterminate because it depends on how the claims are arranged. Consider, for example, three persons with claims of 100, 200, and 300 against an asset worth 500. We want to assign distinct portions of the asset to the claimants so that the overlap between the various portions is minimized. One way to do this is to nest the claim of 100 within the claim of 200 as shown in figure 2. Under this arrangement the first claimant would receive 50, the second 150, and the third 300. Another possibility would be to nest the claim of 100 within the claim of 300 as shown in figure 3. Under this arrangement the amount of overlap is the same as before (200 units are shared by two parties), but the outcome is different: the first claimant receives 50, the second 200, and the third 250. Hence this way of generalizing the contested garment rule is not well-defined when there are more than two claimants.

An alternative approach would be to generalize the run-on-the-bank procedure as follows: compute the expected payment that each claimant would receive if they ran to the bank or the courts, assuming that all lineups are equally likely. This solution is known as the "Shapley value."

Fig. 2. The claim of 100 nested within the claim of 200.

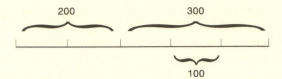

Fig. 3. The claim of 100 nested within the claim of 300.

SHAPLEY VALUE. Line up the claimants in some arbitrary order. Beginning at the front of the line, pay off each claimant in full until the funds are exhausted. The *Shapley value* is the average payment to each claimant over all possible orderings.

We illustrate with a simple example. Three individuals A, B, C have claims of 100, 200, and 300 against an asset worth 400. There are six possible lineups, as shown in table 4.1. The left-most claimant goes first. Thus, in the ordering A B C, claimant A withdraws her full claim of 100 from the common pool, then B withdraws her full claim of 200 from the pool and C gets the remaining 100. The amount that each claimant receives under each ordering is shown in the table. The average over all six orderings is 66 2/3 for A, 116 2/3 for B, and 216 2/3 for C.

TABLE 4.1

The Shapley Allocation When the Claims Are 100 for A, 200 for B, 300 for C, and the Asset Is Worth 400[9]

			Amount Received		
Ordering			*A*	*B*	*C*
A	B	C	100	200	100
A	C	B	100	0	300
B	A	C	100	200	100
B	C	A	0	200	200
C	A	B	100	0	300
C	B	A	0	100	300
	Total		400	700	1300
	Average		66²/₃	116²/₃	216²/₃

[9] The general formula for the Shapley value is defined as follows. Let the n claimants line up in some order. Let P_j be the set of individuals that precede j in line. Let $[a_0 - \Sigma_{i \in P_j} c_i]_+$ denote the amount left over after all of the claimants in P_j have been paid off in full, or zero if the estate cannot cover these claims in full. Then j's payoff in this lineup is the smaller of c_j and $[a_0 - \Sigma_{i \in P_j} c_i]_+$. If P_j contains p individuals, there are $p!$ distinct ways in which they can be ordered and $(n - p - 1)!$ ways in which the individuals who follow j can be ordered. Thus the probability that j immediately follows the set P_j is $\gamma_p = p! (n - p - 1)!/n!$. In this case j's payoff is $a_j(P_j) = \min \{c_j, [a_0 - \Sigma_{i \in P_j} c_i]_+\}$. The expected payment to j over all ways of choosing a set of predecessors of j is therefore $a_j = \sum_{P_j \subseteq N - j} \gamma_{|P_j|} a_j(P_j)$.

In section 3 we argued that if a common asset consists of physically distinct portions, then a fair way to distribute it is to divide each portion equally among those who claim it. This is actually a special case of the Shapley value. To see why, let the claimants line up in some order. Let the first claimant take all of the portions that she has a claim on, the second all of the *remaining* portions that she has a claim on, and so forth. On average, over all possible orderings, every claimant will get an equal share of every portion that she claims.

5. An Inconsistency in the Shapley Value

The Shapley solution is attractive, but has the drawback that it yields inconsistent answers. Consider the following situation. Two people have claims of 200 and 300 against an estate of size 300. The Shapley solution is 100 for the first and 200 for the second. Now let us duplicate this situation. There are now four claimants: two have claims of 200 each, two have claims of 300 each, and the total amount to be distributed is 600. One would expect the solution to be duplicated: the first two claimants should receive 100 each, and the second two claimants 200 each. But the Shapley procedure allocates 116 ²/₃ to each of the lesser claimants and 183 ¹/₃ to each of the greater claimants. This solution is inconsistent with the two-person case.

Is there *any* way of consistently extending the contested garment criterion to more than two claimants? Remarkably enough, such an extension was suggested in the Talmud itself:[10]

> If a man who was married to three wives dies and the kethubah [marriage contract] of one was a maneh [100 zuz], of the other two hundred zuz, and of the third three hundred zuz and the estate [was worth] only one maneh the sum is divided equally. If the estate [was worth] two hundred zuz [the claimant] of the maneh receives fifty zuz [and the claimants respectively] of the two hundred and the three hundred zuz [receive each] three gold denarii [seventy-five zuz]. If the estate [was worth] three hundred zuz, [the claimant] of the maneh receives fifty zuz and [the claimant] of the two hundred zuz [receives] a maneh while [the claimant] of the three hundred zuz [receives] six gold denarii. Similarly, if three persons contributed to a joint fund and they made a loss or a profit they share in the same manner.

Table 4.2 summarizes the three solutions. At first glance they seem to be based on contradictory principles. The first solution divides the estate equally, the third divides it proportionally, while the second is something in between. In fact, all of them are applications of the contested garment rule. To see this, consider any two of the claimants, say the first two. Look at the amounts that they are awarded in some particular solution, say the second one. They divide a

---

[10] In the section on marriage contracts (Kethuboth 93a).

TABLE 4.2
The Solutions (in Zuz) to the Claims Problem in Kethuboth 93a

Amount of Claim		100	200	300
	100	33⅓	33⅓	33⅓
Size of Estate	200	50	75	75
	300	50	100	150

total of 125 in the amounts 50 and 75, and their claims are 100 and 200. This is precisely the division of 125 that would result by applying the contested garment rule to a two-person situation in which the claims are 100 and 200, and the total amount available is 125. The reader may check that in fact *every one* of the solutions in table 4.2 can be explained in this way. That is, every pair of claimants divides the amount that they are allotted according to the contested garment rule.[11]

CONSISTENCY WITH THE CONTESTED GARMENT RULE. An allocation among a group of claimants is *pairwise consistent with the contested garment rule* if every two claimants share the total allotted to them according to the contested garment rule.

Here is how the solution is determined in the general case. Order the claims from the smallest c_1 to the largest c_n. Think of doling out the common asset in small increments. Divide the first increment equally among all claimants, and continue to divide each successive increment equally until either the first claimant receives half of his claim ($c_1/2$) or the asset runs out, whichever happens first. After this, divide each additional increment (if any) equally among claimants 2 through n until the second claimant reaches the halfway mark ($c_2/2$) or the asset runs out. Then divide the next increment equally among claimants 3 through n, and so forth. Proceed in this manner until every claimant has received exactly half of his claim. This happens when the total amount $a_0 = \Sigma c_i/2$.

If a_0 exceeds $\Sigma c_i/2$, the process continues as follows. Give each additional increment to the largest claimant n until the *loss* sustained by this claimant is equal to the loss sustained by the next largest claimant, $n - 1$. If there is more to distribute, divide each additional increment equally between claimants n and $n - 1$ until they sustain the same loss as claimant $n - 2$, and so forth. The reader may check that the solutions constructed in this way are consistent with the contested garment criterion. Moreover, they are the *only* solutions that are consistent with it.

[11] The logic of this passage was first unraveled by Aumann and Maschler (1985).

6. Maimonides' Rule

The contested garment rule is one of several methods suggested in the Talmud for adjudicating various types of claims problems. For example, one of the leading rabbinical authorities in the Middle Ages, Maimonides, argued that the amount should be divided equally among the claimants subject to no one getting more than his claim.

> MAIMONIDES' RULE. Give an equal amount to every claimant or the full amount of his claim, whichever is smaller.[12]

For example, if three individuals have claims 100, 200, and 300, and the estate is worth 400, then Maimonides' solution would be 100, 150, and 150. (Contrast this with the contested garment rule, which yields the division 50, 125, 225.) Maimonides' method is a well-known device for rationing scarce goods. Suppose, for example, that a state enterprise is privatized by offering stock to the public at a fixed price per share.[13] Each person subscribes for the number of shares he wants to buy at the stated price. What happens if the offering is oversubscribed? One approach would be to give everyone a fixed fraction of the shares that they subscribe for (the Aristotelian solution). This has the defect that it encourages the parties to subscribe for more shares than they really want. A second solution is to put a cap on the number of shares that each person can receive. All who subscribe for less than the cap get what they ask for; all who subscribe for more get the maximum allowed amount. The cap is set so that the stock is fully distributed. It may be checked that this is Maimonides' rule. Unlike the proportional rule it does not encourage overbidding. It can, however, be manipulated if the claimants can persuade (or hire) others to subscribe on their behalf. These and other incentive effects will be examined further in section 10.

7. Gain vs. Loss

There are two ways of looking at any solution to a claims problem. One is to focus on the amount each claimant gets, that is, on the gain. The other is to look at how much each claimant fails to get, that is, on the loss. Maimonides' method emphasizes the positive side of the ledger: everyone gains equally subject to no one getting more than he is owed. The same principle could just as well be applied to allocating losses. In other words, the losses would be divided

---

[12] In other words, i's allotment is $a_i = \min\{c_i, x\}$, where the nonnegative number x is chosen so that $\Sigma_i \min\{c_i, x\} = a_0$.

[13] I am indebted to Michael Carter for suggesting this application.

equally subject to no one losing more than the total amount he is owed. Maimonides himself proposed this idea in the following context. Suppose that an
object is auctioned and n people bid. The final bids are $b_1 < b_2 < \ldots < b_n$. If
for some reason the high bidder reneges, the object would be acquired by the
second-highest bidder for the price that he bid (b_{n-1}) and the difference would
be made up by the one who dropped out. On the other hand, if the low bidder
drops out (and the high one does not) the former is presumably not liable,
because the seller realizes the same price as before. Suppose, however, that *all*
of the bidders renege and the object cannot be sold to anyone else. Evidently
they must compensate the seller the amount b_n but it is not immediately clear
how this amount should be divided. Maimonides proposed that every bidder
contribute the same amount, subject to no one paying more than he bid.[14] In
other words, the same principle should apply to the allocation of losses as to the
allocation of gains.

Maimonides' contemporary and intellectual adversary, Rabad, suggested a
different rule for compensating the seller. First divide the lowest bid b_1 equally
among all bidders. Then the lowest bidder leaves the scene and the next increment $b_2 - b_1$ is divided equally among all the remaining $n - 1$ bidders. Then
the next-lowest bidder leaves the scene and the increment $b_3 - b_2$ is divided
equally among the remaining $n - 2$ bidders, and so forth. This solution can be
justified by the following procedural argument. Imagine that the bidders drop
out one at a time. When a given bidder drops out, he causes the price to drop if
everyone who has not yet dropped out bids less (or there is no one left, in which
case the price falls to zero). In either case he must pay the difference between his
own bid and the new lower price. It may be verified that Rabad's solution is the
average that each bidder would pay when all ways of dropping out are equally
likely. In other words, it is a special case of the Shapley value.

Whether gain or loss is the primary focus of attention depends, as we have
already argued, on the psychology of the situation. When it is unclear whether
gain or loss is more important, it makes sense to allocate both gains and losses
according to the same principle. Such a method is said to be *self-dual*.[15] It is
easy to see that the proportional method is self-dual, since if the gains are
allocated proportionally to the claims, then so are the losses. One might suspect
that the proportional method is the only self-dual method, but this is not the
case. In fact the contested garment method is also self-dual. The simplest way
to see this is to refer to figure 1. From the vantage point of the origin O, the
solution path looks the same as it does from the vantage point C, where
the claims have been paid in full. In other words, the loss—as measured by the

[14] See Aumann and Maschler (1985, p. 203).

[15] For any claims problem (c, a_0), the total potential gain is a_0 and the total potential loss is $L = \Sigma c_i - a_0$. Given any allocation method F, the *dual* of F is the method F^* defined as follows: $F^*(c, a_0) = c - F(c, L)$ where $L = \Sigma c_i - a_0$. A method is *self-dual* if $F = F^*$.

shortfall from C—is allocated in the same way that a comparable gain would be from O.

8. Varieties of Equality

On the face of it, there is only one way that a distribution can treat everyone equally. All equal distributions are alike; every unequal distribution is unequal in its own way. Yet the preceding discussion demonstrates that there are many ways in which a division can be said to treat the claimants equally.[16] Conversely, there are many ways in which an allocation may appear to be unequal, yet conform to a more complex and subtle form of equality.

Equality involves three terms:

   (i) the *objects* that are treated equally,
   (ii) the *baseline* from which equality is measured,
   (iii) the *yardstick* of measurement.

Suppose that two individuals receive the amounts a_1, a_2 when their claims are c_1 and c_2, respectively. The *principle of equal gain* requires that $a_1 = a_2$. Here equality means equality of *persons,* the *baseline* from which equality is measured is zero, and the *yardstick* is the amount of money paid out to each. Maimonides' method relies on this principle subject to the natural requirement that no one receive more than his claim. Consider next the *contested garment criterion.* Like Maimonides' method, this concept treats *persons* equally and the measuring rod is *money,* but the *baseline* is the uncontested portion for each claimant.

The dual of Maimonides' method is based on the notion of *equal loss.* Under this conception of equality, persons are treated equally, the baseline is the full amount owed, and the yardstick is money. A variation of this idea is to measure each person's loss, not by the money amount of the shortfall, but by the loss of welfare that it entails. That is, the losses should be apportioned so that everyone suffers the same reduction in welfare from the positions they would enjoy if they received their claims in full. The presumption is that the loss per unit is less of a sacrifice for someone who is well off than for someone who is not. This *equal sacrifice principle* implies that persons with larger claims should shoulder a larger nominal burden, a notion that plays a prominent role in income taxation, as we shall see in chapter 6.[17]

---

[16] This point has been eloquently expounded in Rae's *Equalities* (1981).

[17] Letting U_i denote the utility function of individual i, *equal sacrifice* says that the loss of utility by every two claimants should be the same, that is, $U_i(c_i) - U_i(c_i - a_i)$ should be a constant for all i. In practice it is customary to assume the same utility function applies to all individuals.

TABLE 4.3
Varieties of Equality Implicit in Five Classical Methods

Method	Objects	Baseline	Yardstick
Maimonides	Persons	Zero	Money
Contested Garment	Persons	Uncontested portions	Money
Dual of Maimonides	Persons	Full claim	Money
Equal Sacrifice	Persons	Full claim	Utility
Proportional	Money	Zero	Money

Finally, proportional allocation treats the money itself equally, rather than the persons who claim the money. In other words, the objects of equal treatment are the "dollars" of claim, the baseline is zero, and the yardstick is money—every dollar of claim is recompensed by the same amount. This makes particular sense in situations where the claims are transferable, as they would be in certain kinds of bankruptcy cases for example.

9. Equity, Priority, and Consistency

The preceding discussion shows that equity has a variety of interpretations in even the simplest circumstances. However, there is one feature that all of these interpretations have in common: If every two claimants are treated equitably, then everyone is treated equitably. *Equity is based on pairwise comparisons.* The same holds true for inequity. If a distribution is inequitable, then someone is treated less favorably than someone else, and equity can be increased by transferring some of the good from the more favored to the less favored. Clearly such judgments are also based on pairwise comparisons. In making these judgments, we usually have in mind a standard that allows us to evaluate whether a transfer is called for.

> STANDARD OF COMPARISON. A *situation* (c, a) refers to a person with a claim of size c and a proposed allotment of size a, where $0 \leq a \leq c$. A *standard of comparison* is an ordering of all possible situations.[18]

A standard of comparison has the following interpretation. If someone with claim c and amount a has priority over someone with claim c' and amount a', we mean that the former claimant is *more deserving than* the latter to receive one more unit of the good. A background assumption is that people with equal claims deserve equal amounts, and that receiving more of the good is better than receiving less. Hence if we compare two situations that involve people who

---

[18] Cf. Selten (1978), who uses "standard of comparison" to mean the claim itself.

have equal claims but receive unequal amounts, the one who receives less of the good has priority over the person who receives more.

Each of the classical rules of equity is based on a different standard of comparison. The Aristotelian standard, for example, is the *rate of loss* suffered by each claimant. The larger the percentage by which the claimant is denied his claim, the higher is the claimant's priority for receiving more of the good. The utilitarian standard is the *incremental utility* that each claimant would enjoy from receiving one more unit of the good. The larger the marginal utility for the good, the more deserving the claimant is. The Rawlsian standard is the *inverse of the amount each claimant has*. People with less have priority over those who have more. Under each of these standards, a transfer from a less deserving (lower priority) claimant j to a more deserving (higher priority) claimant i would be justified if j remains less deserving *after* the transfer than i was *before* the transfer.

EQUITY. A distribution is *equitable* with respect to a given standard of comparison if no transfer is justified, that is, if every transfer from a less deserving claimant j to a more deserving claimant i makes j at least as deserving after the transfer as i was before the transfer.[19]

In some cases we can go further. Consider, for example, the Aristotelian standard of equity (rate of loss). When the good is perfectly divisible, there exists an allocation that places all claimants exactly on a par, that is, everyone has an equal rate of loss.

PERFECT EQUITY. An allocation is *perfectly equitable* with respect to a given standard of comparison if no claimant has strict priority over any other.

It is important to observe, however, that perfect equity is not always achievable even when the goods are perfectly divisible. Consider Maimonides' rule, which gives every claimant the same amount provided it does not exceed his claim. The implicit standard here is that A has weak priority over B if either: (i) A's claim is not satisfied and A gets less than or equal to the amount B does, *or* (ii) A's claim is not satisfied, B gets less than A, and B's claim *is* satisfied. Under this standard it is not always possible to distribute the good so that everyone is on a par. Suppose, for example, that two individuals have claims of 300 and 100 against a common asset worth 300. Maimonides' solution would be 200 for the first and 100 for the second. If more became available, it would

---

[19] Formally, the allocation $a = (a_1, a_2, \ldots, a_n)$ is *equitable* relative to the standard of comparison P if $(c_i, a_i) P (c_j, a_j)$ implies that $(c_j, a_j - \epsilon) P (c_i, a_i)$ for all small $\epsilon > O$. Such an allocation exists if P can be represented by a real-valued function $r(c, a)$ that is lower semicontinuous in a for each c. See the appendix, pp. 191–92.

go to the first claimant, because the claim of the second has already been satisfied in full. Thus the first claimant has strict priority over the second. Note, however, that we would not be justified in transferring any amount from the second to the first, because then the second would have strictly higher priority than the first had before the transfer was made. This argument shows that it is not always possible to bring the two claimants onto a perfectly equal footing by transferring resources from someone with lower priority to someone with higher priority. Nevertheless, equity can be achieved *as near as may be* in the sense that the claimant with highest priority has as low a priority as possible among all feasible allocations.

As we saw in chapters 2 and 3, the same property characterizes priority methods for indivisible goods. If the good is doled out one unit at a time to the claimant that currently has highest priority, then taking away one unit from any claimant will certainly give him at least as high a priority as every other claimant. The concept of a priority standard is therefore a common theme in the equitable allocation of both divisible and indivisible goods. Moreover, just as in the case of indivisible goods, the existence of such a standard is a logical consequence of the two fundamental equity principles, which in the present context take the following form.

I. IMPARTIALITY. The allocation depends only on the individuals' claims and the total amount to be distributed.

II. PAIRWISE CONSISTENCY. Whenever two persons with given claims share a given amount, they always share it in the same way irrespective of the other claimants present.[20]

To state the main result of this chapter, we need to define two additional regularity conditions. A rule is *continuous* if whenever the individual claims and the amount to be divided change very slightly, then the solution changes only slightly. It is *strictly monotonic* if whenever the claims are fixed and the amount to be divided increases, everyone gets more.[21] The proof of the following result is outlined in the appendix (Theorem 12).

If a claims allocation rule is continuous, impartial, and pairwise consistent then it is equitable relative to some standard of comparison. If in addition the rule is strictly monotonic, then it is perfectly equitable relative to this standard of comparison.

[20] More formally, F is *pairwise consistent* if, for every n-person claims problem (c, a_0), $(a_1, a_2, \ldots, a_n) = F(c, a_0)$ implies that $(a_i, a_j) = F((c_i, c_j), a_i + a_j)$ for every $i \neq j$.

[21] Formally, a claims allocation method $F(c, a_0)$ is *continuous* if, whenever a sequence of claims problems (c^k, a_0^k) converges to a claims problem (c, a_0), the solutions $F(c^k, a_0^k)$ converge to $F(c, a_0)$.

10. Incentive Effects

In this section we return to an issue that was raised in Section 2, namely, the incentive effects of an allocation rule on the claimants' behavior. This is an important consideration when the claims are generated by voluntary action. Suppose, for example, that Maimonides' criterion were used to pay back the creditors in a bankruptcy filing. Every creditor would receive an equal amount of money up to the full amount he is owed. Unfortunately, this rule might lead to serious distortions in investment behavior, because it would always be safest to be the smallest creditor. It would also create an incentive for creditors to find bogus partners. For example, instead of contributing x dollars to an enterprise, it would make more sense to find a partner and each contribute $x/2$ dollars, for this would lead to a higher rate of repayment in case the enterprise failed. (Or one could wait until after the enterprise fails and then sell off half of one's credit to a friend.) When claims are transferrable, it is clearly desirable to use an allocation rule that is not subject to this type of manipulation.

COLLUSION-PROOF. A claims allocation rule is *collusion-proof* if consolidating the claims of several individuals into one claim does not change the total amount that these claimants receive.

The following result is due to O'Neill (1982), and is proved in the appendix (Theorem 14).

The proportional rule is the unique claims allocation rule that is impartial and collusion-proof.

This result does not say that the proportional rule is completely immune from manipulation. For example, if the claims merely represent *assertions* by the claimants about how much they deserve, then under the proportional rule it is clearly desirable to inflate one's claim as much as possible. When the claims are both verifiable and transferable, however, it makes sense to use a rule that does not encourage the splitting or consolidation of claims among various groups of claimants. Under these circumstances the proportional rule is the most appropriate solution.

11. Summary

In this chapter we have attempted to disentangle three distinct ideas: equal treatment, proportional treatment, and equitable treatment. Equal treatment is an unambiguous and desirable ideal when everyone is similarly situated (equal treatment of equals). But people are often not similarly situated. When they differ—in contribution, need, ability, or blame —equal treatment is generally not appropriate. What then do we mean by the equitable treatment of *dissimilar* individuals? Aristotle's answer is that they be treated commensurate with their differences. For this principle to be workable, the differences must be expressible in a common metric and the good must be divisible. Yet even under these circumstances proportionality is not the only plausible way of treating the claimants equitably. Talmudic solutions, for example, place greater emphasis on treating the claimants equally *subject to* the constraints imposed by their differences. In the abstract this is a perfectly reasonable approach. Moreover, it is sometimes used in everyday situations, for example, in rationing scarce goods by subscription. In other contexts it may have undesirable incentive effects. Maimonides' method would be inappropriate as a bankruptcy rule, for example, because it benefits smaller investors at the expense of larger ones, and hence distorts investment decisions. When entitlement is created by verifiable and fungible claims, the proportional rule makes the most sense because it treats the *units of claim* equally, rather than the persons who possess them.

The larger theme of the chapter is that equity is a subtler concept than either parity or proportionality. What can be said is that equity formulas are usually based, either implicitly or explicitly, on a standard of comparison that ranks the various claimants according to their relative desert. This is the common thread that ties together all of the problems of fair division we have examined so far, and that continue to be the unifying theme in the chapters to follow.

5

Cost Sharing

Cooperation is not a sentiment—it is an economic
necessity.
(*Charles Steinmetz*)

1. Sharing Gains from Cooperation

Whenever a group undertakes a joint enterprise, the prospective benefits are a
form of new property that the group's members must decide how to distribute
for the enterprise to be viable. Firms that enter into a joint production contract,
for example, must agree on how to split the proceeds of their cooperation.
Doctors who share an office must apportion the common expenses of rent,
secretarial help, and equipment. Decisions like these are often reached by direct
negotiation among the parties, and we would certainly not expect any one of
them to agree to an arrangement that leaves him worse off than he was before.
Within these participation constraints, however, many agreements are still
possible. Equity principles are the means by which the parties coordinate on a
particular solution given the constraints imposed by economic rationality. Pure
equity principles, however—like parity and proportionality—do not necessarily satisfy these constraints. How can these principles be modified to give the
parties an incentive to cooperate? This is the subject of the present chapter.

2. A Cost-Sharing Problem between Two Towns

Consider the following illustrative example. Two nearby towns are considering
whether to build a joint water distribution system. Town A could build its own
facility for $11 million without any assistance from B. Town B could build a
separate facility for $7 million without any cooperation from A. A facility that
jointly serves both communities would cost $15 million (see fig. 4). Clearly it
makes economic sense for them to cooperate, since they can jointly save $3
million. These cost-savings represent the common property created by their
joint activity, but for cooperation to occur they must agree on how to divide it.
What equity principles might guide their discussions?

One obvious solution is to share the costs equally ($7.5 million for each). The
argument for equal division is that each town is a corporate entity with the

power to enter into a contract. Since they are equal partners in the enterprise, they should shoulder an equal burden. This argument ignores the possibility that the towns are unequal in other relevant respects however. Suppose, for instance, that town A has 36,000 residents and town B has 12,000 residents. Equal division between the towns implies that each resident of A pays only one-third as much as each resident of B, even though they are served by the same system. This might be considered unfair. An alternate solution would be to spread the costs equally among the persons rather than the towns. Divide the total cost of $15 million by the 48,000 persons served by the system, and assess each individual $312.50. Under this arrangement, town A would pay $11.25 million and town B would pay $3.75 million.

Unfortunately, neither of these proposals takes into account the opportunity costs of the parties. B is not likely to agree to equal division, since $7.5 million exceeds the cost of building its own system. Similarly, A is not likely to agree to equal division per capita, since $11.25 exceeds the costs of building its own system. The problem is to find an equitable division that induces the parties to cooperate. How might this be done?

The answer is to focus on the amounts that the parties *save* rather than the amounts that they pay. If everyone saves relative to their opportunity costs, then everyone clearly has an incentive to participate. Three solutions immediately suggest themselves. One is to divide the $3 million in savings equally among the towns. In this case town A would pay $11 - 1.5 = $9.5 million and town B would pay $7 - 1.5 = $5.5 million. A second, and perhaps more plausible, solution is to divide the savings equally among the residents. Thus everyone would save $62.50, and the total cost assessments would be $8.75 million for town A and $6.25 million for town B. A third possibility is to allocate the savings in proportion to each town's opportunity cost. This yields a payment of $9.17 million for A and $5.83 million for B. (Note that this is the same thing as allocating total cost in proportion to each town's opportunity cost.)

All three of these approaches give the parties an incentive to cooperate, because each town realizes positive savings. The set of all divisions of $15 million with this property is known as the *core* of the cost-sharing game. It consists of all divisions in which A pays at most $11 million and B at most $7 million. Geometrically the core can be represented as a line segment, as shown in figure 4.

3. A Cost-Sharing Problem among Three Towns

Now let's complicate matters by introducing a third town C. Suppose that it would cost $8 million for C to build its own system, whereas to include C in the joint system with A and B would cost an additional $5 million. Clearly it makes economic sense to include C in the project: The total cost if none of the parties

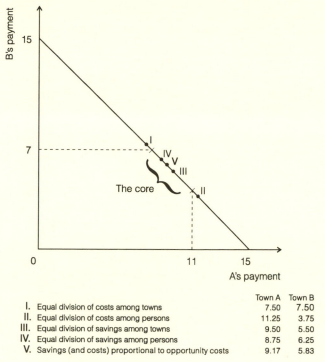

	Town A	Town B
I. Equal division of costs among towns	7.50	7.50
II. Equal division of costs among persons	11.25	3.75
III. Equal division of savings among towns	9.50	5.50
IV. Equal division of savings among persons	8.75	6.25
V. Savings (and costs) proportional to opportunity costs	9.17	5.83

Fig. 4. Five equitable divisions of costs among two towns and their relation to the core.

cooperate is $11 + $7 + $8 = $26 million, whereas the cost is $20 million if they do cooperate. Thus the potential saving is $6 million. Assume that A and C can build their own system for $14 million (a savings of $5 million over their opportunity costs), whereas B and C can build their own system for $13 million (a savings of $2 million over their opportunity costs). The cost associated with each pattern of cooperation is shown in table 5.1.

Let's imagine that the towns divide total costs in proportion to their opportunity costs. Then the allocation is $8.46 million for A, $5.38 million for B, and $6.15 million for C. This solution is not likely to be accepted by A and C, however, because together they are charged $14.61 million, whereas they could build their own joint system for $14 million. In other words, the proportional allocation does not respect the opportunity costs of *groups* of participants, even though it does not exceed the opportunity cost of any single party.

The *core* of this cost game is the set of all divisions of $20 million such that no town, or group of towns, pays more than its opportunity cost. In other words, a core allocation is one that gives every party, and every subset of parties, an incentive to participate. The core is illustrated in figure 5. Each corner of the

TABLE 5.1
Costs of Serving Various Combinations of Three Towns
(in Millions of Dollars)

Grouping of the Towns	Opportunity Costs	Total
A, B, C	11 + 7 + 8	26
A + {B,C}	11 + 13	24
{A,B} + C	15 + 8	23
{A,C} + B	14 + 7	21
{A,B,C}	20	20

large triangle represents a solution in which one of the towns is assessed all of
the costs ($20 million), and the others pay nothing. Each interior point of the
triangle represents a solution in which the towns split the $20 million in some
manner. For example, the point S represents equal division of savings. The
perpendicular distance from S to the base of the triangle is 9 units (A's payment), the perpendicular distance from S to the left-hand side of the triangle is
5 units (B's payment), and the perpendicular distance from S to the right-hand
side of the triangle is 6 units (C's payment). The locations of the other points are
computed similarly. As the diagram shows, none of the three rules discussed in
the preceding section is in the core. Is there some way to treat the parties
equitably and still give them an incentive to cooperate?

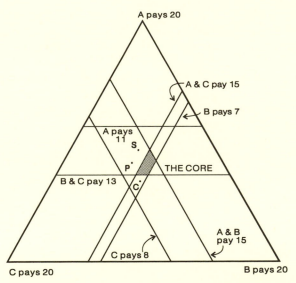

Fig. 5. Three ways of dividing costs among three towns. None is in the
core.

4. The Cooperative Game Model

Before attempting to answer this question let us first formulate the problem more generally. Consider a group of parties who want to divide the cost of a common facility. Each party $i = 1, 2, \ldots, n$ has a *stand-alone cost* $c(i)$ that it would incur if it did not cooperate with the others. Similarly, each subgroup S of parties has a stand-alone cost $c(S)$ that they would incur (as a group) by cooperating with each other, but not with the remaining parties. The function $c(S)$ is defined for all subsets of parties and is called the *cost function or cost-sharing game*. The cost of serving no one, $c(\phi)$, is zero.[1]

> COST SHARING RULE. A *cost sharing rule* allocates the total cost of a project among the members of a group for every possible specification of the cost function.[2]

> CORE. An allocation is in the *core* of the cost-sharing game if no participant, or group of participants, pays more than its stand-alone cost. In other words, a cost allocation is in the core if the cost-savings of every subgroup of participants is nonnegative.[3]

As figure 5 shows, the core of a cost-sharing game may be quite small compared to the set of all possible allocations. In fact, there are perfectly plausible cost-sharing games that have no core distributions. Consider the following variation of the municipal cost-sharing game:

$$c(A) = 11, \qquad c(B) = 7, \qquad c(C) = 8,$$
$$c(A, B) = 15, \qquad c(A, C) = 13, \qquad c(B, C) = 10,$$
$$c(A, B, C) = 20$$

For a distribution to be in the core of this game, A and C together cannot be charged more than 13. Since A, B, and C together pay 20, it follows that B must pay at least 7. Similarly, B and C together cannot be charged more than 10, so A must pay at least 10. Thus together A and B pay at least 17. But this violates the core condition that A and B together pay no more than 15. Hence there is no core allocation.

---

[1] In many applications the cost function is also *subadditive*, that is, for every two disjoint subsets S and S', $c(S) + c(S') \geq c(S \cup S')$. This condition follows if we interpret $c(S \cup S')$ to be the least cost of serving the members of $S \cup S'$, because one way of doing this is to divide them into the two subgroups S and S'.

[2] A *cost sharing rule* is a function $F(c, N)$, defined for every finite set $N = \{1, 2, \ldots, n\}$, and every cost function c on N such that $F(c, N) = (a_1, a_2, \ldots, a_n)$ where $a(N) = \Sigma_{i \in N} a_i = c(N)$ and a_i is the cost allocated to participant i.

[3] The core of a cost function c, written Core(c), is the set of all vectors $(a_1, a_2, \ldots, a_n)$ such that $a(N) = c(N)$ and $a(S) \leq c(S)$ for every subset S of N.

5. The Tennessee Valley Authority

Let's apply these ideas to an actual case. The Tennessee Valley Authority was an ambitious redevelopment project undertaken by the U.S. federal government during the 1930s to control flooding, provide hydroelectric power, and improve the navigational and recreational resources of the Tennessee River Basin through a series of multiple-purpose reservoirs. Economists charged with analyzing the costs and benefits of this project were concerned about how to allocate the common costs among the three purposes. The ideas that they developed have since become standard principles in costing public works projects.

The cost-benefit analysis of such a project can be divided into two parts. First we must decide whether the project should be undertaken at all, and if so on what scale. This is the *efficiency* issue. The second question is how to distribute the costs of the optimal-scale enterprise. This is the *equity* issue. For example, to estimate the optimal scale of the TVA project, we would first estimate the joint demand (as a function of price) for the three services provided by the project—navigation, flood control, and power. Then we would find the project scale that maximizes some measure of social welfare, such as consumers' surplus.[4]

In practice, however, it is difficult to carry out a detailed optimization of this type, because information about the demand for jointly produced services is unavailable or subject to large estimation errors. The customary approach is to carry out the analysis for *target levels* of the planning variables that are thought to be approximately optimal. In other words, instead of estimating demand and cost curves, the analyst makes "point" estimates of benefits and costs.

This was essentially the approach adopted by the TVA economists. They first determined target levels at which navigation, flood control, and power should be provided. Then they estimated the least cost of constructing a reservoir system that would meet the targets. For example, they calculated that providing navigation (objective 1) and flood control (objective 2), but not power (objective 3), would require a system costing $c(1, 2) = \$301,607,000$. To provide just flood control would require a smaller investment of $c(2) = \$140,826,000$, and so forth. For each subset S of the three objectives the economists estimated the stand-alone cost $c(S)$ of meeting those objectives at the targeted levels. This cost function is shown in table 5.2, and its core is illustrated in figure 6.

The concept of the core was, in fact, first proposed in connection with the TVA case by J. S. Ransmeier (1942). He suggested the following criteria for evaluating a cost allocation method:

> The method should have a reasonable logical basis. . . . It should not result in charging any objective with a greater investment than would suffice for its develop-

---

[4] This approach is known as "Ramsey pricing" (Ramsey, 1927; Manne, 1952; Baumol and Bradford, 1970).

TABLE 5.2
Cost Function Estimated by the TVA for Navigation (1), Flood Control (2), and Power Generation (3), in Thousands of 1938 Dollars

Services	φ	{1}	{2}	{3}	{1,2}	{1,3}	{2,3}	{1,2,3}
Cost	0	163,520	140,826	250,096	301,607	378,821	367,370	412,584

Source: Ransmeier (1942, p. 329).

ment at an alternate single purpose site. Finally, it should not charge any two or more objectives with a greater investment than would suffice for alternate dual or multiple purpose development. (Ransmeier, 1942, p. 220.)

In other words, the costs allocated to the various objectives should not exceed the stand-alone cost of any *combination* of objectives. This is precisely the definition of the core.

The core can be interpreted in two ways. On the one hand, it provides an incentive for the parties to cooperate. If each aspect of the project (each objective) benefits a distinct constituency or group, and if everyone's consent is required for the project to go forward, then the group will not agree on a cost-sharing formula unless it is in their interest to do so, that is, unless it leaves all of them better off than they would otherwise be. If an allocation is not in the core of the cost function, however, there is some subset of parties that collectively pays more than the cost of serving them alone (i.e., more than their stand-alone cost). They could do better by withdrawing from the joint project, forming their own smaller consortium, and providing the required services for themselves at

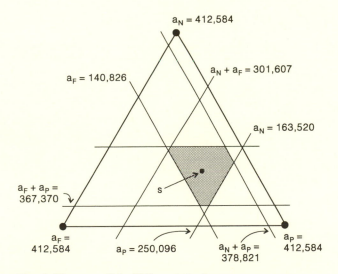

Fig. 6. The core of the TVA cost-sharing game.

lower total cost. In this sense the core is a *strategic* criterion that provides an incentive for the agents to cooperate.

The core may also be interpreted, however, as a criterion of *equity*. Consider a particular objective such as hydropower. The incremental cost of providing hydropower is the difference between the cost of the project with hydropower and the cost of the project without it, that is, \$412,584,000 − 301,607,000 = \$110,977,000. If hydropower (i.e., the users of hydropower) are charged less than this amount, we could say that hydropower is being subsidized by the other objectives. More generally, a subset S is *subsidized* if collectively the members of S are not charged enough to cover the incremental cost of serving them.

> SUBSIDY FREE. The *incremental cost* of serving a subset S is the difference between the cost of serving everyone and the cost of serving everyone but the members of S. A cost allocation is *subsidy-free* if no subset is charged less than its incremental cost.[5]

It is easy to see that subsidy-free charges exist for any cost function, because *any* charges are subsidy-free so long as they are high enough. The goal, however, is to cover total costs exactly while not subsidizing any group. This is equivalent to requiring that the charges be in the core of the cost-sharing game.[6]

6. The Decomposition Principle

Now let's consider a different type of example. Suppose that four homeowners want to build an electrical line to connect their houses with an existing trunk power line, as shown in fig. 7.

A reasonable way to proceed is to decompose the cost of the project into its constituent parts. Everyone uses the line from the tie-in point O to the first house A. Everyone except A shares the line from A to B. Only D uses the leg BD and only C uses the line BC. Assume that all homeowners who share a given line divide the cost equally. Then the total cost allocation would be as shown in the right-hand column of table 5.3.

In the general case, suppose that n people share a common facility that consists of m distinct parts or elements. The cost of element j is c_j. The cost of serving a subset S of users is the total cost of all the elements that they use. In other words, $c(S) = \Sigma c_j$, where the sum is over all elements j such that at least one member of S uses j. In this case we say that the cost function *decomposes* into distinct elements.

---

[5] This is also known as the "incremental cost test" (Zajac, 1978).

[6] By assumption, costs are fully distributed: $a(N) = c(N)$. If the allocation is subsidy-free, then $a(N - S) \geq c(N) - c(S)$ for every subset S. By subtracting the second inequality from the first equality it follows that $a(S) \leq c(S)$ for every subset S, so a is in the core.

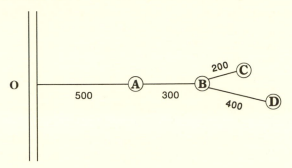

Fig. 7. Cost of connecting four houses to a trunk power line.

TABLE 5.3
Decomposition of Electrical Line Costs

		Cost Elements				
		OA	AB	BC	BD	Charge
Persons	A	125				125
	B	125	100			225
	C	125	100	200		425
	D	125	100		400	625
	Total Cost	500	300	200	400	1,400

DECOMPOSITION PRINCIPLE. If a cost function decomposes into distinct cost elements, divide the cost of each element equally among those who use it. The charge to each user is his share of each cost element, summed over all elements.[7]

If a cost function decomposes into distinct elements, the decomposition principle yields a solution that is in the core.

The proof is straightforward. The stand-alone cost of any coalition of parties *S* is the total cost of all elements used by one or more members of *S*. In the full group, the cost of each of these elements is borne by all parties that use it (including the members of *S*). Furthermore, the members of *S* pay nothing for the elements they do not use. Hence *S*, as a group, pays no more than its stand-alone cost. Therefore the cost allocation is in the core of the cost game.

The decomposition principle makes good sense in a variety of situations. Consider, for example, the problem of setting landing fees at a public airport.

[7] In other words, the charge to user i is $a_i = \Sigma c_j / s_j$, where s_j denotes the number of users of j and the sum is over all elements j that i uses.

Assume for simplicity that the landing fees cover just the cost of building and maintaining the runways, and that other common costs (e.g., terminal facilities) are covered by other types of fees. Equity demands that the landing fees reflect the burden that each type of aircraft puts on the system. Jumbo jets should be assessed more than twin-engine Cessnas, for example, because larger planes require longer runways. Suppose that there are m different types of aircraft that use the airport. Order them according to the length of runway that they need. Type 1 needs a short runway, type 2 needs a somewhat longer runway, and so forth. Schematically we can think of the runway as being divided into m sections. The first section is used by all planes. The second is used by all but the smallest planes, the third by all but the smallest two types of planes, and so forth. Let the cost of the first section be c_1, the cost of the second section c_2, and so forth. According to the decomposition principle, we would divide the cost of the first section equally among all planes, the cost of the second section equally among all planes except those of the first type, and so on. The result is a system of charges that reflects the amount that each aircraft contributes to total cost. Table 5.4 shows an example based on cost data from Birmingham Airport in 1968–69.

7. The Shapley Value

The decomposition principle involves three distinct ideas. The first is that those who do not use a cost element should not be charged for it. The second is that

TABLE 5.4
Aircraft Landings, Runway Costs, and the Shapley Value
for Birmingham Airport, 1968–69

Aircraft Type	Number of Landings	Incremental Cost (£)	Shapley Charge for Landing (£)
Fokker Friendship 27	42	65,899	4.86
Viscount 800	9,555	10,826	5.66
Hawker Siddeley Trident	288	18,475	10.30
Britannia	303	2,000	10.85
Caravelle VI R	151	236	10.92
BAC 111 (500)	1,315	706	11.13
Vanguard 953	505	4,354	13.40
Comet 4B	1,128	2,353	15.07
Britannia 300	151	8,473	44.80
Corvair Corronado	112	2,118	60.61
Boeing 707	22	2,236	162.24
Total	13,572	117,676	

everyone who uses a given cost element should be charged equally for it.[8] The third is that the results of different cost allocations can be added together. We shall now show how to apply these ideas to any cost-sharing situation, whether or not it actually decomposes into distinct cost elements.

Consider a group of parties N called *players* who may cooperate in a joint project whose total cost is $c(N)$. For each coalition (subset) S of players, let $c(S)$ be the total cost that the players in S would incur if they carried out the project by themselves. A player i is a *dummy* if he contributes no additional cost to any coalition, that is, if the cost of serving any subset of players is the same whether i is included or not. The three aspects of the decomposition principle can then be expressed as follows.

I. DUMMY. A dummy player is charged nothing.

II. SYMMETRY. If two players enter symmetrically into the cost function, they are charged equally.

III. ADDITIVITY. If the cost function decomposes into the sum of two functions c' and c'', that is, if $c(S) = c'(S) + c''(S)$ for every coalition S, then the cost allocation for c is the sum of the allocations for c' and c''.

To illustrate these ideas consider the following example. A town is planning to develop a recreation area for public use. The area will include one or more of the following projects: a playing field (1), a swimming pool (2), and slides and jungle gyms for children (3). The town council has obtained estimates for the capital and operating cost of these facilities, both by themselves and in combination. (See table 5.5.) The capital cost of developing the playing field is negligible, so it is a dummy in the capital cost function. However, its upkeep involves substantial operating cost. By contrast, the jungle gyms and slides require substantial capital outlays but negligible operating costs. In other words, project 3 is a dummy in the operating cost function.

The costs happen to work out so that the annualized capital cost of installing a swimming pool is the same as the annualized capital cost of building jungle gyms ($10,000 for each). It also happens that the cost of maintaining the pool is the same as the cost of maintaining the field ($3,000 for each). There are potential gains from doing the projects in combination, however, because the contractor will give a better price for constructing the swimming pool and jungle gyms as one project than doing them separately. Moreover, maintaining the pool and playing field together costs less than maintaining each separately because of reduced labor costs. The council has decided to implement all three projects at an annual amortized cost of $20,000, but it needs to determine the

[8] Implicit in this definition is the assumption that everyone who uses a cost element uses it to more or less the same extent. An alternative assumption is that each user is charged in proportion to his *degree* of usage. See Shapley (1981) and Kalai and Samet (1988).

TABLE 5.5
Sharing Capital and Operating Costs of a Recreation Area

	Annualized Capital Cost	Annual Operating Cost	Total Cost
c(1)	$ 0	$3,000	$ 3,000
c(2)	10,000	3,000	13,000
c(3)	10,000	0	10,000
c(1,2)	10,000	4,000	14,000
c(1,3)	10,000	3,000	13,000
c(2,3)	16,000	3,000	19,000
c(1,2,3)	16,000	4,000	20,000

share of the cost to attribute to each project in order to set user fees for the pool and the playing field.

The above three principles determine the answer as follows. Consider first the capital cost function. Since 1 is a dummy, its share of capital cost is zero (principle I). Furthermore, the cost function is symmetric in projects 2 and 3, so they have equal shares (principle II). Thus the capital charges are $0 for project 1, $8,000 for project 2, and $8,000 for project 3. Next, consider the operating cost function. Here project 3 is a dummy, so its share of operating cost is zero. Moreover, the cost function is symmetric in projects 1 and 2, so their shares of the total operating cost are equal. Hence the operating charges are: $2,000 for project 1, $2,000 for project 2, and $0 for project 3. The additivity principle then implies that the total charges should be: $2,000 for project 1, $10,000 for project 2, and $8,000 for project 3.

This example was designed to illustrate the three principles in a particularly transparent way; in general, they do not lead to the answer quite so easily. Nevertheless, they uniquely determine the following rule, which we have already come across in chapter 4.

SHAPLEY VALUE. Given a cost-sharing game on a fixed set of players, let the players join the cooperative enterprise one at a time in some predetermined order. As each player joins, the number of players to be served increases. The player's *cost contribution* is his net addition to cost when he joins, that is, the incremental cost of adding him to the group of players that has already joined. The *Shapley value* of a player is his average cost contribution over all possible orderings of the players.

We illustrate the computation for the recreation area example using just the total cost data (i.e., column 3 of table 5.5). There are six possible orderings of the players (projects) as shown in table 5.6. In the first ordering, player 1 joins first and incurs the stand-alone cost $c(1) = \$3,000$. Then player 2 joins, which increases costs from $3,000 to $c(1, 2) = \$14,000$. Thus the cost contribution of player 2 in this ordering is $11,000. Finally, player 3 joins, which increases

TABLE 5.6
Computation of the Shapley Value
for the Recreation Area Problem

	Cost Contribution of Player in Each Order		
Order	1	2	3
123	$ 3,000	$11,000	$ 6,000
132	3,000	7,000	10,000
213	1,000	13,000	6,000
231	1,000	13,000	6,000
312	3,000	7,000	10,000
321	1,000	9,000	10,000
Column Total	12,000	60,000	48,000
Column Average	2,000	10,000	8,000

costs from $14,000 to $c(1, 2, 3) = \$20,000$. Hence his cost contribution in this ordering is $6,000. The other rows of the table are computed similarly. The average of each player's contribution, over all six orderings, is shown in the bottom row. It will be seen that it is identical to the allocation that we computed by applying the three principles directly to the data in table 5.5. This result holds in general: *The Shapley value is the unique cost allocation rule that satisfies principles I–III.*[9]

When the cost function decomposes into cost elements, the Shapley value yields the same result as the decomposition principle, hence it is in the core. There are perfectly plausible examples, however, where the cost function does not decompose and the Shapley value fails to be in the core. Consider the municipal cost sharing problem discussed in section 3. This cost function does not decompose, because a water distribution system that serves each town separately is not made up of components from the joint system; it involves a complete redesign of the system. Table 5.7 shows the cost contribution of each player in each of the six possible orderings. Their average (the Shapley value) is computed in the last row of the table. It is not in the core because together players A and C pay $14.16 million, which exceeds their opportunity cost of $14 million.

8. Equitable Core Solutions: The Nucleolus

We therefore turn to the question of how to select an equitable allocation in the core. The answer builds on the ideas developed in the preceding chapters: first

[9] Shapley (1953).

TABLE 5.7
The Shapley Value for the Cost-Sharing Game
among Three Towns

Player			A	B	C
A	B	C	11	4	5
A	C	B	11	6	3
B	A	C	8	7	5
B	C	A	7	7	6
C	A	B	6	6	8
C	B	A	7	5	8
	Total		50	35	35
	Average		8.33	5.83	5.83

identify an appropriate solution when there are just two players, then extend it
many-player situations using the consistency principle.

In the two-player case the core is just a line segment (see fig. 4), so the natural
solution is to choose the *midpoint*. Under this arrangement both players save the
same amount relative to their stand-alone costs. This is known as the *standard
two-person solution*. This does not extend in an obvious way to more than three
players, because equal division of cost-savings may not be in the core, as the
example of figure 5 shows. Consider, however, the point labeled $a*$ in figure 8,
which is an enlargement of the core of figure 5. This corresponds to the cost
allocation: \$7.75 million for town A, \$6.5 million for town B, and \$5.75 for
town C.

To motivate this solution, suppose that the payment to town A is held fixed at
7.75. The range of charges for B and C that lies within the core is represented by
the horizontal dotted line segment through $a*$. Its left endpoint x is the maxi-

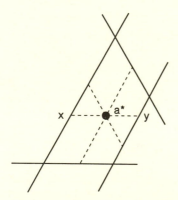

Fig. 8. Close-up of the core of the municipal cost-sharing game.

mum amount that town C can be charged while staying in the core, and the right endpoint y is the maximum amount that B can be charged while staying in the core. Notice that a^* is the midpoint of this line segment. In other words, towns B and C split the difference between the solutions that are most (respectively least) favorable to each, *given* that town A is fixed at the value 7.75. Similarly, it can be checked that towns A and C split the difference between the most and least favorable solutions when town B is held fixed at the value 6.50, and towns A and B split the difference between the most and least favorable solutions when town C is held fixed at 5.75.

More generally, whenever the core of the cost game is nonempty, there exists an allocation in the core such that *every two parties split the difference between the most and least favorable solutions to themselves given that the other players' allocations are held fixed. In other words, there exists a core allocation that is pairwise consistent with the standard two-person solution.* [10]

In more complex games there may actually exist more than one allocation with this property. However, we can single out one of them by the following argument. For each subgroup S let $e(S)$ be the total amount that the members of S save as a group relative to their stand-alone cost $c(S)$. We may take this as the standard for comparing how well the various subgroups fare under the proposed allocation, that is, $- e(S)$ is a measure of disadvantage or priority. The allocation $a_1, a_2, \ldots, a_n$ minimizes disadvantage among all proper subgroups if the *smallest* of the values $e(S)$ is as *large* as possible, among all remaining coalitions the *next smallest* value of $e(S)$ is as large as possible, and so forth. [11]

> NUCLEOLUS. Given a subadditive cost function $c(S)$ on a group of players N, the *nucleolus* is the unique allocation of total cost that lexicographically maximizes the distribution of cost-savings among all proper subsets of N. Moreover, the nucleolus is pairwise consistent with the standard two-person solution.

Under the cost allocation (7.75, 6.5, 5.75) the cost-saving of each proper subgroup of towns is as follows:

$$A \quad 11 - 7.75 = 3.25 \qquad \{A, B\} \quad 15 - 7.75 - 6.50 = 0.75$$
$$B \quad 7 - 6.50 = 0.50 \qquad \{A, C\} \quad 14 - 7.75 - 5.75 = 0.50$$
$$C \quad 8 - 5.75 = 2.25 \qquad \{B, C\} \quad 13 - 6.50 - 5.75 = 0.75$$

---

[10] The set of all such allocations is known as the "prekernel" of the cost game (Davis and Maschler, 1965).

[11] For every allocation a, and every proper subset S of N, the *cost savings* for S is $e(S) = c(S) - a(S)$. The number $-e(S)$ is a measure of the disadvantage of coalition S. Arrange the $2^n - 2$ numbers $e(S)$ from smallest to largest and let this vector be denoted by $\theta(a)$. The *nucleolus* is the allocation of total cost $c(N)$ that lexicographically maximizes $\theta(a)$ subject to $a_i \leq c(i)$ for all i. In other words, for every allocation a' satisfying $a_i' \leq c(i)$ for all i, the first component in which $\theta(a)$ and $\theta(a')$ differ has a larger value in $\theta(a)$ than in $\theta(a')$. If c is subadditive the conditions $a_i \leq c(i)$ are superfluous and can be dropped.

Thus the distribution of cost-savings, ranged from lowest to highest, is .50, .50, .75, .75, 2.25, 3.25. It can be shown that every other allocation yields a distribution of cost-savings that is lexicographically inferior to this one.[12]

The nucleolus cropped up in disguised form in the preceding chapter. Recall that a *claims problem* involves a group of individuals, each of whom has a numerical claim c_i against an amount of common property a_0. To translate this into the present framework, we may think of c_i as claimant i's stand-alone cost, because this is how much i stands to lose if there is no agreement. The amount that i *saves* by entering into the agreement is a_i, and the difference $c_i - a_i$ is the amount that i *loses*. The set of all allocations that satisfy $0 \leq a_i \leq c_i$ is the core of the cost-sharing game. When there are just two claimants, the standard solution is to choose the *midpoint* of the core. The reader may check that this is precisely the contested garment rule from the Babylonian Talmud. In chapter 4, we showed how to extend the contested garment rule to any number of claimants using the consistency principle. It turns out that this extension is precisely the nucleolus of an appropriately defined game.[13] While we are certainly not claiming that the sages of the Talmud were aware of cooperative game theory, let alone the nucleolus, this example shows that the principles underlying the nucleolus are very ancient indeed.

9. Summary

In this chapter we have been concerned with the equitable division of costs and benefits in cooperative enterprises. Individuals only have an incentive to participate if they are charged less than their opportunity costs. The same holds for subgroups of individuals. These incentive constraints define the core of the cost-sharing game. As we have seen, simple equity formulas such as equal or proportional division may not be in the core. The problem, therefore, is to find a solution in the core that is as equitable as possible. When costs can be decomposed into distinct cost components, each used exclusively by a subset of the claimants, the natural solution is the Shapley value. When there is no such decomposition, the Shapley value may still be employed but it is not necessarily in the core. An alternative approach is to apply the equal cost-savings standard to subgroups of claimants. There exists a unique allocation called the *nucleolus* that is equitable as near as may be according to this standard.

---

[12] This example shows why it is necessary to consider the lexicographic maximum, rather than just maximizing the minimum cost saving over all subgroups. For example, if we transfer t in cost from A to C or vice versa, where $t < .25$, then the minimum cost-saving is still .50, but the next-smallest saving (.75) decreases by t.

[13] Let $a_0 \geq 0$ be the amount to be divided, and $c_i > 0$ the amount of i's claim, where $\Sigma c_i \geq a_0$. Define the "cost function" $c(S) = \min \{a_0, \Sigma_{i \in S} c(i)\}$. The core of this cost-sharing game is the set of all allocations a such that $0 \leq a_i \leq c_i$ and $\Sigma a_i = a_0$. The nucleolus of c is the consistent extension of the contested garment rule defined in chap. 4 (Aumann and Maschler, 1985).

6

Progressive Taxation

> For all they did cast in of their abundance; but she
> of her want did cast in all that she had, even all her
> living.
>   (*Mark XII, 44*)

1. Historical Background

When Benjamin Franklin wrote that the only two certainties are death and taxes, he could not have meant income taxes, which were all but unknown in his day. A few Italian city states had experimented with a progressive income tax in medieval times, and Britain adopted a temporary income tax during the Napoleonic Wars. But the income tax did not come into widespread use until the late nineteenth century. Great Britain did not make the income tax a permanent part of its fiscal apparatus until the 1870s, though a series of temporary income taxes were in force after 1842. Japan followed suit in 1887, Prussia and the Netherlands in the 1890s. In the United States, Congress established an income tax in 1894, only to have the Supreme Court overturn it a year later on the grounds that the Constitution prohibits any taxation that is not linked directly to political representation. The difficulty is contained in the same sentence that governs the apportionment of representation (Article I, section 2; see chapter 3): "Representatives and direct taxes shall be apportioned among the several states that may be included within this Union according to their respective numbers." A head or poll tax would be acceptable under this criterion; a tax levied on income would not, or so the high court held. This lacuna in fiscal policy was closed in 1913 with the ratification of the Sixteenth Amendment, which reads: "The Congress shall have the power to lay and collect taxes on incomes, from whatever source derived, without apportionment among the several States, and without regard to any census or enumeration."

Historically, the development of the income tax was a response to the changing sources and distribution of economic wealth. Prior to the industrial revolution, income was derived primarily from landholdings, so a natural object of taxation was rent from real property. In seventeenth-century England, for example, property income was generally assessed at a flat rate, with an exemption for persons below a certain economic level. In addition, there were customs and excise taxes on consumption goods, especially luxury goods such as salt, silk, tobacco, tea, chocolate, etc. Direct taxes were levied on persons and households. A per capita charge or "poll tax" was assessed according to a complicated schedule based on the person's social rank, profession, and possessions. Finally, there was a house tax, commonly known as "hearth money," which was originally levied on the number of hearths or stoves in the residence, and later as a fixed amount on each house plus a graduated surcharge based on the number of windows.[1] All of these taxes were based in one way or another on a person's "ability to pay" as revealed by profession, landholdings, residence, consumption patterns, and so forth. The notion of taxing income directly was considered by various theorists, but rejected on the ground that collecting the requisite information would be costly and constitute an unwarranted invasion of privacy.[2]

Beginning in the nineteenth century, however, the rise of commercial interests and the diffusion of the money economy—combined with increasing pressures on state treasuries to finance an ever-wider array of public services (and foreign wars)—compelled governments to impose taxes directly on income. At first these taxes were adopted as "temporary"measures, and they were, by modern standards, at very low rates. Gradually, however, they became an entrenched part of fiscal policy, and they also became markedly progressive.

2. The Progressivity Principle

A tax is strictly *progressive* if the amount of tax paid as a proportion of income rises with income. Progressivity is a feature of many types of assessments besides taxation. Membership dues in professional associations are often progressive. The American Political Science Association, for example, currently has the following dues schedule: $55 for those with annual incomes under $30,000; $75 for those with incomes between $30,000 and $40,000; $85 for those with incomes between $41,000 and $50,000; $90 for those with incomes between $51,000 and $60,000; $95 for all higher incomes. Progressivity is also common in the allocation of unexpected losses or shortfalls. When a firm falls on hard times and must cut employees' wages, it would not be unusual for them to cut the wages of higher-salaried workers by a larger percentage than lower-salaried workers.[3]

---

[1] For an informative history of progressive taxation in Great Britain, see Shehab (1953).

[2] See Adam Smith (1776, vol. 2, book V, chap. 2.)

[3] In 1991 USAir announced the following schedule of paycuts for its employees: Workers who make less than $20,000 per year receive no reduction. Workers who make between $20,000 and $50,000 take a cut of 10 percent on the amount they earn above $20,000. Those who make between $50,000 and $100,000 take a 10 percent cut on the amount between $20,000 and $50,000 (i.e., a cut of $3,000) plus 15 percent of the amount they earn over $50,000. Those who make over $100,000 take a cut of $10,500 plus 20 percent of the amount they earn in excess of $100,000 (Washington Post, October 14, 1991).

The rationale for progressive assessments is clear enough: those who are better off should pay at a higher rate because they can absorb the loss more easily. The purpose of this chapter is to examine the progressivity principle from various angles using taxation as the frame of reference. Among other questions we shall be interested in the following. How progressive are income taxes in practice? Second, what degree of progressivity is justified on equity grounds? Third, what is the effect of progressive taxation on economic variables like investment and work effort, and to what extent does progressivity need to be tempered or modified to avoid substantial losses in efficiency?

3. The U.S. Federal Income Tax

We shall focus on income taxes in the United States, which are fairly representative of patterns in other industrialized countries. Since World War II, the United States federal tax code has undergone half a dozen major reforms. The most recent overhaul was in 1986, when the top rate was reduced to 33 percent and various deductions and loopholes were closed. At the same time the number of marginal rates (known as tax brackets) was reduced to three: 15 percent, 28 percent, and 33 percent. These rates define the *nominal tax schedule*—the amount of tax owed on each dollar of taxable income. Taxable income is not, however, the same thing as economic income. It is arrived at by deducting from income a basic allowance or *exemption* for the taxpayer and each dependent, plus various expenses that are considered either "necessary" (such as medical expenses) or socially desirable (charitable contributions).[4] The *effective tax rate schedule* is the fraction of economic income that each income class pays in taxes. This schedule is strictly progressive if the rate increases with income.

As figure 9 shows, the federal personal income tax in the United States is quite markedly progressive, in spite of recent reductions in the marginal rates paid by upper-income households.[5] The following features are noteworthy. There is a minimum level of income (about $3,300 in 1988) below which the tax rate is zero. This may be interpreted as a subsistence level, though it is certainly a very minimal level of subsistence. Above this threshold, the effective tax rate rises steadily but at a decreasing rate, tapering off at about 30

[4] The 1988 exemption is $1,950 for the taxpayer and each dependent. An additional exemption is granted if the taxpayer is over 65 and another if he is blind. Deductions and credits are allowed for qualifying medical expenses, child care expenses, taxes paid to state and local authorities, payments to retirement plans, donations to charitable causes, mortgage interest payments, and various other expenditures.

[5] Throughout this discussion we restrict ourselves to taxes levied by the federal government directly on household incomes, not on sales taxes, personal property taxes, and corporation taxes. When all of these are added together the tax structure is much less progressive; indeed according to some estimates it is flat or regressive (Pechman, 1987). For a more complete theoretical treatment of incidence and efficiency issues in taxation see Atkinson and Stiglitz (1980).

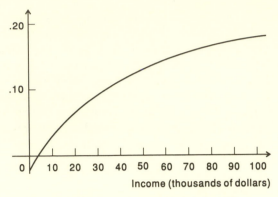

Fig. 9. The effective U.S. tax schedule in 1988.

percent. The tax rate schedules of many European countries and Japan have a similar shape, though the minimum level and top marginal rates vary considerably from one country to another.[6] Is there some general equity principle that explains why these schedules look the way they do, or are they merely ad hoc?

In the next three sections we shall examine this question from several different angles. First we shall consider various justifications for progressivity on *equity* grounds. Then we shall see whether it can be supported on *economic* grounds. Finally, we shall ask how close these theories come to explaining how tax rates are structured in practice in the United States.

4. Redressing Inequality

A traditional argument for progressive taxation is that it redresses the disparities in income and wealth that are a by-product of the market system. According to this rationale, progressive taxation is a corrective measure that the public demands to reduce inequality.[7] The plausibility of this explanation hinges, of course, on how much impact the income tax actually has on reducing inequality. To address this issue we need to have some numerical measure of inequality both before and after taxation.

A convenient way of summarizing the income distribution is the *Lorenz curve*, which shows the fraction of total income received by each percentile of the population, ranged from lowest to highest income bracket. Figure 10 shows the Lorenz curve of income before tax in the United States in 1988. The poorest 30 percent of the population garnered about 5 percent of pre-tax income, the poorest 50 percent about 15 percent of pre-tax income, and so forth.

[6] Young (1990).
[7] Blum and Kalven (1953).

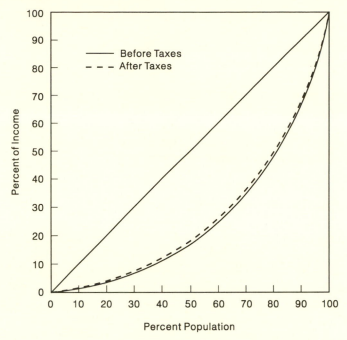

Fig. 10. Lorenz curve of income distribution in the United States before and after taxes, 1988. (Source: Congressional Budget Office, 1988, Tables A-5 and A-7.)

A rough-and-ready measure of the amount of inequality is the area between the diagonal and the Lorenz curve, divided by the area of the triangle formed by the diagonal and the bottom and right-hand sides of the square. This ratio is known as the *Gini index* of the income distribution. If everyone had the same pre-tax income, the Lorenz curve would coincide with the diagonal and the Gini index would be zero (i.e., there would be no inequality). The opposite extreme occurs when all income is concentrated in the hands of one individual, in which case the Gini index is one.

To what extent does the federal income tax lower inequality? The answer is: not by very much. The dotted line in figure 10 shows the distribution of income after federal taxes.[8] The Gini index decreases from .511 to .492, which represents a very slight decrease in inequality. Although the figure is not detailed enough to show this, the major effect of taxation is to reduce the share of total

[8] This does not include transfer payments (e.g., income supplements and other benefits), which further reduce income inequality, though not by much. The Gini index after both taxes and transfer payments is approximately .47, which is a further reduction of about 4%. (These estimates are based on the Congressional Budget Office (1988).) For simplicity we ignore here the effects of taxation on the distribution of pre-tax income, a subject that is examined in sections 8–9.

income enjoyed by the richest one-tenth of the population by about 2 percent, and to increase the share of total income enjoyed by the lower- to middle-income groups by a comparable amount. The effects on the poorest one-tenth of the population and the next-to-richest one-tenth of the population are about neutral.

The inescapable conclusion is that the federal income tax in its current form does not change the income distribution by more than a token amount. The reason is that the tax is only mildly progressive, and the total tax take represents less than 12 percent of pre-tax income. Thus it does not have enough bite to make much of a dent in the income distribution.

5. The Benefit Theory

A second theory of tax equity is that citizens should pay in accordance with the benefits they enjoy from public services financed by taxes. This is the *willingness to pay* or *benefit theory* of taxation. It does not necessarily imply, however, that taxes should be progressive. One could argue, for instance, that all persons enjoy the same protection under the state, so equity requires that all should pay equally. On the other hand, one could just as easily argue that everyone does *not* enjoy the same degree of protection by the state. And even if they did, the cost of protection varies depending on who is being protected. The rich enjoy the protection of their property as well as their persons, which suggests that they should pay more. This "payment for protection" argument suggests a two-part tax in which there is a head tax on individuals and a flat tax on real property. Indeed, both were prominent features of the tax system before the income tax was introduced.

The limitation of this argument is that it takes too narrow a view of the services provided by the state. What about education, transportation, parks, police, law courts, and the myriad of other services that are offered by the modern state? One approach to this problem is simply to ask individuals how much they value these publicly financed activities and then tax them accordingly. This approach to taxation was first suggested by the Swedish economist Erik Lindahl. We suppose that each individual has a demand schedule for publicly provided goods and services, just as he does for other types of goods. This demand curve can be expressed as the quantity of public goods that he or she would be willing to buy at various prices. The crucial difference between public and private goods, however, is that private goods are enjoyed exclusively by the person who possesses them, while public goods are enjoyed simultaneously by everyone. An army or a highway network is very different from a handgun or a car, because the former benefit everyone, the latter only their owners. Still, it remains true that (just as for private goods) the economically optimal quantity of public goods is that at which supply equals demand.

To be concrete, let's say that we want to determine how many policemen to employ in the community. Let q be the total number of policemen on the force and let $p_i(q)$ be the amount that citizen i would personally be willing to pay to hire one more policeman given that the current number is q. The total willingness to pay for one more policeman is the sum of all individuals' willingness to pay, $\Sigma p_i(q)$, because one extra policeman on duty benefits everyone. Finally, suppose it costs $c(q)$ to hire this extra policeman. It makes sense to hire him if and only if the public's willingness to pay exceeds cost, that is, if $\Sigma p_i(q) > c(q)$. The optimal level of the force is the quantity q^* at which total willingness to pay just equals incremental cost: $\Sigma p_i(q^*) = c(q^*)$.

The situation is illustrated graphically in figure 11. We suppose for simplicity that there are just two citizens, 1 and 2. For each quantity q of the public good, we add the two demand curves vertically to obtain the total demand curve DD. The point E at which total demand equals marginal cost is the optimal level of the public good q^*. At this level, individual 1 pays $p_1 q^*$ and individual 2 pays $p_2 q^*$, that is, each individual's tax equals his stated willingness to pay per unit times the optimal quantity.

LINDAHL TAX. The *optimal level* of a public good is the quantity q^* at which the willingness to pay for one more unit of the good, summed over all individuals, equals the marginal cost of supplying it. The *Lindahl tax* for each individual is the optimal quantity times his willingness to pay for one more unit at this quantity.[9]

Assuming that willingness to pay for more police increases with income (which seems reasonable), then the Lindahl tax increases with income. Under certain conditions the tax *rate* rises with income, that is, the Lindahl tax is progressive.[10]

Simple and elegant as this solution may be, it has the drawback that individuals have no incentive to reveal their true demand, because they know that the smaller their stated willingness to pay, the smaller their tax will be. So everyone is tempted to bias his willingness to pay downward, and the optimal level of the public good will not in fact be provided. Indeed, if the number of taxpayers is very large it makes sense to report almost zero willingness to pay, because one will then enjoy the public services provided by others at little or no expense to oneself. This *free-rider problem* undermines the Lindahl approach as a practical means of distributing the tax burden. To make it workable, one would have to

[9] The taxes $(p_1, p_2, \ldots p_n)$ are a *Lindahl equilibrium* if there exists a quantity q^* such that, for every i, $p_i = p_i(q^*)$ and $\Sigma_{i=1,n} p_i = c(q^*)$.

[10] Let $u(q, y)$ be the utility for amount of public good q and level of income y, the same for everyone, where we assume that u is quasi-concave and differentiable. Let the n individuals have incomes $y_1, y_2, \ldots, y_n$. At the Lindahl equilibrium, the unit price charged to i satisfies the condition $p_i = (\partial u(q, y_i)/\partial q)/(\partial u(q, y_i)/\partial y_i)$ for every i. Thus $p_i q/y_i$ equals the elasticity of substitution between q and y_i. If this is increasing in y_i for each q, then the tax $t_i = p_i q$ divided by pretax income $x_i = p_i q + y_i$ is increasing in y_i, which implies that the tax is progressive.

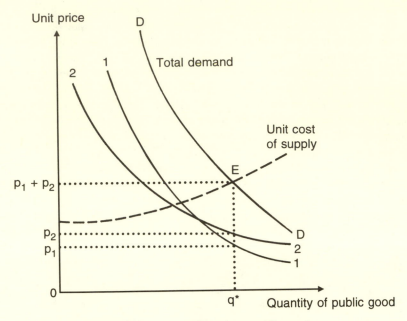

Fig. 11. Lindahl taxes for two people and one public good.

estimate the willingness to pay for public services of a *representative* person in each income class, and apply a uniform tax rate to everyone in the same class.

Even if we could make such an estimate, however, it is not clear that the result would accord with our everyday intuition about justice. For, as John Stuart Mill pointed out, it suggests that the most dependent and neediest members of society are the ones that should pay the most.

> If we wanted to estimate the degrees of benefit which different persons derive from the protection of government we should have to consider who would suffer most if that protection were withdrawn: to which question if any answer could be made, it must be that those would suffer most who were weakest in mind or body. . . . If there were any justice, therefore, in the theory of justice now under consideration [the benefit theory], those who are least capable of helping or defending themselves, being those to whom the protection of government is the most indispensable, ought to pay the greatest share of its price: the reverse of the true idea of distributive justice, which consists not in imitating but in redressing the inequalities and wrongs of nature. . . . Government must be regarded as so preeminently a concern of all, that to determine who are most interested in it is of no real importance.[11]

[11] *Principles of Political Economy,* book V, chap. 2.

6. Ability to Pay and Equal Sacrifice

These considerations led Mill to conclude that the proper basis for distributing the tax burden is not benefit received but ability to pay. Equity in taxation means that everyone should bear an equal burden. This does not mean that everyone should pay the same *amount* in taxes. Someone with an income of $15,000 (in current U.S. dollars) would probably find a tax of $1,000 quite onerous, while someone with an income of $500,000 would scarcely feel it at all. In assessing the equity of a tax distribution, said Mill, it is the loss of well-being that matters, not the sum of money itself. "Equality of taxation, therefore, as a maxim of politics, means equality of sacrifice. It means apportioning the contribution of each person towards the expenses of government so that he shall feel neither more nor less inconvenience from his share of the payment than every other person experiences from his. This standard, like other standards of perfection, cannot be completely realized, but the first object in any practical discussion should be to know what perfection is."[12]

How then should the extent of sacrifice be measured? The classical utilitarians thought of well-being or utility as a property that attaches to economic circumstances. More income implies greater well-being because it provides additional means with which to realize one's objectives and satisfy one's desires. Intuitively one can imagine that diminishing returns eventually set in: the increase in well-being that results from having an extra dollar of income decreases the more income one has. But how can we measure this effect?

One way to answer this question is to look at the chances that people would take to be in different income classes. Consider the following simple thought experiment. Due to events beyond your control, your income will either be $20,000 per year or $100,000 per year. Both outcomes are equally likely. Now suppose that someone offers you the opportunity to increase the lower option from $20,000 to $30,000, or to increase the higher option from $100,000 to $110,000, but not both. Which would you prefer? Empirical evidence suggests that many people would prefer to increase the lower amount. From this we could infer that the marginal gain in utility from an extra $10,000 is greater for someone making $20,000 per year than for someone making $100,000 per year. Similarly, we could argue that a head tax of $10,000 probably represents a greater loss of utility for a low-income person as compared to a high-income person.

Now let's examine the implications of this idea for the distribution of the tax burden. Assume for simplicity that everyone has the same utility $U(x)$ for income level x. Alternatively, we could assume that $U(x)$ is the utility function of an average or "representative" person. Under normal conditions $U(x)$

12 Ibid, p. 804.

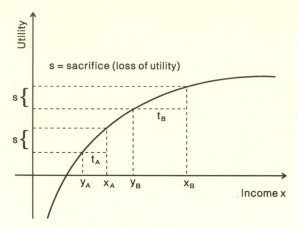

Fig. 12. The equal absolute sacrifice principle.

is concave, that is, the marginal gain in utility from each additional dollar of income decreases with higher levels of income (see fig. 12). Suppose that individual A has pre-tax income x_A and pays tax t_A. Before taxes A's utility level is u. After taxes his utility is $u - s$, where s is the loss in utility. Now consider B, who has a higher level of pre-tax income x_B. As the figure shows, the tax t_B on x_B must be substantially larger than t_A if both are to suffer the *same* loss in utility s.

EQUAL ABSOLUTE SACRIFICE TAX. Let $t(x)$ be a tax schedule that gives amount of tax owed as a function of income level x. The schedule $t(x)$ *equalizes absolute sacrifice* if it imposes an equal loss of utility on all income classes relative to some utility function $U(x)$.[13]

When the marginal utility of income is decreasing, equal absolute sacrifice implies that taxes increase with income, but it does not necessarily imply that the tax *rate* increases with income. Consider the logarithmic utility function $U(x) = \log x$, which Mill regarded as a reasonable approximation of the relationship between utility and income. In this case, a fixed percentage decrease in income represents the same loss of utility at every income level. Thus everyone sacrifices equally if they pay the same percent of their income in tax. In other words, equal sacrifice can be used to justify a flat-rate tax. Indeed, for some utility functions it can lead to a strictly regressive tax.[14] For utility functions that are estimated directly from empirical data, however, the results support a progressive schedule, as we shall show in the next section.

[13] That is, $t(x)$ equalizes absolute sacrifice if $U(x) - U(x - t(x)) = s$ for some nonnegative constant s and all $x > 0$. Thus the tax schedule takes the form $t(x) = x - U^{-1}[U(x) - s]$.

[14] Equal absolute sacrifice implies a strictly progressive schedule if the elasticity of marginal utility $-xU''(x)/U'(x) > 1$. This is consistent with empirical data (Friend and Blume, 1975).

The equal sacrifice principle set the stage for a lively discussion of tax equity that occurred around the turn of the last century. In 1889 the Dutch economist, A. J. Cohen Stuart, suggested that "equal sacrifice" should be interpreted to mean that everyone suffers the same *percentage* loss in utility. If the utility function is logarithmic, this criterion results in a tax schedule of form $t(x) = x - c(x/c)^{1-r}$ for $x \geq c$, which is known as a *Cohen-Stuart tax schedule*.[15] Below income level c (which can be interpreted as a minimum subsistence level) the tax rate is zero, and above c the tax rate is strictly increasing, gradually approaching 100 percent for very large incomes.

A second variation on the sacrifice theme was developed by Edgeworth, Sidgwick, and other leaders of the utilitarian school. They held that taxes should be distributed so as to minimize *aggregate sacrifice* summed over all taxpayers. At first sight this idea makes sense. Imagine for a moment that we are standing behind the veil of ignorance and do not know what economic position we will occupy in society. Imagine further that all income levels are equally likely (up to some maximum value). How would we wish to distribute taxes given that we do not yet know who we will be? If we are expected utility maximizers, we would want to distribute the tax burden so that the expected loss of utility (before we know who we are) is as small as possible. This is exactly Edgeworth's proposal.

Unfortunately it leads to some rather extreme results. Assume as before that the marginal utility of income is strictly decreasing. Each dollar of tax imposes the least sacrifice on those with the lowest marginal utility of income, that is, on the richest taxpayers. The solution is therefore to concentrate the tax entirely at the upper end of the income scale. Above some threshold level x^* (which is determined by the total amount of tax to be raised) we should tax away all additional income at a 100 percent marginal rate; below that level we should not tax income at all. This solution is known as the *leveling tax* because its effect is to lop off all incomes above the level x^*. The difficulty is that it completely eliminates the incentive to earn more income above this level. This sets a vicious circle in motion. The natural response of upper-income taxpayers would be to adjust their pre-tax incomes down to the threshold value x^*, since this is all that they are allowed to keep anyway. (This assumes that they derive no utility from work *per se*, which is probably incorrect for many people.) To raise the required amount of revenue, the government would have to lower the threshold. Individuals would then respond by working even less. In the limit,

---

[15] Let $U(x)$ be the utility of income level x, and let r be a constant between zero and one that represents the rate of loss of utility. The tax schedule $t(x)$ *equalizes rate of sacrifice* if $U(x - t(x))/U(x) = 1 - r$, that is, if $t(x) = x - U^{-1}[(1 - r)U(x)]$. In the particular case where $U(x) = A\log x + B, A > 0$, a simple calculation shows that $t(x) = x - c(x/c)^{1-r}$ where $c = e^{-B/A}$ is the level of income at which utility is zero. This approach requires us to specify the zero-point of the utility function, so it is more demanding than equal absolute sacrifice, which is independent of *both* the zero-point and the scale of $U(x)$.

no one would work and tax revenue would be zero. "The acme of socialism is thus for a moment sighted," remarked Edgeworth, "but it is immediately clouded over by doubts and reservations."[16]

7. The Effect of Progressive Taxation on Work Effort

To clear up these doubts, we need to analyze the equity of the tax structure in tandem with its impact on work effort. It stands to reason that the higher marginal tax rates climb, the less incentive taxpayers will have to earn more income, because there is less take-home pay from every pre-tax dollar earned. In fact, matters are not so simple. Contrary to first appearances, taxation may actually *increase* work effort rather than reduce it.

To see why, consider a person who earns $40,000 per year. We assume that his income is derived entirely from wages and that his wage rate is fixed, but he can adjust the number of hours worked through overtime. Let's say that our hypothetical worker pays 25 percent in tax, so he takes home $30,000. Suppose further that his marginal tax rate is 35 percent, so he keeps 65 cents for every additional dollar earned. Now suppose that taxes go up: on $40,000 he now pays 30 percent and his marginal rate is 40 percent. Will he be inclined to work more or less? It all depends. Since he takes home only $28,000, he is less well off than before and might work a little more to make up for lost income. But he only gets to keep 60 cents for every extra dollar that he earns, so he might prefer to work less.

This example reveals two countervailing effects of taxation on the labor supply. On the one hand, it reduces the taxpayer's after-tax wage rate, which shifts his choice in favor of more leisure and less labor. This is the *substitution effect*. On the other hand, it reduces his level of income, which induces the taxpayer to work harder in order to make up for the loss. This is the *income effect*. The two effects work in opposite directions, and it cannot be said *a priori* which of them dominates. Whether an individual increases or decreases his work effort in response to higher tax rates depends on the slope of his indifference curve between labor and leisure and the structure of the tax rates.

Consider figure 13, which shows a hypothetical taxpayer's trade-off between income and leisure. Point *M* is the maximum amount he can earn before taxes given his wage rate. If he does not work at all, his income is zero (point *N*). The slope of the budget line *MN* is determined by his wage rate. The optimal combination of income and leisure occurs at the point *X*, where the indifference curve is tangent to the taxpayer's budget line. Now introduce a flat-rate tax of 25 percent. The new budget line is *M'N* and the optimal combination of income and leisure is *Y*. This represents an *increase* in work and a *decrease* in leisure. This conclusion is highly sensitive, however, to the form of the utility function.

[16] Edgeworth (1897, p. 121).

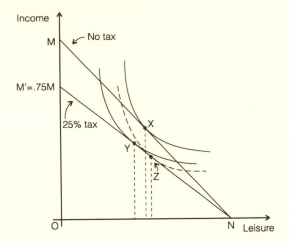

Fig. 13. The impact of a flat tax on work effort: two cases.

If his indifference curve were the dashed line, for example, then the optimal combination would be Z, which represents a *decrease* in pre-tax income and an *increase* in leisure. Hence the effect on the labor supply is ambiguous even for a flat-rate tax.

8. Optimal Taxation

We shall now apply these observations to our earlier discussion of tax equity. The essential idea is that, to achieve a distributive goal such as maximizing total utility, we must take into account the responses of taxpayers to the rate structure. As usual we take some representative taxpayer's utility function as the basis for the analysis. The naive solution is to set the marginal tax rate at 100 percent for all incomes above some threshold x^*, and at 0 percent for all incomes below x^*. (The argument is the same as for minimizing total sacrifice, as discussed in section 6). As we have already seen, however, this conclusion is not correct when taxpayers respond to the rate structure. If they face marginal rates of 100 percent, the unambiguous effect is to remove the incentive to earn more than the threshold amount x^*. Pre-tax income falls, which means the government must lower x^*, which leads everyone above the new level to lower their incomes, and so forth until no one works and income is zero. Clearly this outcome does not maximize total utility after taxes. The question therefore is: what is the optimal structure of rates if society's goal is to maximize total utility after-taxes subject to raising a given amount of revenue?

To analyze this question, let us assume that each person's wage rate is fixed in the short run by such factors as education, talent, and choice of occupation.

Workers adjust the amount they work to maximize the utility that they derive from income and leisure. In other words, faced with a given tax schedule, each worker adjusts the number of hours he works until the marginal utility from earning one more hour's worth of *after-tax income* (his wage less the fraction taken in tax) just equals the disutility from giving up one more hour of leisure. This determines the number of hours worked, and the pre-tax and post-tax income of each worker, as a function of his wage rate. (Figure 13 is illustrative.) The outcome depends, of course, on the choice of tax schedule. The idea is to find the tax schedule that meets some social objective, like maximizing total utility, *given* the adjustment in work effort by taxpayers. Such a schedule is said to be *optimal* for the given objective.

To illustrate the types of results obtainable (and the sensitivity of the conclusions to the objective function) consider the following example. Assume that every worker has the same Cobb-Douglas utility function for income Y and leisure L, $U(Y, L) = \sqrt{YL}$. Assume further that the logarithm of the wage rate is normally distributed in the population. The left-hand columns of table 6.1 show the structure of tax rates that maximize total utility. In the right-hand columns are the tax rates that maximize the utility of the lowest income group.

Several points about these results are worth noting. First, in the utilitarian case, the marginal tax rate is more or less constant and the tax schedule is approximately linear over much of the income range. Second, in the Rawlsian case, tax rates are substantially higher than in the utilitarian case. Third, in both cases taxes are progressive over part of the income distribution (the effective rate increases with income), but at higher income levels marginal rates are decreasing. In fact, if the number of individuals is finite, the highest wage earners face a marginal rate equal to zero. The reason is roughly the following: suppose that the top marginal rate were strictly positive. Consider the taxpayer with the highest pre-tax income, say x^*. If we were to reduce the marginal tax rate that applies to income above x^*, then the top earner would be induced to earn a little more, and no one else would want to earn less. Therefore more tax would be collected at the top of the income scale, which could be used to reduce rates further down the line.[17]

This discussion highlights the importance of analyzing the impact of an equity criterion on the behavior of the people it targets. The results need to be interpreted with caution, however, since they are very sensitive to the assumed form of the utility function and the distribution of wage rates. Most important, they depend on the *form* of the equity criterion itself. Suppose, for example, that instead of maximizing total utility (or minimum utility) we want all taxpayers to sacrifice equally, where sacrifice refers to the difference between a taxpayer's utility level in the absence of taxation and his utility level in the

[17] Seade (1977).

TABLE 6.1
Optimal Tax Rates for Utilitarian and Rawlsian Objectives. Individual Income-Leisure Tradeoff Is Given by $\sqrt{YL}$ and Wage Rates Are Lognormally Distributed.

Relative Wage Level	Utilitarian Objective		Rawlsian Objective	
	Average Tax Rate	Marginal Tax Rate	Average Tax Rate	Marginal Tax Rate
Median	6	21	10	52
Top Ten Percent	14	20	28	34
Top One Percent	16	17	28	26

Source: Atkinson and Stiglitz, 1980, table 13-3.

presence of taxation. Because taxpayers are able to substitute between income and leisure, the loss in utility is not as great as in a world where no adjustment occurs. The *amount* of adjustment depends on the interplay between the substitution and income effects, which must be analyzed using a particular utility function. There is at least one case, however, where these two effects cancel out. If utility is *separable* in income and leisure—that is, if the marginal utility of extra leisure is independent of the level of income and vice versa—then there is no net adjustment: labor supply and pre-tax income remain unchanged by an equal sacrifice tax. In this situation the naive analysis of equal sacrifice discussed in section 5 above yields the optimal tax schedule.[18] In sum, the form of the tax schedule and its impact on the labor supply depend very much on the equity criterion we seek to implement, in addition to taxpayers' wage rates and their preferences for income versus leisure.

9. The Effect of Taxation on Risk-Taking

We turn now to the impact of taxation on another economic variable: investment behavior. Consider the following example. You can invest $10,000 today with an even chance of either losing it all or tripling its value in a certain time period. Absent taxation, the expected value at the end of the period is $15,000, a gain of 50 percent. Suppose that the alternative is a safe security that will yield a 30 percent gain for sure. Which investment you find most attractive depends on your degree of risk aversion. A risk-neutral investor would prefer the first option while a risk-averse investor might well prefer the second.

Now let us consider how a progressive tax might alter this choice. Suppose that gains are taxed at a rate of 60 percent because they push you into a higher bracket, while losses can be written off at a rate of only 40 percent because they push you into a lower bracket. The after-tax gain from the safe investment is

[18] Berliant and Gouveia (1993).

now $1200 and the expected after-tax gain from the risky one is $1000. Hence the latter is *less* attractive than the former for both a risk-neutral and a risk-averse investor. The reason is that increasing marginal rates skew the outcome by taking a bigger bite out of gains than can be offset in losses.[19]

It would seem, therefore, that a progressive tax reduces the attractiveness of risky investments as compared to riskless ones, but this is not necessarily true. Two other effects must be considered. First, taxation reduces the overall income level of the taxpayer, which may change his attitude toward risk. This *income effect* holds whether the tax is flat-rate or progressive; what matters is the magnitude of the tax, that is, the extent to which it reduces after-tax income. Moreover, whether it increases or decreases risk-taking depends on the shape of the utility function. Second, higher rates reduce the *range* of expected after-tax income, which tends to *increase* risk taking. These effects interact in a complex way, and their net impact depends on the degree of risk aversion, the progressivity of the tax, and its magnitude.[20]

We say that a tax schedule is *risk-neutral* for a given individual if it does not change the individual's investment choices under uncertainty. Since individuals differ in their degree of risk aversion, there will, in general, be no tax function that is neutral for everyone. However, if we make the simplifying assumption that all individuals are alike in their degree of risk aversion but differ in their income, then the question has a simple answer that dovetails with the discussion of equity, namely, *a nonnegative tax schedule is risk-neutral if and only if it equalizes either absolute or proportional sacrifice.*[21]

If utility varies as the logarithm of income, then equal absolute sacrifice implies a flat-rate tax, whereas equal rate of sacrifice implies a Cohen-Stuart tax (as we saw in section 6). Empirical studies suggest, however, that the marginal utility of income decreases more rapidly than the logarithmic model implies. The rate at which marginal utility decreases can be estimated from data on household investment behavior, that is, from the proportion of wealth held in risky assets (such as stocks) compared to the proportion held in relatively riskless ones (such as savings accounts). In a classic study of this type, Friend and Blume (1975) estimated that the elasticity of marginal utility is more or less

---

[19] We assume throughout this discussion that losses can be fully offset by other income, a condition that is known as *full-loss offset*.

[20] Domar and Musgrave (1944); Bamberg and Richter (1984).

[21] Let $U(x)$ represent utility for income x in the absence of taxation. Let $t = f(x)$ be the tax schedule. Then $V(x) = U(x - t)$ is the taxpayer's utility for after-tax income. The schedule is *risk-neutral* if the taxpayer makes the same choices with taxation as in the absence of taxation. Since von Neumann–Morgenstern utility is uniquely defined up to a positive linear transformation, this amounts to saying that $V(x) = U(x - t) = AU(x) - B$ for some $A > 0$. There are two cases to consider. If $A = 1$, then $U(x) - U(x - t) = B$, which means that t equalizes absolute sacrifice. If $A \neq 1$, let $b = B/(1 - A)$. It is easily verified that $[U(x - t) + b]/[U(x) + b] = A$. By assumption, $t \geq 0$ and U is increasing, so $A < 1$. Thus the tax equalizes the rate of sacrifice at rate $1 - A$. This result is due to Buchholz (1988).

constant and greater than unity, which implies that the utility function takes the form $U(x) = -x^{-p} + B$ for some positive exponent p and arbitrary constant B. This is known as an *isoelastic* utility function. With such a utility function taxpayers suffer the same *absolute loss* in utility s if the tax function takes the form $t(x) = x - [x^{-p} + s]^{-1/p}$. All taxpayers suffer the same *rate of loss* r if the tax schedule takes the form $t(x) = x - [(1 - r)x^{-p} + r(x/c)^p]^{-1/p}$, where $c = e^{-B}$ is the minimum level of income that is subject to taxation (the "subsistence level").

The interest of these tax schedules from an empirical standpoint is that they fit quite closely to the way that rates are graduated in practice. Consider, for example, the 1988 U.S. tax schedule shown in figure 14. This can be very well approximated by an equal rate of sacrifice schedule in which the rate of sacrifice is .0235, the threshold level of taxation is \$3,300, and the exponent in the utility function is $p = 0.507$, a value that is consistent with the empirical findings of Friend and Blume. The fit is extremely close over the range of estimation \$0–\$100,000, though the two curves diverge for very high incomes because the equal sacrifice tax rate gradually approaches 100%.

The goodness of fit may be coincidental, of course, and it certainly does not prove that legislators consciously tried to implement an equal sacrifice schedule, either on grounds of equity or economic efficiency. What it does show is that the twin goals of equity and risk neutrality are not necessarily incompatible, and both point in the direction of some progressivity in rates. Moreover, a schedule based on these principles would be reasonably consistent with current practice in the United States.[22]

It should also be pointed out that the 1988 tax distribution shown in figure 14

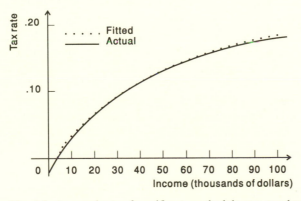

Fig. 14. An equal rate of sacrifice tax schedule compared to the U.S. effective schedule, 1988. [c = \$3,300, p = 0.507, r = 0.0235]

[22] A good fit is also obtained for tax schedules in other industrialized countries, including Germany, Italy, and Japan (Young, 1990).

TABLE 6.2
U.S. Federal Personal Income Tax Rates, 1964–1988,
by Real Income Level in 1964 Dollars

Income (1964 Dollars)	1964	1969	1976	1985	1988	Mean
1,000	0.8	0	−1.0	−0.9	−1.0	−0.4
5,000	7.7	6.2	7.5	6.1	4.8	6.5
10,000	10.3	9.7	10.8	9.2	8.9	9.8
15,000	12.7	11.3	13.5	11.2	11.3	12.0
20,000	13.6	13.6	14.7	13.2	13.7	13.8
50,000	19.2	20.1	26.5	21.2	21.0	21.6
100,000	26.1	27.7	31.6	24.2	24.3	26.8

Source: Pechman, *Federal Tax Policy,* 1st–5th editions.

is representative of the situation that has prevailed over the past 25 years or more. Despite the fact that the U.S. tax code has undergone at least half a dozen major reforms during the period 1964–1988, and the top rate has dropped from 91 to 33 percent, the distribution of rates has remained surprisingly stable (see table 6.2) due to various offsetting factors. Indeed, except for the two top income groups, which were temporarily pushed into higher brackets due to inflation in the 1970s, the tax rate in each income class has varied by only about three percentage points during the entire period.

No doubt this stability is due in part to social inertia: once a particular distribution of rates becomes established, it is difficult to dislodge because it is viewed as a kind of status quo property right by various income groups. This cannot be the entire explanation, however, since taxes can always be changed through the political process. It seems reasonable to conjecture that a distribution that has remained in place for so long probably reflects public opinion about what the appropriate amount of progressivity is. In other words, while individuals differ in their opinions about the proper degree of progressivity, the political process can be expected to reflect the median voter's position on this issue, which may in fact be fairly stable. It would be interesting to test this hypothesis by sampling voter preferences for different tax distributions, just as the army sampled soldiers' opinions to see who should be discharged first.

10. Summary

In this chapter we have examined four normative arguments for distributing the tax burden, and compared them with recent practice in the United States. The first argument is that progressive taxes are a form of compensatory justice that redresses inequalities in the income distribution. If this is the rationale for progressive taxation, however, its overall impact (at least in the United States) is quite small. A second argument is that people should be taxed in accordance with their willingness to pay for public services. In theory this solution is attractive, and under some conditions it is consistent with progressivity in rates. In practice, however, it is difficult to find out how much people are willing to pay for public services. A third approach is to levy taxes to promote some social objective such as maximizing total utility (the utilitarian principle) or maximizing minimum utility (the difference principle), where the analysis is carried out for some representative individual's utility for income and leisure. The naive pursuit of such an objective leads to confiscatory rates and serious economic distortions. When incentives on the labor supply are included in the analysis, the resulting tax structure is still progressive over part of the income range (at least for some scenarios) but marginal rates decline toward the top.

The fourth theory that we examined would distribute taxes so that everyone sacrifices equally, either in absolute or relative terms. Such a tax is also called for if the objective is not to distort investment incentives. The analysis is based on a representative individual's utility function for income, which can be estimated indirectly from data on investment behavior. The resulting tax schedule is progressive, whether based on equal absolute or equal rate of sacrifice. It is also broadly consistent with the recent distribution of taxes in the United States, though it would imply rates that gradually approach 100 percent at the top of the scale, which is not current practice.

The conclusion is that, while no other theory explains precisely why tax rates look the way they do, various theories support some degree of progressivity, which is in fact an established feature of income taxation in many countries.

7

Fair Bargains

A hypothesis or theory is clear, decisive, and positive, but it is believed by no one but the man who
created it. Experimental findings, on the other hand,
are messy, inexact things which are believed by everyone except the man who did that work.
(*Harlow Shapley*)

1. Bargaining Over Common Property

Distributive decisions involve a variety of actors. Though institutions often
make the choices, their authority is significantly constrained by law, custom,
and public opinion. The kidney allocation formula, for example, was developed by a committee consisting of medical specialists and representatives from
donor and patient groups, after seeking opinions from the general public about
the kinds of criteria that should and should not count. The army's discharge
formula was based mainly on opinions expressed by the soldiers themselves.
The distribution of the tax burden is formally decided by legislative vote, but it
is heavily influenced by public opinion and pressures from special interest
groups. Seats in the U.S. House of Representatives are allocated according to a
statutory formula passed by Congress, though their discretion is significantly
constrained by judicial standards of one person, one vote. In these cases the
claimants' views influence the distributive decision to some degree, but they are
not the sole arbiters of the outcome.

There are some allocative situations, however, in which the distribution is
decided directly by the claimants. A cost or profit sharing agreement between
partners in a joint enterprise is of this character. So is an international agreement
about sharing common property like the deep ocean bed, the high seas, or
broadcasting bandwidths. These allocations typically result from direct bargaining among the stakeholders. The purpose of this chapter is to explore what,
if anything, is meant by a *fair* bargain, and why fair bargains matter.

2. The Bargaining Set

Imagine a group of claimants sitting around a table trying to decide how to
allocate some good among themselves. They may allocate it in any way they see

fit so long as all agree on the outcome. Thus from a procedural point of view the decision must be unanimous. We shall also assume that the good is divisible, or if it is not, that they divide chances at getting the good. An *agreement* is a division that everyone approves. If they fail to reach unanimous agreement, the property is forfeited. What form might such an agreement take, and what role does equity play in shaping the outcome?

We begin by examining this question from the standpoint of classical bargaining theory. The cornerstone of this theory is the *utility* that the claimants have for the good being negotiated. Assume that each claimant prefers more of the good to less, and they do not care how much the *others* receive. In other words, each claimant's utility is strictly increasing in his own portion, and is independent of the others' portions. In addition, we want the utility functions to reflect the bargainers' attitudes toward risk. Risk is a factor in bargaining for two reasons. First, if the good is indivisible, the parties are bargaining over chances at getting the good rather than the good itself, so their attitudes toward chance events matter. Second, even if the good is divisible, there is an element of risk in bargaining because there is always a chance that it will break down (e.g., someone "walks out"), in which case the parties get nothing. We make the standard assumption that the parties evaluate uncertain prospects according to their expected utility, where prospects with higher expected utility are preferred to prospects with lower expected utility.[1] For convenience we shall also assume that the disagreement distribution has zero utility and that, for each bargainer, receiving all of the property has utility. These conditions determine each person's utility function uniquely.

BARGAINING SET. Given an amount of some divisible good to be allocated among a group of claimants, the *bargaining* set B consists of all utility payoffs that the claimants can realize from a full or partial allocation of the good.[2]

EXAMPLE: Two individuals are owed money by a debtor. Individual 1 is owed $60,000, and individual 2 is owed $180,000, but the debtor has only $90,000. The two creditors collect the $90,000 in a legal judgment. The court decrees that the creditors must decide how to divide the money or forfeit it.

An agreement or bargain is expressed as a pair of fractions a, b where a is

---

[1] Let $pa \oplus (1 - p)b$ denote the prospect of receiving the portion a with probability p and the portion b with probability $1 - p$. Its expected utility is $pu(a) + (1 - p)u(b)$. Under the assumptions of von Neumann–Morgenstern utility theory, the prospect $pa \oplus (1 - p)b$ is preferred to the prospect $p'a' \oplus (1 - p')b'$ if and only if $pu(a) + (1 - p)u(b) \geq p'u(a') + (1 - p')u(b')$.

[2] We assume throughout that the utility functions are continuous, concave, and strictly increasing in each good, and that the zero point is chosen to be $u_i(0) = 0$ for every i. Given an amount $a_0 > 0$ and a set of n claimants with utility functions $u_1(a_1), u_2(a_2), \ldots, u_n(a_n)$, the *bargaining set* is $B = \{(u_1(a_1), u_2(a_2), \ldots, u_n(a_n)): \Sigma a_i \leq a_0 \text{ and } a_i \geq 0 \text{ for all } i\}$. Under our assumptions B is a closed, bounded, convex subset of R^n_+. For any payoff vector $u \in B$, and any vector v such that $0 \leq v \leq u$, v is also in B, because the utility functions are continuous, strictly increasing, and $u_i(0) = 0$.

the fraction of the money for claimant 1, b is the fraction of money for claimant 2, and $a + b \leq 1$. Assume that creditor 1's utility for money is proportional to the amount he receives (i.e., 1 is *risk-neutral*), whereas creditor 2 has a declining marginal utility for money (2 is *risk-averse*). To be concrete, let 1's utility for the fraction a be $u_1(a) = a$ and let 2's utility for the fraction b be $u_2(b) = \sqrt{b}$. The bargaining set consists of all pairs $(u_1(a), u_2(b))$ such that $a + b \leq 1$ and a and b are nonnegative (see fig. 15).

3. The Coordination Problem

What division might the bargainers agree to? Clearly they have an interest in achieving an *efficient* allocation, which in this case means that none of the good is thrown away. The efficient allocations correspond to the payoffs that lie on the northeast boundary of the bargaining set. While an efficient outcome is desirable, however, it is not certain that the bargainers will be able to agree on one. The difficulty is that, typically, there is a *continuum* of efficient outcomes. Unless the claimants can agree on *exactly one* of them, there will be no bargain. The problem for the bargainers, therefore, is not simply to demand as much as they can for themselves; it is to correctly *anticipate* what the others are going to agree to. Their expectations must coordinate on the same solution. How do the bargainers solve this *coordination problem?*

One answer to this question is to assume that the bargainers engage in a structured interaction or game. Consider the following scenario when there are just two bargainers. First one makes an offer, which the second either accepts or rejects. If it is rejected, the second bargainer makes an offer, which the first either accepts or rejects. If it is rejected, the first again makes an offer, which the second either accepts or rejects, and so forth. After each rejection, there is a small probability that the bargaining breaks down permanently (this is where the risk factor comes in). The process continues until either an agreement is reached or a breakdown occurs. This is known as the *alternating offers game.*

If the bargainers are perfectly rational and their utility functions are common knowledge, they can anticipate exactly how the offers and counteroffers are going to unfold, and they will be able to reach agreement right away.[3] Thus they can solve the coordination problem because, given the structure of their interaction, each can anticipate what the other is going to do. Of course, the validity of this approach depends on the assumption that the bargainers interact in exactly the way specified in the model, and that they know each others' utility functions, neither of which is likely to hold in practice.

A second way that the bargainers can solve the coordination problem is to look for a payoff distribution that everyone agrees to be fair. In other words,

---

[3] In the next chapter we shall analyze this game in greater detail.

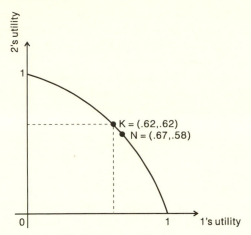

Fig. 15. The bargaining set for two creditors dividing $90,000.

they look for a solution that can be justified on objective grounds. One form of justification is to reason deductively from general equity principles, as in the derivation of formulas for allocating representation (chapter 3) and common costs (chapter 5). Another is to cite prominent authorities, like the rules of Aristotle and Maimonides for dividing contested property (chapter 4). A third approach is to appeal to precedent—to what is usual, customary, and expected in distributive problems of this sort (taxation has something of this flavor). All three of these approaches serve a similar purpose: they narrow the set of plausible outcomes, which helps to coordinate the parties' expectations about what the others are likely to accept. They also shift the discourse from making claims and demands to offering justifications and reasons, which is usually more constructive and more likely to convince others.

4. Classical Bargaining Solutions: Nash and Kalai-Smorodinsky

Let us now consider what equity principles might be deployed to justify a particular solution. In previous chapters these principles were expressed in terms of the physical *amounts* that the claimants receive in relation to their claims. Bargaining theory takes a different approach by defining equity in terms of the claimants' *utility payoffs*. In other words, the discussion is grounded in the levels of welfare that the parties can attain, not on the amounts that they actually receive. This means that equity is evaluated solely in terms of the bargaining set.

Let's see whether an equitable solution suggests itself by looking at the bargaining set in a particular case. Consider the point labeled *K* in figure 15, where the utility payoffs for both claimants are equal (.6180 for each). Concretely this corresponds to the agreement in which the first claimant gets about $56,200 and the second claimant gets about $33,800. The justification for this agreement is that each claimant is indifferent between his designated fraction and a .6180 chance at getting the whole $90,000. In other words, both parties are treated equally relative to the same (risky) prospect. Moreover, although this notion of equity is based on interpersonal comparisons of utility, it does no violence to utility theory because the comparisons do not depend on how the utility functions are scaled. It says simply that *a bargaining outcome is equitable if each claimant is indifferent between his portion and a fixed chance at getting all of the goods.* In general there is a unique efficient outcome with this property, known as the *Kalai-Smorodinsky solution.*[4]

A less obvious candidate for a fair payoff distribution is the point labeled *N* in figure 14. This has the approximate coordinates (.6667, .5773) and corresponds to an agreement in which the first claimant gets $60,000 and the second gets $30,000. To understand the basis of this solution, consider what would happen if we transfer a little money from one claimant to the other. Suppose, for example, that we transfer $1000 from claimant 2 to claimant 1. The payoffs from this new division are (.6778, .5676). Note that total utility has increased from .6667 + .5773 = 1.2440 to .6778 + .5676 = 1.2454, so we might argue that the transfer should be made. This argument is suspect, however, because it depends on the choice of *units* in which each person's utility function is measured.

One way around this problem is to consider the *percentage* by which the claimants' utilities change. This comparison is meaningful because percentage changes in a person's utility are independent of the absolute units in which that person's utility is measured. Under the transfer mentioned above, claimant 1's utility increases from .6667 to .6778, a gain of about 1.1 percent, while 2's utility decreases from .5774 to .5676, a loss of about 1.7 percent. Since the percentage loss outweighs the percentage gain we could say that the transfer is *not* justified.

Now let us consider a transfer of $1000 in the other direction. Claimant 1's utility decreases by about 1.67 percent while claimant 2's utility increases by 1.65 percent. Once again the percentage loss outweighs the percentage gain, so we could say that this transfer is also unjustified. It turns out, in fact, that *no* transfer of any size is justified; moreover, ($60,000, $30,000) is the only efficient allocation with this property.

NASH STANDARD. The *Nash standard of comparison* is the percentage change in a claimant's utility when he receives a small additional amount of the good.

---

[4] This solution was first characterized axiomatically by Kalai and Smorodinsky (1975), and first suggested in an early paper by Raiffa (1953).

A transfer between two claimants is *justified* under the Nash standard if the gainer's utility increases by a larger percentage than the loser's utility decreases; otherwise it is not justified. A division is *equitable* if no transfer is justified. *For any group of claimants there exists a unique division of the good that is equitable with respect to the Nash standard, and the associated payoffs are known as the Nash bargaining solution. The Nash solution maximizes the product of the claimants' utilities over all feasible payoff distributions.*[5]

The Nash standard of comparison identifies a unique outcome in any bargaining set, whether or not it arises from allocations of physical property. Similarly, the Kalai-Smorodinsky criterion identifies a unique outcome in any bargaining set, namely, the one for which the ratio of each claimant's payoff to his maximum possible payoff is the same for all claimants. Each of these criteria defines a *bargaining rule,* that is, a function that selects a unique set of payoffs in any given bargaining set. These rules are based on different ways of comparing the utilities of the bargainers, but they do no violence to the assumptions of utility theory, because they are independent of the units in which the claimants' utility are measured, that is, they are *scale-invariant.* Second, both rules yield *efficient* outcomes: there exists no other outcome in which someone is better off and no one is worse off. Third, they are *impartial:* the outcome depends only on the utilities of the claimants for the various outcomes, not on any other distinguishing features. The crucial difference between the two rules is that Nash is consistent, whereas Kalai-Smorodinsky is not.

> CONSISTENCY. A bargaining rule is *consistent* if the payoffs to every subgroup
> of bargainers satisfy the rule when the payoffs to all other bargainers are held
> fixed.

We shall illustrate this idea with a variation of the above example. Suppose there are three parties who are bargaining over their fractions of a common "pie." An agreement will be of the form (a, b, c), where a is the fraction for the first party, b is the fraction for the second, c is the fraction for the third, and $a + b + c \leq 1$. Assume that the associated payoffs are $u_1(a) = a$, $u_2(b) = \sqrt{b}$, and $u_3(c) = \sqrt{c}$. Thus 1 is risk-neutral while 2 and 3 are equally risk-averse. First consider the Kalai-Smorodinsky rule: We want to find a division such that $a + b + c = 1$ and $a = \sqrt{b} = \sqrt{c}$. The unique solution of these equations is $(^1/_2, ^1/_4, ^1/_4)$.

Now suppose that claimants 1 and 2 look at how much they get in relation to each other. Together they receive three-quarters of the pie. According to the Kalai-Smorodinsky criterion, they share this amount fairly if there is a fixed probability p such that $u_1(a) = pu_1(^3/_4)$ and $u_2(b) = pu_2(^3/_4)$, that is, if $a = (^3/_4)p$ and $\sqrt{b} = p\sqrt{(^3/_4)}$. The unique efficient solution of these equations is approx-

5 See the appendix, pp. 210–12.

imately $a = .5687$ and $b = .1813$, which is not the solution that they agreed to. In other words, if both claimants accept the Kalai-Smorodinsky as being equitable, then the first claimant can plausibly demonstrate that his payoff is too small relative to the second's, given that the third party's payoff is fixed. The Kalai-Smorodinsky rule is therefore inconsistent.

The Nash rule, on the other hand, is consistent. This follows because the Nash solution maximizes the product of the claimants' utilities, so it certainly maximizes the product of the utilities of any subgroup *given* that the utilities of everyone outside the group are held fixed. An even more remarkable fact is that the Nash rule is the *unique* bargaining rule that is consistent, efficient, impartial, and scale-invariant.[6] It would therefore appear that the Nash standard is the most satisfactory way of defining a fair bargain.

5. Framing Effects

Nevertheless, there is a flaw in this argument. Consider again the situation in which the two creditors divide $90,000. The Nash solution suggests that the first should get $60,000, while the second should get only $30,000. It seems odd to call this outcome "fair" when the second claimant is owed *three times* as much money as the first. Surely we would expect this information to have a bearing on the agreement that the parties reach. Even though the claims are not legally enforceable, they create a powerful framing effect that influences the parties' perceptions of the plausibility of various outcomes. This additional information is not part of the Nash calculation, which depends only on the claimants' utility functions and the disagreement allocation. The reason that the Nash solution awards the first creditor more money than the second is simply that the former is more risk-averse than the latter.[7]

Under certain conditions, differences in risk aversion may indeed have some bearing on the bargaining outcome, as we shall see in the next chapter. Moreover, it makes intuitive sense that the more risk-averse bargainer is at a disadvantage: since he is less willing to accept the risk of a breakdown in the negotiations, he may be more inclined to give in. But there is no reason to believe that the outcome depends *only*, or even mainly, on differences in risk aversion. Common sense, buttressed by empirical data on how subjects bargain, suggest that the context of the bargain—whether it is a child custody suit, a wheat agreement, an arms treaty, or the sale of a used car—shapes the outcome to a significant extent. The details of the situation create framing effects that influence what the bargainers believe to be fair and what they

---

[6] See the appendix, Theorem 20.

[7] The inadequacy of classical bargaining theory for describing norms of distributive justice has been pointed out by Yaari and Bar-Hillel (1984) and Roemer (1986b).

believe others will accept.[8] Purely utilitarian definitions of equity are inadequate because they fail to take into account the full range of information
available to the bargainers. Moreover, since the utility functions are usually not
common knowledge, equity principles based on them are ineffectual. We must
look at the *context* within which a bargain occurs, and the information that is
accessible to the bargainers, to understand the form that equity arguments will
take.

6. Equity Criteria Based on Tangible Claims

Consider again the two creditors who must decide how to split the $90,000 they
jointly collect from the debtor. How would we actually expect the bargaining to
proceed? Each will try to anticipate what the other is going to accept; at the
same time, each will try to influence what the other believes he will accept. The
tools at their disposal are solutions that are supported by principle and precedent. Since they are unlikely to know much about the other's degree of risk
aversion, we can expect that they will couch their arguments not in terms of
utilities but in the light of information that is directly accessible, namely, the
amounts they lent the debtor.

The smaller creditor might try to argue, for example, that they should split
the $90,000 equally. In support of this position she might point out that the
amounts they are owed cannot be legally enforced, so they should have no
bearing on the issue. The second creditor might counter (especially if he were a
Talmudic scholar) that equal division is appropriate, but $90,000 is not the
amount in dispute. He would observe that the first is owed only $60,000, so he
has sole claim to the remaining $30,000. Hence the fair solution is for him to
take the $30,000 and then split the $60,000 equally. (Recall from chapter 4 that
this is the contested garment principle.) On the other hand, if he were an
Aristotelian, he would argue that the only acceptable solution is to split the
money in proportion to the claims.

These are the kinds of arguments that each would be likely to make in
pressing his case. Which solution prevails depends on the plausibility of the
arguments and the degree to which they are backed up by authority and precedent. In other words, plausibility depends on who the bargainers are and on the
cultural assumptions they share. In western society, for example, the customary
solution would be to split the assets in proportion to the claims. Thus the first
creditor would receive $22,500 and the second would receive $67,500. This
solution is not the only equitable one, but given its prominence as a cultural
norm, the bargainers will find it hard to agree on anything else. *Norms of equity
are powerful because they condition the bargainers' expectations about what*

---

[8] This point has been documented empirically by Yaari and Bar-Hillel (1984).

the outcome will be. These norms of equity are framed in terms of the tangible aspects of the situation (e.g., the size of the claims), not the bargainers' utility functions and their attitudes toward risk.

7. Experimental Results on Bargaining

The importance of norms and precedents in conditioning expectations is borne out by laboratory experiments. In a typical experimental setup, two subjects bargain over how to divide a fixed sum of money or another good that can be redeemed for money. The rules are that, if the subjects can agree on how to divide the good within a specified time period, they receive the agreed-upon division; otherwise they receive nothing. For example, Nydegger and Owen (1974) performed the following experiment. Twenty subjects were paired at random, and each of the ten pairs was given one dollar to divide if they could agree on how to divide it. The result was that all of the bargainers divided the dollar equally. Notice that this is not necessarily what the Nash model would lead us to expect. If subjects differ appreciably in their attitudes toward risk, then the more risk-averse subjects should be willing to accept less than half of the money. But no variation in the outcomes was observed; they all split the money evenly, a pattern that has been confirmed in numerous other experiments.

One explanation of these findings is that subjects choose the fifty-fifty split because it is the most prominent and obvious solution. It is a "focal point" (Schelling, 1960). There are in fact two different reasons why fifty-fifty is a focal point. First, it is the only symmetric solution in a symmetric bargaining situation. Every other division is in competition with its mirror image. Second, equal division is a social norm. It is the customary solution when the claimants have equal claims, just as proportional division is customary when the bargainers have unequal claims.

A second explanation is that each subject's utility is linear in money when the amounts are small. Hence the results accord with bargaining theory, which predicts that they split the money evenly when their utility functions are linear.

The simple experiment of dividing the dollar is unable to distinguish between these two explanations because the context is not rich enough. Subsequent experiments shed more light on the matter however. Roth and Murnighan (1982) analyzed the following situation: two subjects were given one hundred lottery tickets to divide. Each subject's chance of winning a prize was proportional to the number of lottery tickets that he received in the bargain, but the money value of the prizes was different for the two players. Player 1's prize was worth $20 whereas player 2's prize was worth $5. Thus, if the two players divided the tickets in the proportions 20/80, then 1 had a 20 percent chance of winning $20 and 2 had an 80 percent chance of winning $5, so the expected money payoff was the same for each.

In this situation there are *two* focal points: split the money equally and split the lottery tickets equally. Bargaining theory, however, predicts only the latter solution. The reason is that standard theory assumes that each individual's utility function is *linear* in the probability of winning. In other words, each individual is supposed to have twice as high a utility for $2x$ lottery tickets as compared to x tickets, for any x between zero and one hundred. The monetary size of the prizes should not matter, because they simply rescale the utility functions, and the bargainers are not supposed to compare their utilities on a cardinal scale. Each division of the tickets amounts therefore to a division of their utilities, so the Nash solution is to divide the tickets equally.

The experimental results show, however, that the solutions occupy a spectrum between splitting the tickets evenly and splitting the money evenly (see fig. 16).

More precisely, when neither subject was told the value of the other side's prize, most of them split the tickets evenly. But when the value of both prizes was common knowledge, most of the divisions represented a compromise between the two focal points. Thus when additional information was provided that the bargainers considered to be salient (in this case the monetary value of the prizes), they used this information as a standard of comparison, which changed the bargaining outcome even though it did not change the bargainers' utility functions.

One might conjecture that *any* additional information that creates competing focal points would result in a more diffuse pattern of outcomes. This is not so however. It is crucial that the bargainers consider the information to be *salient* to the situation. For example, Roth, Malouf, and Murnighan (1981) conducted a variant of the above experiment in which the bargainers divided one hundred lottery tickets, and the prize was a certain number of *chips* having monetary value. Both of them knew the *number* of chips in each prize, which was substantially different for the two players, but each of them knew only the monetary value of his *own* chips.

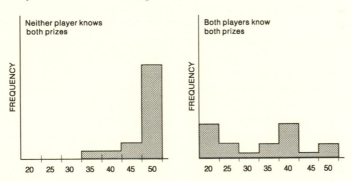

Fig. 16. The distribution of outcomes in terms of the percentage of lottery tickets obtained by the $20 player. (Source: Roth and Murnighan, 1982.)

As in the previous case this created two competing focal points: divide the lottery tickets evenly (giving them an equal chance of winning the prize but not an equal expected payoff in chips), or divide the tickets so that the expected payoff in chips was equal. This had no statistically significant effect on the outcomes, however. The player whose prize appeared to be smaller (i.e., consisted of fewer chips) frequently tried to argue that he should receive more lottery tickets to compensate for his disadvantage, but (unlike the case where the money prizes differed) the other player tended not to accept these arguments. Moreover, the one making the arguments tended, in the end, to back off from them. Thus salience is a crucial element in establishing the credibility of the yardstick with which equity is measured.

What, though, makes one yardstick more salient than another? In previous chapters we have argued that the salience of a standard of comparison is a function of three factors; rational argument, authority, and precedent. Each of these factors lends credibility to a given way of framing the problem, and solidifies the players' beliefs about what the outcome is likely to be. When there are several competing standards, and no clear arguments or authorities to support one over the other, it is reasonable to expect that precedent will play a substantial role in determining which standard is viewed as the norm.

In a fascinating series of experiments, Roth and Schoumaker (1983) examined to what extent bargainers could be *conditioned* to favor one standard over another through the reinforcement effect of precedent. Each pair of subjects divided one hundred lottery tickets with prizes of $40 and $10, respectively. Each subject played twenty-five games in succession. Unknown to each subject, however, the first fifteen plays were against a programmed opponent who insisted on a solution that was close to one of the two focal outcomes (either equal expected money payoffs or equal chances). After the first fifteen rounds, the subject was paired against a succession of other subjects who had been playing against a *similarly* programmed opponent. Furthermore, the solutions that each subject had agreed to in the previous five rounds were published for both to see. The conjecture was that the experience of the subjects in the programmed rounds would create mutual expectations that would tend to lock them into whatever solution they had become accustomed to playing. A third group of subjects played the full twenty-five rounds without programmed opponents to serve as control.

The results confirmed the hypothesis that the expectations formed in the early rounds strongly influenced the players' bargaining behavior in subsequent rounds. Almost all of the players who became accustomed to an opponent who insisted on equal chances in the first fifteen rounds continued to make equal chances agreements in the remaining ten rounds. This was true even though for the $10 player such an agreement was distinctly unfavorable compared to the alternative focal point (equal expected money payoffs). Similarly, the players who had become accustomed to an opponent who insisted on equal expected money payoffs continued to make agreements that were biased toward an equal money solution even though this outcome was relatively unfavorable for the $40 players.

These experiments provide rather convincing evidence (if we needed any) that knowledge of the players' utility functions is not enough to predict the outcome of a distributive bargain. The outcome is strongly influenced by what the bargainers expect it to be *a priori* but these expectations do not normally involve the claimants' utility functions for the simple reason that people typically do not know others' utility functions. Instead, expectations are shaped by the visible qualifications that the claimants bring with them, and the distributive norms that apply to the situation at hand.

8. Empirical Evidence from Sharecropping Practices

The importance of social norms is also apparent in bargains between economic agents, where the stakes are considerably higher. Sharecropping is a particularly interesting example because it is practiced in almost all agricultural societies, and has been extensively studied by economists. The terms of a sharecropping contract specify the fraction of the harvest to be received by the tenant and the landlord, where the labor is supplied by the tenant and the land by the owner.[9] Such a contract is attractive from the landlord's point of view because it encourages the tenant to work hard and produce a large crop. It is also attractive from the tenant's point of view because he does not have to make capital outlays, and it protects him to some degree from adverse events such as low prices and bad weather.[10]

According to classical bargaining theory, the fractions that the tenant and landlord agree to should depend on their utility functions and on their alternatives should they fail to agree. The landlord's alternatives include finding another tenant, leasing out the land, or putting it to some other use. The tenant's alternatives include working on someone else's land, hiring out his labor locally, moving to another area, or seeking other forms of employment. These alternatives put bounds on the bargains that each party is willing to accept, but typically they also leave some latitude for negotiation. An able worker should be able to strike a better bargain than a less able one. A landowner with especially fertile land should be able to strike a better bargain than his less fortunate neighbors. We would also expect that risk-averse parties tend to obtain less favorable terms than those who are risk-neutral, all else being equal. If the postulates of bargaining theory are correct, we would therefore expect to

[9] The division of responsibility for providing seed, fertilizer, equipment, and various other inputs is also specified in the contract.

[10] For a discussion of the incentive properties of sharecropping contracts see Bell and Zusman (1976), and Newbery and Stiglitz (1979).

TABLE 7.1

Frequency Distribution of Cropsharing Rules in Selected Regions of India, 1975–76

State				Crop Shares (Tenant: Owner)										
	3:1	2:1	10:6	3:2	9:7	1:1	18:22	7:9	2:3	6:10	7:13	1:2	6:17	1:3
Paddy														
West Bengal	6.4	4.7	1.2	1.8	0.0	66.9	3.5	0.0	3.8	0.0	0.6	6.4	0.6	4.1
Bihar	0.0	0.5	0.0	1.0	0.0	86.5	0.0	1.6	0.0	2.6	0.0	6.2	0.0	1.6
Orissa	3.4	0.0	6.9	6.9	3.4	79.4	0.0	0.0	0.0	0.0	0.0	0.0	0.0	0.0
Wheat														
Uttar Pradesh	0.6	0.0	0.0	0.0	0.0	83.8	0.0	0.0	6.0	0.0	0.0	6.0	0.0	3.6

Source: Bardhan (1984), table 9.2.

see substantial variability in the terms of the deals that are actually struck.

Empirical studies show, however, that cropsharing rules tend to be remarkably uniform within each agricultural community. For example, Bardhan (1984) conducted an extensive survey of sharecropping formulas used in northern and eastern India. He found that in over 60 percent of the villages there was a single sharing formula, and in over 90 percent of the villages there were at most two sharing formulas. Moreover, *by far the most frequent rule in all areas and for all crops was equal division* (see table 7.1).

These data lend further credence to the idea that bargainers reach agreement, not on the basis of their utility for various allocations, but by coordinating on a prominent or focal solution. Fifty-fifty is certainly the most prominent way to divide a pie into two pieces, and it is easy to justify on grounds of fairness. This is not to say that bargainers will always choose such a solution, or that differences in risk aversion play no role in their choices. The evidence suggests, however, that nominally fair solutions appear to be very powerful even when the claimants have a lot at stake, and are therefore motivated to bargain hard. Nor is this a violation of economic rationality. A rule like equal division is not economically inefficient so long as the outcome is within the bounds established by the parties' opportunity costs—including the costs of gathering information about alternatives to agreement. In many cases this leaves a wide range of agreements that are economically rational. The greater the degree of indeterminacy, however, the greater the risk that the negotiations will break down because the negotiators are unable to settle on any one of them. In other words, the *lack* of an established rule is costly because it increases the probability that the bargainers fail to reach agreement even though it is in their interest to do so. In this sense, norms of equity increase efficiency by coordinating peoples' expectations and reducing the transaction costs of bargaining.

9. Summary

In this chapter we have reviewed various concepts of equity in the theoretical literature on bargaining. These concepts are framed in terms of the bargainers' utilities for the good (their degree of risk aversion) rather than their degree of entitlement to them. Within this framework the equity properties developed in earlier chapters suggest that the Nash solution is the most satisfactory. Nevertheless, the Nash solution (and other utility-based solutions) fail to predict how real bargains are resolved because they leave out crucial contextual information that the parties use to make interpersonal comparisons. Utility is not a practical means for making such comparisons for the simple reason that it is not accessible information. Instead, the agents look for cues in the situation itself. Visible evidence of claim, need, and desert frame discussions about equity, and provide the toeholds by which the bargainers reach agreement.

8

Fair Process

Fair play: equity in the conditions or opportunities
afforded to a player.
 (*Oxford English Dictionary*)

1. Games of Fair Division

In this chapter our focus shifts from simple distributive bargains to more complex situations in which different *kinds* of goods must be allocated. Two issues arise in this setting that were not particularly important in earlier cases. First, we would like the allocation to be both equitable and *efficient*. In other words, we want to give the goods to those who value them most highly *subject to* the condition that everyone receives a fair share. This raises some difficult conceptual issues, for the portions allotted to different individuals will generally look quite different (given that their tastes are different). It is not clear that we can tell whether the claimants are treated fairly simply by comparing what they receive. Second, the introduction of efficiency creates a procedural problem. Preferences are usually private information, and we cannot expect people to honestly reveal them unless it is in their interest to do so. The challenge, therefore, is to design procedures that *induce* the claimants to reveal enough information about their preferences so that an equitable and efficient solution can be implemented.

To set the stage, imagine that a group of claimants holds a bundle of property in common that they wish to divide equitably among themselves. The property may consist of various kinds of goods: homogeneous and divisible (money); heterogeneous and divisible (land); homogeneous and indivisible (silverware); or heterogeneous and indivisible (houses, paintings, diamonds). We shall assume that each claimant is entitled to a prespecified share of the property, but because it consists of heterogeneous or indivisible goods it cannot be divided in proportion to the shares. An allocation *procedure* is a method or process for selecting an allocation. Traditional examples include auctions, divide and choose, and various forms of mediation and arbitration. Though these procedures differ in detail, they all have a common purpose, namely, to induce the claimants to reveal information about their preferences.

Some procedures, like mediation, are relatively informal and loosely structured. In the usual format, the mediator meets with the various parties to gather confidential information about their preferences, then recommends a solution based on her conception of what is fair (and efficient) given what she has been told. She would probably not want to specify her criteria very precisely in advance, because this might cause the parties to bias their answers. She may also need to go through several rounds before uncovering a solution that everyone finds acceptable. Informal procedures like this can be quite effective, even though the rules are not clearly articulated and the claimants are not obliged to follow the mediator's recommendations.[1]

There is another class of procedures, however, that require no intervention by a third party. They are *self-enforcing* in the sense that they yield fair outcomes when the claimants act in their own self-interest and play by the rules of the game. These are sometimes known as *games of fair division*. In general, a *game* involves a group of *players,* each of whom is assigned to a *role*. For each role there is a prescribed set of *actions* or *moves* that the role-player can take at each successive stage of the game. An *allocation game* is a game whose outcome is an allocation of some or all of the common property. The game is "fair" if it yields normatively fair outcomes when played by intelligent players. To evaluate the fairness of such a process, we therefore need to have in mind some standard by which to evaluate the fairness of the result.

Over the course of the next two chapters we shall explore these two issues in tandem: the design of allocation procedures, and the development of standards for judging outcomes. We begin by considering two traditional games of fair division: auctioning indivisibles, and divide and choose. These games are best suited to situations involving small numbers of claimants (two, three, or perhaps half a dozen). In the following chapter we shall turn our attention to the case of large numbers of claimants and the role of competitive markets in allocating goods both equitably and efficiently.

2. Auctioning Indivisibles

Let's begin with the case in which the common property consists of several indivisible goods plus a single divisible good such as money. Assume that the claimants are equally entitled to the property, and that they assign different money values to the indivisible goods. A natural way to achieve both equity and efficiency would appear to be the following: give each indivisible good to the claimant who puts the highest *value* on it, and let him compensate the others by an amount equal to their share of the value.

This solution is not as straightforward as it seems at first, however. Consider the following example. Alistair and Beatrice have been left equal shares of an estate that consists of a 100-acre farm and $50,000 in cash. For the present, we

---

[1] If the third party can make a binding decision, then she *arbitrates* the solution. For a game-theoretic analysis of various arbitration methods see Crawford (1979b, 1985) and Brams, Kilgour, and Merrill (1991).

shall think of the farm as being indivisible. (In other words, although it could be divided, it would lose most of its value if it were.) Assume that Beatrice values the farm more than Alistair does in the following sense: she is indifferent between receiving the farm or $300,000, whereas he is indifferent between receiving the farm or $100,000. Thus they have substantially different tastes. We shall also assume that they have substantially different private resources: Alistair is wealthy, while Beatrice has nothing aside from her inheritance.

The procedure described above works as follows. First the heirs divide the money in the estate equally. Then they write down the money values that they attach to the farm. The farm goes to the one who names the largest value, and the winner pays the other one-half of the sales price.

This procedure has two interpretations. On the one hand it defines a *principle* of fair division, namely, the farm should go to the person who values it most, and the other claimant should be compensated by an amount equal to his share of this value. It also defines a *process* by which such a division can supposedly be achieved. Unfortunately, the process does *not* have the alleged outcome when the claimants play the game intelligently, as we shall soon see.

First we need to define the rules of the game a bit more precisely. Since transfers of money are involved, the players must offer proof that they can make good on the amounts that they promise to pay. The process will therefore work as follows. In stage one, each player puts into an envelope the amount of money that he proposes to pay to the other in return for the farm. In stage two, the envelopes are opened. The highest bidder gets the farm, and the amount in the high bidder's envelope is paid to the other, whose own envelope is returned. If there is a tie for high bid, it is resolved by the toss of a fair coin.[2]

Let us analyze the outcome of this procedure when the two heirs bid for the farm. Suppose that they bid a and b, respectively, where we assume that all bids must be in a whole number of dollars. The bids are *in equilibrium* if neither heir can obtain a strictly preferred outcome by unilaterally changing his bid. Clearly, b cannot exceed $25,000 because B has no funds other than her share of the money in the estate. Suppose now that a is *less* than or equal to b. Then A could do better by outbidding B by one dollar, which A is able to because he has additional funds. This contradicts the assumption that the bids are in equilibrium, so we conclude that a is *strictly larger* than b. Suppose next that a is strictly *greater* than $b + 1$. Then A could do better by reducing his bid to exactly $b + 1$ dollars, since he would still get the farm but pay less for it. Thus in equilibrium we must have $a = b + 1$, which means that A wins the bid. It must also be true that $b = $25,000$. For if b were *less* than $25,000, then (since $a =$

---

[2] This procedure generalizes to the case of n claimants with equal or unequal shares as follows. Let claimant i have share s_i, where $0 < s_i < 1$ and $\Sigma s_j = 1$. Each claimant puts an amount of money in an envelope. We interpret this to be the bidder's reported valuation of the item *less* his own share. Thus if i puts m_i dollars in the envelope, we say that i's *imputed valuation* of the item is $v_i = m_i/(1 - s_i)$. The rule is that the bidder with the highest imputed valuation gets the item, and the amount he put in the envelope is allocated among the others in proportion to their shares.

$b + 1)$ B could match A without exceeding her resources. B has an incentive to do so, because this gives her a 50 percent chance of getting the farm and paying a dollars for it, which she strictly prefers to losing the farm and being paid a dollars in compensation. Therefore, in equilibrium, B bids the limit of her resources ($25,000), A outbids B by one dollar ($25,001), and the final allocation is: A gets the farm and is $1 out-of-pocket; B gets $50,001.[3]

This allocation is *efficient* because B cannot buy the farm from A at a price that A is willing to accept and B can afford. But it is not clear that the allocation is *equitable*. In particular, it does not implement the principle of division that was used to justify it, because neither claimant wrote down his "valuation" of the farm. This lapse could perhaps be overlooked if this outcome were the only efficient one. In this case, however, *every* allocation of the property is efficient. If B gets the farm and some (or all) of the money, B is not willing to sell the farm to A at a price he is willing to pay. Similarly, if A gets the farm and some (or all) of the money, B is not able to buy the farm at a price that A is willing to accept. Thus in every case there are no potential gains from trade, and the allocation is economically efficient (Pareto optimal). The auction implements one among many efficient allocations, but there is no reason to think that it is the most equitable one.

Indeed, there is some reason to think otherwise, because the auction tends to discriminate against claimants with small private endowments. B is at a disadvantage because, although she values the farm highly, she does not have other goods to offer A in compensation. Even her interest in the common property is not enough to overcome this disadvantage.

One way to put the claimants on a more equal footing would be to insist that they bid only with money (or other divisible goods) distributed from the estate. In the above example this means that both are constrained to bid $25,000 or less. Given their valuations, it is clear that both will in fact bid $25,000, which results in a tie. Assume that ties are resolved by the toss of a fair coin. Thus there is a 50 percent chance that A gets the farm and B gets the money, and a 50 percent chance that B gets the farm and A gets the money. Note that both of these allocations are efficient.[4]

---

[3] A variant of this method, due to Knaster, was reported by Steinhaus (1948) in his landmark paper on fair division. In Knaster's version, the high bidder pays the total sales price into a common fund. Then each heir (including the high bidder) takes out of the fund his fractional share times the amount *he* bid on the object. This may leave a surplus in the common fund, which is divided among all of the heirs in proportion to their shares. Like the method discussed in the text, this process encourages strategic bidding.

[4] It is not true *in general* that the outcome of the auction is efficient when the players are restricted to bid with money from the estate. Suppose, for example, that the claimants' valuations are reversed: B values the property at $100,000 and A values it at $300,000. When both are constrained to bid at most $25,000, the equilibrium outcome is that both bid the limit: $25,000. Thus, with 50 percent probability, B gets the farm and A gets the money. But for any price between $100,000 and $300,000 A would be willing and able to buy the farm and B would be willing to sell it, so both would be better off.

From an *ex ante* standpoint one could say that this resolution of the problem is fair, but it seems unlikely that the heirs would actually agree to it. The reason is that there are other ways of sharing or dividing the supposedly "indivisible" good that both of them would probably prefer to taking a fifty-fifty chance on the two outcomes described above. First, the farm could be physically divided. Even though it loses some of its value, both heirs might prefer this option to taking a 50-50 chance at getting the farm or the money. Second, the farm could be divided in other ways, say by converting it to a joint stock company and issuing corporate shares ("equity") that entitle the holders to a *pro rata* portion of the profits. (If there is a house it could be time-shared.) Third, the farm could be sold and the proceeds divided. Every one of these techniques converts the farm into a form of property that can be divided equally. Depending on how risk-averse the heirs are, it is conceivable that they would prefer *any one* of these alternatives to a fifty-fifty chance of getting either the money or the farm.

3. Superior and Inferior Modes of Division

In general, a technique that converts indivisible common property into a divisible commodity will be called a *mode* of division. The three most common modes of division are: time-sharing (rotation), conversion by sale, and dividing chances at getting the good (randomization). Let us assume that, once a mode of division has been agreed upon, the claimants divide the property in proportion to their predetermined shares. We shall say that one mode is *ex ante superior* to another if every claimant prefers division by the first mode to division by the second mode, and at least one claimant strictly prefers it. The two modes are *equivalent* if every claimant is indifferent between the two outcomes.

To illustrate these ideas let us return to the division of the farm. There we identified four plausible modes of division: I divide the land; II divide the profits; III sell the land; IV hold a lottery. Their relative desirability depends on the heirs' preferences. For example, if both heirs are sufficiently risk-averse, they might think mode IV is inferior to all the others. They would probably prefer mode I to mode II if there are no economies of scale from large landholdings; otherwise it could be the other way around. If they do not get along with each other, they might prefer mode III to all of the others.

If the goal is to achieve an outcome that is both equitable and efficient, we may need to carry the analysis one step further. It is possible, for example, that mode I is preferred to mode II by everyone *ex ante,* but that after trading to an efficient allocation some prefer the outcome under mode II to the outcome under mode I. This suggests the possibility of comparing modal divisions *ex post* as well as *ex ante.* For this idea to have much power, we need to make some assumption about which trades will in fact occur from a given initial allocation.

A natural candidate is the set of *competitive allocations*.[5] We could say that one mode is *ex post superior* to another if every claimant prefers all competitive outcomes under the first mode to all competitive outcomes under the second. Finally, we could say that one mode is *unambiguously superior* to another if everyone prefers the first to the second both *ex ante* and *ex post*. It is reasonable to expect that, in some cases, the heirs will agree that one mode is superior to the others even in this demanding sense.

4. Divide and Choose

We turn now to another complication that often arises in the division of common property. If some of the goods are heterogeneous, we cannot divide it in proportion to the shares. An example would be a farm in which the land is of uneven quality. One way to deal with this situation is to convert the property into a homogeneous good by one of the devices discussed above (issuing corporate shares, distributing lottery tickets, or selling it). Another option would be to divide the property so that, even though the portions are different, each claimant prefers his portion to the others.

A traditional method of this type is divide and choose. One claimant is designated to be the divider and the other to be the chooser. The divider splits the property into two portions, then the chooser selects one and the divider takes the other. Children often use this method for sharing a piece of cake. It is an allocation game because the permissible actions at each stage are clearly defined, and the end result is an allocation of the property.

Moreover, it is fair because the outcome is envy-free. This can be argued under two different models of how the players might act in such a game. In one model, the divider is assumed to play conservatively because he is unsure of the chooser's tastes. Since he is uncertain which piece the chooser will select, he plays it safe by creating two portions that he values equally, so it does not matter to him which one she selects. This results in an envy-free allocation, because the chooser does not strictly prefer the portion she passed over, and the divider is indifferent between the two.

In the second model, the divider is well informed about the chooser's tastes and optimizes his choice of division based on this information. That is, he creates one portion that is as desirable as possible from his own point of view subject to its being, from the chooser's point of view, a little *less* desirable than

---

[5] An allocation is *competitive* from a given initial allocation if there exists a set of prices, one for each good, such that each person's portion is most-preferred within the set of all portions that he is able to buy given the value of his initial allocation. Such an allocation exists provided that the utility functions are continuous, strictly increasing, and strictly quasi-concave, and everyone begins with a positive amount of every good (Debreu, 1962).

the complementary portion. Assuming that the chooser selects rationally, this outcome is also envy-free.[6]

A Variant of Divide and Choose

Divide and choose can also be applied to common property that consists exclusively of homogeneous divisible goods. Consider the following simple example. *A* and *B* have a pound of cake and a pound of ice cream to divide. Pound for pound *A* likes ice cream better than cake. *B* is indifferent between ice cream and cake but (unlike *A*) she would prefer a mixture to eating only cake or only ice cream. Let's suppose that *B*'s optimal mixture of ice cream and cake is fifty-fifty. We shall assume that, if *A* is chosen to be divider, his optimal strategy is to create two pieces—one consisting of almost all the ice cream, and the other consisting of all the cake plus a tiny dollop of ice cream. This division is designed so that *B* slightly prefers the latter portion, while *A* greatly prefers the former portion. Hence the resulting allocation is envy-free. It could be argued, however, that it is unfair because it leaves B *worse off* than if they had divided the cake and ice cream equally, which seems the natural thing to do.

This observation can be generalized as follows. Suppose that the common property consists of several kinds of goods, each of which is homogeneous and perfectly divisible. Suppose further that the two claimants are equally entitled to these goods. The *transparently equitable* solution is to divide each of the goods equally between them. The disadvantage of this solution is that it may be inefficient; by exploiting differences in the claimants' tastes, both of them could be better off. This argument is only justified, however, if both of them actually are better off as compared to the transparently equitable solution. As we have just seen, the classical divide and choose procedure fails this simple test.

> ACCEPTABLE. An allocation of common property between two claimants is *acceptable* if neither claimant is worse off than under an equal division of the goods.

The following variation of traditional version of divide and choose yields an outcome that is acceptable to both parties (Crawford, 1980).

> CRAWFORD'S DIVIDE AND CHOOSE. The divider creates two labeled portions, one that he designates for himself and the other that he designates for the chooser. If the chooser rejects this division, each of them receives one-half of all the goods.

---

[6] The existence of envy-free divisions under various assumptions is discussed in Crawford (1977), Berliant, Dunz, and Thomson (1992), and Brams and Taylor (1992).

It can be shown that, *if the claimants play this game rationally, it yields an allocation that is efficient, acceptable, and envy-free.*[7]

5. The Divider's Advantage

It would appear that this procedure solves the fair division problem in a satisfactory way, but a serious difficulty remains, because the divider is in a much better position than the chooser to exploit the differences in these preferences. In other words, a claimant can do at least as well in the role of divider as in the role of chooser (assuming that both act rationally) and often he can do better. To see this, suppose that A is divider, B is chooser, and A designates the portion a for himself and b for B. Let e, e denote equal division. If A divides rationally, then A prefers a to e while B is indifferent between b and e. (Otherwise A could transfer a small amount from portion b to portion a, thereby creating a bigger portion a' for himself and a smaller one b' for B that B thinks is at least as good as e.)[8]

Now let them switch roles. As divider, B can offer exactly the same division a, b that A did, so she can certainly do at least as well as before. A will accept, since a is at least as good as e. However, B may be able to do considerably better than this by cutting the pieces in a different way. Thus a person is always at least as well off in the role of divider as chooser, and is often better off. This phenomenon is known as the *divider's advantage.*[9]

---

[7] Assume that each claimant's preferences can be represented by a utility function that is continuous, strictly increasing, and quasi-concave. Let u and v be the utility functions for A and B, respectively, and let the total bundle of goods be denoted by a_0. Without loss of generality, let A be the divider and B the chooser. A's optimal strategy is to propose a division (a, b) such that $u(a)$ is maximized subject to $v(b) \geq v(e)$, where $e = a_0/2$ denotes equal division. Under our assumptions the maximum exists and the corresponding allocation(s) are efficient. Let us also assume that B chooses A's proposed allocation, since in B's opinion it is no worse than equal division. Since A likes his portion at least as well as equal division, the division is acceptable. It remains to be verified that it is envy-free. Suppose not. If B strictly prefers A's portion, then B strictly prefers a to b and B also prefers b to e. Quasiconcavity therefore implies that B strictly prefers $(a + b)/2$ to e, which is impossible, because $(a + b)/2 = e$. A similar argument shows that A does not strictly prefer B's portion to his own. Therefore the allocation is efficient, acceptable, and envy-free.

[8] If no division Pareto dominates e, e we assume that A divides equally. We also assume that whenever the chooser is indifferent between the divider's offer and equal division, he obliges the divider by accepting his proposal.

[9] It must be stressed that the divider's advantage rests on the assumption that the players' utility functions are common knowledge and that everyone acts rationally based on this knowledge. If these assumptions do not hold, there are situations in which the chooser may have an advantage. Suppose, for example, that A is dividing a piece of cake that is topped off with icing and a cherry. Assume that both of their utility functions are additive (that is, the sum of utilities of the pieces equals the utility of the whole), but A does not know B's tastes. If A wants to play it safe, he would

To see how large the divider's advantage can be, consider the following variation of the example discussed in section 2. There is $200,000 in the estate and 100 acres of land. A values land at $1,000 per acre and B values it at $3,000 per acre. All of this is assumed to be common knowledge to the parties. If A is divider his optimal choice is approximately

$$a: \text{ 16 acres } + \$200,000; \qquad b: \text{ 84 acres.}$$

B slightly prefers her designated portion b to equal division, so A gets all of the money and some of the land. If on the other hand B is divider, her (approximately) optimal choice is

$$a': \$150,001; \qquad b': \text{ 100 acres } + \$49,999.$$

A slightly prefers the portion a' to equal division so he accepts it. (We assume that the heirs are not spiteful.) By being divider, B therefore gets a substantially more valuable portion.

> ROLE-NEUTRALITY. An allocation game is *role-neutral* if the equilibrium pay-offs do not depend on how the claimants are assigned to the roles in the game.[10]

Role-neutrality is analogous to saying that the playing field is level: the players can be expected to do equally well no matter what end of the field they must defend. As we have just seen, Crawford's variant of divide and choose is not role neutral, and in this sense it is not equitable. Is there any way to make it so?

6. Removing the Divider's Advantage by Lottery

The first solution that springs to mind is to determine the divider by the toss of a fair coin. This game has three stages: first the coin is tossed, second the divider creates two labeled portions, third the chooser selects one and the divider takes the other. This variation of Crawford's divide and choose is obviously role-neutral before the toss occurs, because the roles are completely undifferentiated. The difficulty is that the game may be *inefficient* in the sense that there are other fair games that both parties would prefer to play. This would be the case, for example, if the players are very risk-averse and neither is inclined to take the chance of being the chooser. However, the game may be inefficient even if the

---

divide the cake into two pieces that, while not identical, are equally desirable from his own point of view. Of these two pieces, B would almost certainly prefer one to the other (assuming that her tastes differ from A's). It follows that B is likely to receive a portion that she values at more than one-half the total, while A receives a portion that he values at exactly one-half of the total.

[10] The appropriate definition of equilibrium depends on the context. In the divide and choose game we mean *subgame perfect equilibrium*, that is, the players' strategies are in equilibrium at the beginning of the game and at every subsequent stage of the game.

parties are risk-neutral. By "risk-neutral" we mean that each is indifferent between receiving one hundred acres with 50 percent probability and receiving fifty acres for sure. Similarly, each is indifferent between receiving $100,000 with 50 percent probability and $50,000 for sure, and so forth. It is convenient to scale the utilities so that receiving *none* of the property has utility zero, and receiving *all* of the property has utility one, for each of the claimants.

Figure 17 shows the utility payoffs for all possible distributions of land and money among the two claimants (including only *some* of the land and money). Point $E = (.50, .50)$ represents equal division. Point $A = (.72, .50)$ represents the outcome when A is divider, whereas $B = (.50, .70)$ is the outcome when B is divider. The expected utility from an equal chances lottery is the midpoint of the outcomes A and B, that is, $C = (.61, .60)$. This is inefficient because all outcomes to the northeast of C leave both claimants better off.

This phenomenon is quite general: a lottery is typically an *inefficient* way of compromising between two allocations. To see why, consider any distributive bargaining problem that involves divisible goods. The bargaining set consists of all payoff combinations to the claimants that arise from feasible allocations. Under normal assumptions this set will be convex, and it will often be strictly convex. Suppose now that one theory recommends that the outcome be point A, which is efficient, while another theory recommends that the outcome be point B, which is also efficient (fig. 17 is illustrative). Suppose that we compromise by tossing a coin between A and B. The expected payoffs from this compromise are the midpoint of the line connecting A and B. Assuming that the bargaining set is strictly convex; some other outcome will be strictly preferred by both parties. Moreover, this will often be the case even if the set is not strictly convex

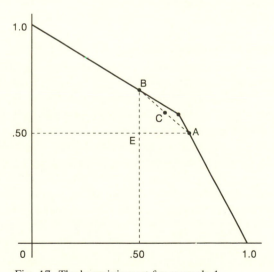

Fig. 17. The bargaining set for example 1.

and A and B are far enough apart. Thus, compromising by lottery may be fair, but it is typically inefficient.

7. Successively Splitting the Difference: The Raiffa Solution

Fortunately, there are other ways of compromising that are both fair and efficient. We shall illustrate one such approach using Crawford's divide and choose as the motivating example. Construct the following two-stage procedure:

1. One of the players is designated to be divider, who proposes a portion for the chooser. If it is rejected, a fair coin is tossed to determine who will be divider in stage two.

2. The (new) divider proposes a portion for the (new) chooser. If it is rejected, the goods are divided equally and the game is over.

Let us analyze how this game should be played. We assume, as always, that both players are rational and they know each other's preferences. (Moreover, each knows that the other knows, each knows that the other knows that he knows, and so forth.) If Alistair is divider in stage one, then he reasons as follows. If she rejects his proposal and they go on to stage two, then his expected utility from the lottery is .61 and her expected utility is .60. So in stage 1 he must offer her a portion that has a utility of at least .60. Moreover, he can do this by offering her all of the land. Thus, if Alistair is divider in stage one, then the outcome is $A' = (.667, .600)$. This is the most that *he* can get given that *she* gets at least as much as in C (the fallback position). Similarly, if Beatrice is divider in stage one, then she offers Alistair a portion that results in the point $B' = (.610, .634)$. This is the most *she* can get given that *he* gets at least as much as in C (see fig. 18).

It is still true, of course, that the two-stage procedure is biased in favor of the divider: B' is better for Beatrice than C; likewise, A' is better for Alistair than C. Thus we have obtained efficiency, but possibly at the expense of equity. Note, however, that the disparity between the two outcomes A' and B' is less than the disparity between A and B. This suggests that we should carry the process a step further by holding a lottery to be divider in stage one of the two-stage game. The expected outcome from this lottery is the average of A' and B', namely, $C' = (.638, .617)$. Note that this outcome is efficient.

This solution can be justified by the following argument. First the claimants agree that each of them gets one-half of the maximum utility gain that each would get if he received *all* of the property. This takes them to point $E = (.50, .50)$. Then they agree that each gets one-half of the *remaining* maximum gain as measured from point E to the Pareto frontier. This takes them to point C. Then they agree that each gets one-half of the remaining gain as measured from point C to the Pareto frontier. This takes them to point C', which is actually on the Pareto frontier.

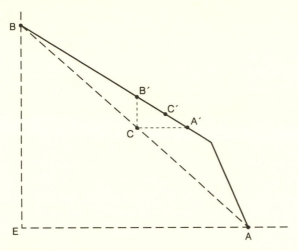

Fig. 18. A close-up of the bargaining set in fig. 17, with the Raiffa solution illustrated.

If the Pareto frontier consists of straight-line segments, then the process converges in a finite number of steps to a unique efficient point. If the boundary is curved, the sequence of outcomes *approaches* a unique efficient point in the bargaining set, but never reaches it. This solution is known as the *Raiffa solution*.[11] The procedure described above amounts to a way of *motivating* the claimants to choose the Raiffa solution on their own.

The procedure may be stated more generally as follows. Let G_1 be the game in which an even chances lottery is held to determine the divider, and the claimants play divide and choose with equal division as the fallback. Let G_2 be the game in which an even chances lottery is held to be divider, and the claimants then play divide and choose with the game G_1 as the fallback. In this fashion one defines a sequence of games G_1, G_2, G_3, . . . , G_n. Each such game involves a chance move at the beginning, so it is role-neutral. Moreover, as n becomes large, the expected outcome approaches (or is equal to) the Raiffa solution. Thus, in the limit, the game G_n is both efficient and role-neutral, and implements a solution that compromises fairly between the more extreme outcomes that result when one or the other claimant exerts his power as divider.

8. Alternating Offers: The Nash Solution

We now describe a third way of removing the divider's advantage. The idea is to let the privilege of being divider *alternate* between the two claimants. Select someone to go first, say A. On the first day he proposes a division, with one

[11] Raiffa (1953).

piece designated for himself and the other for B. She can either accept or reject the proposal. If she rejects it, then on the following day she gets to make a proposal, which he either accepts or rejects, and so forth. The offers and counteroffers alternate in this way on succeeding days until someone accepts. This is called the *offer-counteroffer procedure*. It treats the parties more even-handedly than ordinary divide and choose, because the chooser is given the power to reject the other's division and become divider himself. It can also be thought of as a stylized model of the give-and-take often seen in real bargaining.

What prevents the offers and counteroffers from going on indefinitely? Why doesn't A propose that he receive the whole estate whenever he is divider, and B do the same? The answer is that the process breaks down if they remain too intransigent. Imagine, for example, that whenever an offer is rejected, there is a small probability p that bargaining will not resume on the following day (say because someone "walks out"). In this case the goods are divided equally. Under these circumstances, the parties have an incentive to be more reasonable in their demands.

Define the utility *gain* of an offer as the difference between the utility of the offer and the utility of the fallback position, which is .5 by assumption. If a prospective offer holds out a potential gain of u tomorrow (relative to equal division), then this prospect has an expected gain today of only $(1 - p)u$ because of the probability p that the process breaks down in the meantime.

Let us say that A makes an offer on the first day that has utility gain u to himself and utility gain v to B if accepted right away. She is then faced with a choice: If she refuses, she can make a proposal on the second day that is more desirable for her and less so for him. Suppose that her planned proposal would involve a gain (if accepted on the second day) of u' to him and v' to her, where $v' > v$. Because there is a probability that negotiations will not resume on the second day, however, the present expected value of this prospective proposal is qv' for her and qu' for him, where $q = 1 - p$. Thus she prefers to accept A's offer now if and only if $v \geq qv'$.

This reasoning presupposes, however, that A actually will accept her offer on day two. If he does not, the negotiations will be drawn out even longer, and the present value of her counteroffer will be even less than qv'. For A to accept her offer on day two, he must find it more attractive than waiting until day three and renewing his previous offer.[12] This implies that $u' \geq qu$. In *equilibrium* these two conditions are satisfied as equalities, that is, $u' = qu$ and $v = qv'$. In this case B will accept A's offer on the first day, because the cost of delay equals any advantage she would get by waiting until the second day to make an alternative proposal.

[12] Here we make the simplifying assumption that each party does plan to renew its previous offer in later periods. Such an equilibrium is said to be *stationary*. It can be shown that any subgame perfect equilibrium of this infinitely repeated game is in fact stationary (Rubinstein, 1982).

If we apply this reasoning to the above example, and the probability of breakdown is $1/5$, then in equilibrium Alistair offers Beatrice almost all of the land (99.15 acres) and keeps the remainder for himself. Her counter proposal is to offer Alistair approximately $190,678 and to keep the remainder for herself. With a breakdown probability of one in five it is not worth waiting, however, so she accepts his offer immediately.

As the probability of breakdown becomes very small, it can be shown that the outcome converges to the solution in which Alistair gets all the money ($200,000) and Beatrice all the land (100 acres). This is precisely the Nash solution, that is, it maximizes the product of the claimants' utility gains relative to equal division. Moreover, this result holds in general:

As the breakdown probability approaches zero, the equilibrium outcome of the offer-counteroffer procedure approaches the Nash solution relative to the disagreement outcome of equal division.[13]

9. Bidding to Be Divider: The Egalitarian Solution

Yet a fourth way of equalizing the roles of divider and chooser is to auction off the right to be divider. By allowing the claimants to bid for the privilege, the "rent" attached to being divider is competed away and divider and chooser are placed on an equal footing.[14] The bidding process works as follows:

Step 1. Each heir "bids" a fraction between zero and one.

Step 2. The heir who bids the largest fraction becomes divider. (If they bid the same fraction then one of them, say the elder, is designated to be divider.) The divider creates two portions, one that he designates for himself and the other that he designates for the chooser.

Step 3. The chooser accepts or rejects her designated portion. If she rejects, then she gets to take the fraction of the goods that *she* bid, and the divider takes the remainder.

Note that this is similar to a "second price" auction in which the highest bidder wins the object, but pays the amount bid by the second-highest bidder. We shall illustrate how the procedure works using our previous example. Suppose for the sake of argument that B bids three-fifths and A bids two-thirds. Then A wins the bid, and he divides the goods into two portions, one designated

[13] Let a_0 be the initial bundle and let $e = a_0/2$. The *Nash solution relative to equal division* is the unique division (a^*, b^*) that maximizes $(u(a) - u(e))(v(b) - v(e))$ subject to $a + b \leq a_0$ and $a, b \geq 0$. For each small probability of breakdown p let (a_p, b_p) be the (subgame perfect) equilibrium division that results from the offer-counteroffer game. Then (a_p, b_p) converges to (a^*, b^*) as p converges to zero (Binmore, 1987; see also Rubinstein, 1982).

[14] This idea is due to Crawford (1979a).

for B and the other for himself. If B finds that her portion contains at least three-fifths of the estate in her estimation, she chooses it. Otherwise, she rejects the division and claims three-fifths of the land and three-fifths of the money.

It turns out that A can make B an offer that she will accept, and that is still attractive for him, namely

a: $200,000; b: 100 acres.

B's portion b is as desirable for her as three-fifths of the entire property, so she has nothing to lose by choosing it (given that she will get only three-fifths of the property if she turns it down). This leaves A with the portion a, which is as desirable to him as two-thirds of the entire property.

B can do even better, though, if she raises her bid. Suppose that she bids just under two-thirds. Then A would still be divider, and he would have to create a portion that *she values* at nearly two-thirds of the whole property. The portion 100 acres plus $33,000 meets this condition. This would leave him with only $167,000, which he values at substantially less than two-thirds of the whole. Thus he is motivated to underbid B slightly, which forces her to offer him a portion worth nearly two-thirds of the whole. This mutual adjustment process goes on until an equilibrium is reached. In this particular example, the unique equilibrium outcome is for both to bid the fraction five-eighths, and the resulting division is

Alistair: $187,500;   Beatrice: 100 acres + $12,500.

This allocation is fair in the sense that both A and B are indifferent between their portions and the same fraction ($5/8$) of the whole property. Such an allocation is said to be *egalitarian*.[15]

This procedure can be generalized to any number of claimants as follows. Each claimant bids a fraction between 0 and 1, and the high bidder becomes divider. Ties are resolved by some precedence convention such as age. The divider then proposes an allotment for each player. If all accept the game ends. If a claimant objects, the *lowest* bidder takes the fraction of all the goods that she bid, then the next-lowest bidder takes the fraction that she bid (or everything left on the table, whichever is smaller), and so forth until all the goods have been allotted. (The divider goes last.) It may be shown that the equilibrium outcome of this procedure is both efficient and egalitarian in the sense that everyone is indifferent between his portion and some common fraction of the whole property (Demange, 1984).

Like offer-counteroffer and successive compromise, bidding to be divider improves on the traditional divide and choose method in three senses. First, each claimant can assure himself of a share whose utility is at least as great as

---

[15] More generally, an allocation is *egalitarian-equivalent* if there exists some fixed bundle of goods such that everyone is indifferent between his allotted portion and the fixed bundle (Pazner and Schmeidler, 1978). This idea will be discussed in greater detail in chapter 9.

equal division. Second, if the claimants know each other's preferences for the goods, and if each acts to maximize the utility of his own share, the outcome is efficient. Third, the process creates a level playing field by removing the divider's advantage. Moreover, unlike offer-counteroffer, the process works for any number of claimants.

10. Summary

In this chapter we have explored various ways in which traditional games of fair division can be said to be fair. We concluded that one type of process—auctioning indivisibles—leads to inequitable outcomes when the parties have substantially different private endowments. This effect can be mitigated by restricting the resources with which the claimants bid, but then the outcome may not be efficient. An alternative approach that all parties may prefer is to convert the indivisible goods into divisible ones. This can be done by choosing a suitable mode of division and giving each claimant his proportional share of the converted property. Usually several different modes of division are possible, and some may be Pareto superior to others.

A second traditional procedure, divide and choose, is well suited to situations in which the property is heterogeneous. This process is fair in that it yields allocations that are envy-free. Moreover, this conclusion does not depend on the assumption that the players are perfectly rational or that their preferences are common knowledge. A difficulty with the traditional form of divide and choose is that it may not produce a result that both parties prefer to an equal division of the property *ex ante* (assuming such a division exists). This problem can be corrected by modifying divide and choose so that equal division is the fallback position if the chooser does not accept the divider's proposed allocation.

Unfortunately, neither the modified nor the original version of divide and choose creates a level playing field, because it gives a substantial advantage to the divider. We explored four different ways of eliminating the divider's advantage: (i) each claimant has an equal chance at being divider; (ii) one is chosen at random to be divider, but if his division is rejected there is a new random draw to determine who is divider (and iterations of this idea); (iii) the claimants alternate in making offers and counteroffers; (iv) they bid to be divider. Each of these procedures improves on traditional divide and choose by creating a level playing field. Moreover, except for the first approach, each yields an efficient outcome when the players act rationally and their preferences are common knowledge. The efficiency and equity of the outcome is highly sensitive, however, to the assumption of rationality and common knowledge. When players do not have full information or make mistakes, the results can be very far from the ideal predicted by these models.

9

Equity, Envy, and Efficiency

It is hard to endure envy, but much harder to have
nothing worth envying.
   (*Latin proverb*)

1. Fair and Efficient Exchange

This chapter continues our discussion of equity and efficiency, but instead of
focusing on procedure, we shall ask what outcomes are fair from an *a priori*
standpoint. The basic premises are the same as before: there is a bundle of
common property on the table and a group of persons who claim various shares
of it. For simplicity we shall assume that the property consists solely of homogeneous, divisible goods. (If some of the goods are heterogeneous or indivisible they can be converted to homogeneous, divisible ones by one of the modes
of division described in the preceding chapter.) We take it as given that the
claimants' shares are just and appropriate under the circumstances. Thus it
would be *fair* to give each claimant his share of each of the goods, because these
are the portions to which the claimants are *entitled*. If they have diverse tastes,
however, they can do better. We say that an allocation is *efficient* if no other
allocation makes everyone at least as well off and someone better off. It is
acceptable if no one strictly prefers his a priori share to what he is allotted. The
question that we shall examine in this chapter is: which among the acceptable
and efficient allocations are fair from a normative point of view?

2. Transparent Inequity

To motivate the discussion consider the following example. Three heirs are left
equal shares of an estate that consists of 600 acres of land, 1200 shares of stock
in a family business, and $300,000 in cash. Assume for simplicity that each heir
has a constant trade-off rate between the various goods, where the rates are as
follows:

A $500 per acre, $500 per share;
B $1,500 per acre, $250 per share;
C "   "   .

Equal division allots each heir 200 acres of land, 400 shares of stock, and $100,000 in cash, but this is inefficient. For example, B and C would be willing to buy A's share of land for a price between $500 and $1500 per acre. Similarly, A would be willing to buy the others' stock for anywhere between $250 and $500 per share. Within these bounds there is a wide range of allocations that are both acceptable and efficient. Consider, for example, the following sequence of trades. First B agrees to give A 400 shares in return for 40 acres and $45,000. Both parties are better off as a result of this exchange. In a separate trade, C agrees to give A 300 shares in return for 160 acres and $55,000. Again both parties to the trade are better off than before. Of course C made a more favorable bargain than B did, and as a result C now has *more of every good* than B does.

Although this situation arose through a perfectly natural chain of events, it is unlikely that an arbitrator would have suggested it as a fair solution *ex ante,* because it has no justification independently of the process by which it was arrived at. Indeed there are prima facie reasons against it. Not only is B worse off than $C,$ it is clear to everyone that this is the case. Their shares are *transparently unequal.* If such a solution were recommended by an arbitrator, B would no doubt feel ill-treated. This is not because the allocation is irrational (as we have just seen it results from a rational sequence of trades), but because it treats equals unequally.

TRANSPARENT INEQUALITY. An allocation is *transparently unequal* if some claimant's portion contains more of every good than another claimant's portion.

A transparently unequal allocation generates envy that is evident to everyone. Other allocations may generate envy but only the envious claimant knows it. For example, if B gets 200 acres plus $250,000 and no stock, while C gets 400 acres and no money or stock, then B envies C but it is not evident to anyone else unless they know B's preferences in detail. No envy is therefore a more restrictive criterion of equity than transparent inequality. We would argue, in fact, that it is too restrictive, because it is inappropriate when the claimants have unequal shares. The virtue of transparent inequality is that it extends naturally to this case.

TRANSPARENT INEQUITY. An allocation is *transparently inequitable* if for some two claimants i and $j,$ the ratio between i's allotment and i's share is greater than the ratio between j's allotment and j's share.

3. Egalitarianism

The three criteria considered so far—acceptability, efficiency, and no transparent inequity—narrow the field, but in most cases they do not determine a unique solution. We therefore want to look for principles that further delimit the set of fair and efficient outcomes.

Consider the following example, which surfaced in the preceding chapter. Two heirs A and B are bequeathed equal shares of an estate consisting of 100 acres of homogeneous land and $200,000 in cash. A values this land at a constant rate of $1000 per acre, while B values it at $3000 per acre. Consider the following allocation:

$$A \quad \$150,000 \qquad 0 \text{ acres;}$$
$$B \quad \$\ 50,000 \qquad 100 \text{ acres.}$$

This solution is clearly efficient, because B values land more than A. It is envy-free, because A is indifferent between his own portion and B's, while B prefers her portion to A's. Finally, it is acceptable because A is indifferent between his initial entitlement ($100,000 plus 50 acres) and his allotted portion ($150,000) while B prefers her portion to her initial entitlement. Therein lies a problem however: B seems to be much better off relative to her initial position than A is. In saying this, of course, we are implicitly making interpersonal comparisons of welfare. Is there some way to pin down this intuition more precisely without violating the canons of utility theory?

One way of arguing that B is better off than A is to observe that B puts a higher money value ($350,000) on her portion than A puts on his portion ($150,000). One might argue that an equitable solution is one in which the claimants value their portions equally in monetary terms.

MONEY EGALITARIAN. An allocation is *money egalitarian* if each claimant is indifferent between his portion and the same sum of money.[1]

In our example there is a unique money-egalitarian allocation that is also efficient, namely,

$$A \quad \$200,000 \qquad 25 \text{ acres;}$$
$$B \qquad 0 \qquad 75 \text{ acres.}$$

This is equitable in the sense that both claimants value their portions at $225,000. The difficulty is that it is unacceptable to B, who would prefer to receive her initial entitlement. This problem can be surmounted by using the common property itself (rather than money) as the standard for comparing the claimants' levels of welfare.

EGALITARIAN. An allocation of divisible property is *egalitarian* if every claimant is indifferent between his portion and the same fraction of the entire property.

Consider, for example, the following allocation:

$$a \quad \$187,500 \qquad 0 \text{ acres;}$$
$$b \quad \$\ 12,500 \qquad 100 \text{ acres.}$$

---

[1] This idea extends to unequal shares as follows: each claimant i is indifferent between his portion and ms_i, where $m > 0$ is a fixed sum of money and $s_i > 0$ is i's share.

A is indifferent between his portion a and $5/8$ of the money ($125,000) plus $5/8$ of the land (62.5 acres). Similarly, B is indifferent between her portion b and $5/8$ of the money plus $5/8$ of the land. Hence the allocation is egalitarian. It is also efficient, because B does not want to sell land at a price that A is willing to pay. Indeed it is the unique allocation that is both egalitarian and efficient.[2] More-over, unlike the money-egalitarian allocation, both claimants are better off than they were under equal division, so the allocation is acceptable. This idea generalizes in a natural way to the case of unequal shares.

EQUITARIAN. An allocation of divisible property is *equitarian* if every claimant is indifferent between his portion and a fraction of the entire property that is proportional to his share.[3]

Suppose, for example, that A is bequeathed three-fourths of the property, and B is left only one-fourth of the property. Thus A is entitled to $150,000 plus 75 acres, and B is entitled to $50,000 and 25 acres. This allocation is not efficient, because B is willing to buy some of A's land at a price that A is willing to accept. Consider, however, the following reallocation:

$$
\begin{array}{lll}
a^* & \$200,000 & 53^1/_8 \text{ acres;} \\
b^* & \$0 & 46^7/_8 \text{ acres.}
\end{array}
$$

It may be checked that A is indifferent between his portion a^* and $27/32$ of the entire property, while B is indifferent between her portion b^* and $9/32$ of the entire property. Therefore the allocation is equitarian, because these fractions are in the same proportion as their bequeathed shares. The allocation is also efficient; indeed it is the unique efficient allocation that is equitarian. Finally, both heirs are better off than they would have been by simply dividing the property in proportion to their shares.

Given a bundle of divisible common property, and a group of claimants with predetermined shares, there exists an efficient, equitarian allocation of the property and every such allocation is acceptable.[4]

We give the argument for the case of equal shares; it generalizes easily to the unequal shares case. Consider an allocation $a_1, a_2, \ldots, a_n$ that is both effi-

[2] Suppose there exists another allocation (a', b') that is egalitarian and efficient. By definition, both claimants are indifferent between their portions and some fixed fraction f of the land and money. This fraction cannot be higher than $5/8$, because both claimants would be better off than under the allocation (a, b) which is efficient. The fraction f cannot be lower than $5/8$, because then a, b would be strictly better than (a', b'), so the latter would not be efficient. Therefore $f = 5/8$ and the two allocations are identical.

[3] In other words, the allocation $(a_1, \ldots, a_n)$ is *equitarian* if each claimant i is indifferent between a_i and $s_i f a_0$, where a_0 is the initial bundle, s_i is i's share, and f is a fraction between 0 and 1.

[4] This result follows if the claimants' utility functions are continuous and strictly increasing in every good. For some of the results in this chapter we require in addition that the utility functions be strictly quasi-concave and differentiable.

cient and egalitarian. By definition, every claimant i is indifferent between his portion a_i and some fixed fraction f of the whole property a_0, where $0 \leq f \leq 1$. Suppose, by way of contradiction, that some claimant i prefers his equal share of the property $e = (1/n)a_0$ to his designated portion a_i. Then f must be smaller than $1/n$, because everyone strictly prefers more goods to less. Therefore *every* claimant prefers equal division e to fa_0, and by assumption every claimant is indifferent between fa_0 and his portion. Therefore everyone strictly prefers equal division to the proposed allocation. Hence the proposed allocation cannot be efficient, which is a contradiction.

4. A Difficulty with Egalitarianism

It would seem that we have now identified a satisfactory solution to the problem of fair and efficient allocation, but in fact we have not. The difficulty may be illustrated by the following example. A woman leaves equal shares of her estate to her three children, Alistair, Beatrice, and Colombine, all of whom are partial to martinis. The property consists of 522 bottles of gin and 522 bottles of vermouth. Alistair insists that his martinis be mixed in the ratio three parts gin to one part vermouth. Beatrice insists that her martinis be in the ratio one part gin to two parts vermouth. Colombine is not fussy and will take her drinks in any mixture; all she cares about is volume. Under equal division, each is entitled to 174 bottles of gin and 174 bottles of vermouth. From these initial entitlements, each can make up the number of bottles of martinis shown in table 9.1.

TABLE 9.1
Equal Allocation of Gin and Vermouth

| | Initial Entitlements | | | |
	Gin	Vermouth	Proportions	Martinis
Alistair	174	174	3 : 1	232
Beatrice	174	174	1 : 2	261
Colombine	174	174	unrestricted	348
Total	522	522		841

This allocation is wasteful because the initial endowments (except for C's) are not in the right proportions. Consider instead the allocation in table 9.2. This allocation is efficient, because all three heirs have portions that permit them to mix martinis as they like them without wasting any ingredients. It is also egalitarian. To check this, let us compute the number of bottles of martinis that each could make from $522f$ bottles of gin and $522f$ bottles of vermouth, where f is a fraction between 0 and 1. The answer is: Alistair, $696f$ bottles;

TABLE 9.2
An Efficient Allocation of Gin and Vermouth

	Gin	Vermouth	Proportions	Martinis
Alistair	216	72	3 : 1	288
Beatrice	108	216	1 : 2	324
Colombine	198	234	unrestricted	432
Total	522	522		1,044

Beatrice, $783f$ bottles; Colombine, $1044f$ bottles. Setting $f = {}^{12}/_{29}$ we obtain: Alistair, 288 bottles; Beatrice, 324 bottles; and Colombine, 432 bottles, which is exactly the allocation shown in table 9.2. Hence it is egalitarian.

Now we come to the difficulty, which the reader may already have noticed: Columbine receives more of both goods than her sister does. The solution is *transparently unequal*. Egalitarian or not, it would be very difficult to justify this solution to the claimants given that they have equal entitlements. It can be shown, in fact, that *whenever three or more claimants with equal shares divide a given bundle of goods, there exists a situation (a choice of utility functions) such that the egalitarian solution is transparently inequitable.*[5] This result casts doubt on the appropriateness of the egalitarian standard.

5. Competitive Allocations

We began this chapter with the assumption that the claimants are legitimately entitled to their shares of the common property, and the issue is which distributions (if any) preserve the fairness inherent in these shares while increasing welfare. An outcome that we have not yet considered is the one that would naturally result if the claimants trade in a competitive market.

> COMPETITIVE ALLOCATION. An allocation is *competitive* from the initial entitlements if there exist relative prices for the goods, such that each claimant prefers his portion among all portions that he can buy given the value of his initial entitlement.[6]

We shall illustrate this concept using the last two examples. In the example of section 3 there are two heirs, each with an initial entitlement of $100,000 and 50 acres of land. A has a tradeoff rate of $1000 per acre, and B has a tradeoff rate of $3000 per acre. Suppose that the price of land is quoted at $2000 per acre. At this price B wants to buy as many acres as she can, and with her endowment of

---

[5] This result is due to Moulin and Thomson (1988).

[6] Throughout this section and the next we shall assume that the claimants' preferences are such that a competitive allocation from the initial entitlements exists. For this it is sufficient that the utility functions be continuous, strictly increasing in every good, and strictly quasi-concave (Debreu, 1962).

$100,000 she can buy exactly 50. *A* wants to sell his 50 acres and this is all he has to sell. Thus the market clears at this price for land; moreover $2000 per acre is the *only* price at which it clears. The unique competitive allocation is therefore: *A* gets all the money and *B* gets all the land.

Next consider the example from section 4. We want to find a tradeoff rate between gin and vermouth that clears the market. If the tradeoff rate is not one-to-one, however, Columbine will unload all of her gin or vermouth on the market (whichever is relatively cheaper) and this will cause a market imbalance. Therefore the only tradeoff rate that clears the market is one bottle of gin for one of vermouth. Alistair's optimal choice is to sell half the vermouth (87 bottles) and buy 87 bottles of gin. This leaves him with his preferred ratio of 3 gin to 1 vermouth. Beatrice's optimal choice is to sell one-third of her gin (58 bottles) and buy 58 bottles of vermouth. For the market to clear, Columbine must sell 29 bottles of gin and buy 29 bottles of vermouth. Since this is within her set of optimal choices, the market can clear, and the unique competitive allocation is:

	Gin	Vermouth
Alistair	261	87
Beatrice	116	232
Columbine	145	203

6. The Equity of Competitive Allocation

An important feature of the competitive allocation mechanism is that it allocates goods efficiently without requiring that market participants know the others' preferences. Each person simply buys a bundle that he prefers within the set of all bundles that he could buy given the value of his initial holdings. This is a purely *procedural* justification for competitive allocation. We now propose to show that there are *equity* arguments in its favor as well. Indeed, every competitive allocation satisfies the three basic fairness principles introduced so far.

I. Every Competitive Allocation from Proportional Division is Acceptable

This follows because every claimant chooses a bundle of goods that he most prefers within the set of allocations that he can afford to buy with his initial entitlement, so he must be at least as well off as before.

II. There is No Transparent Inequity in a Competitive Allocation

Each claimant's budget equals the total value of his initial endowment evaluated at the prevailing prices. Thus i's budget is s_i/s_j times j's budget. Furthermore, each claimant's competitive portion has a value equal to his budget. Therefore i's competitive portion has a total value equal to s_i/s_j times the total value of j's competitive portion. Hence i could not receive more than s_i/s_j times the amount of every good that agent j does, so the competitive allocation is not transparently inequitable.

III. If the Entitlements are Equal, the Competitive Allocations are Envy-Free

Consider any two claimants i and j. Certainly i can afford j's portion because their initial endowments, which are equal, have the same total value. Now in a competitive allocation, i purchases the portion that he likes best within the set of portions that he can afford. Therefore he must like it at least as well as j's portion, since j's portion is also affordable for i.

We are now going to show that competitive allocation has the key equity property identified in earlier chapters.

> CONSISTENCY. A criterion of equity is *consistent* if every subgroup finds that the way they divide the amount allotted to them is equitable. In other words, if an allocation is equitable for the group then it looks equitable to every one of its subgroups.[7]

Consistency can be viewed as a condition of social stability. For suppose that society has adopted a concept of equity that is *not* consistent. Then in some situation there will exist a subgroup of individuals who find that the way they divide the amount of property allotted to them (as a subgroup) is unfair. In other words, it does not accord with the normative concept that everyone in this society subscribes to. Not only will this group feel unfairly treated, they may take action to change the situation. They are able to do so because at issue is how the property *allotted to them as a subgroup* is divided, which we may reasonably suppose is under their control. If they try to reallocate it, however, inequities for other subgroups may result. In short, unless *every* subgroup agrees that they divide the property allotted to them in an equitable way, the division is *unstable*.

We now introduce a very weak notion of impartiality. Suppose that society contains two distinct subgroups of individuals that are *equivalent* in the sense that there is a one-to-one correspondence between the two groups, and corresponding members have the same preferences and the same shares. If these two groups are given equivalent bundles to divide, then surely it is fair if they divide the bundles in the same way.

> REPLICABILITY. It is equitable for equivalent groups to divide equivalent bundles in the same way.

Note that the condition is quite weak, because it does not say that equivalent groups *must* adopt equivalent allocations; it simply says that they *may* adopt

[7] Formally, let $a = (a_1, \ldots, a_n)$ be an allocation of the bundle a_0 among n claimants according to some criterion. The criterion is *consistent* if, for every subset of claimants J, a_J is an allocation of the bundle $a_0' = \Sigma_{i \in J} a_i$ among the claimants in J according to the criterion.

equivalent allocations without violating equity. Virtually all of the allocation criteria that we have considered are replicable. For example, if an allocation for a particular group is envy-free, and if an equivalent group also adopts this allocation, then the distribution is envy-free for the two groups together. If an allocation is egalitarian for a group, and it is adopted by an equivalent group dividing an equivalent bundle, then the distribution is egalitarian for the two groups together. If an allocation is competitive for a given group and a set of prices *p,* and it is adopted by an equivalent group dividing an equivalent bundle, then the allocation is competitive for the two groups together relative to the prices *p.* The central result of this chapter is the following.

> *Competitive allocations from initial entitlements are acceptable, efficient, consistent, and replicable. Moreover, every criterion of equity with these four properties consists solely of competitive allocations.*[8]

We have already remarked that competitive allocations exhibit no transparent inequity and (in the case of equal entitlements) no envy. Thus the above result has the following corollary:

> *An allocation criterion that is acceptable, efficient, consistent, and replicable does not produce transparently inequitable outcomes, and when the claimants have equal shares, all of the allocations are envy-free.*

7. The Competitive Standard of Comparison

Since competitive allocations are consistent, and in particular pairwise consistent, it stands to reason that they are based on interpersonal comparisons of some sort. But exactly what is being compared? To analyze this question, let us first consider the case of two individuals who are entitled to equal shares. In a competitive allocation from equal division, the prices of the goods are proportional to the claimants' marginal utilities for these goods, and at these prices the claimants' holdings have equal value. Conversely, if the claimants' marginal utilities are in proportion to prevailing prices, and their holdings at these prices have equal value, the allocation is competitive. What is being compared, then, is *the value of the claimants' holdings at competitive prices.* Assuming that prices are public information, the equity or inequity of the allocation can therefore be evaluated *directly from the allocation itself* without making any assumptions about the claimants' preferences. A similar conclusion holds when

---

[8] We assume that the utility functions are differentiable in addition to being continuous, strictly increasing, and strictly quasi-concave. For a proof see the appendix, Theorem 25. This theorem was first proved for the situation where the claimants have equal shares by Thomson (1988).

the claimants have unequal shares. In a competitive allocation from proportional division, the value of each claimant's allotment is proportional to his share. Hence the equity of the allocation can be evaluated directly from the allocation and the prevailing market prices. This is a substantial advantage of competitive allocation over egalitarianism and other such conceptions of equity, because it is based on a *visible* standard of comparison.

8. Enlarging the Pie

Like most other allocation methods, however, competitive allocation does not satisfy all reasonable criteria of fairness. One common-sense idea, for example, is that everyone should be better off (or at least not worse off) if the size of the pie increases.

> MONOTONICITY. If the quantity of some or all goods increases, every claimant can be allocated a new portion that he likes at least as well as his old portion.

This is the analog of house monotonicity in apportionment. Unfortunately, when multiple goods are to be distributed, it is difficult to satisfy. In particular, competitive allocation is not monotonic. Consider the following variation of the example in section 4. A and B are entitled to equal shares of 600 bottles of gin and 600 bottles of vermouth. A insists that his martinis be in the ratio 3 parts gin to 1 part vermouth, while B insists that her martinis be in the ratio 1 part gin to 2 parts vermouth. It may be checked that the unique market clearing price from the initial equal division is 3 bottles of vermouth for every bottle of gin. This yields the competitive allocation

$A:$ 360 gin + 120 vermouth; $B:$ 240 gin + 480 vermouth.

Now suppose that there is more to go around, say 900 bottles of gin and 600 bottles of vermouth. Each heir is initially entitled to 450 bottles of gin and 300 bottles of vermouth. Since gin is now more abundant, its price relative to vermouth is lower. The market-clearing price is now 4.5 bottles of gin for every bottle of vermouth, and the unique competitive allocation is

$A:$ 720 gin + 240 vermouth; $B:$ 180 gin + 360 vermouth.

Note that B is not only worse-off than before, she actually receives less of *both* goods. The reason is that the relatively greater abundance of gin drives down its price to such an extent that B, who is in the position of selling gin, does not get enough vermouth in return to compensate for the fact that she has more gin to dispose of.

This difficulty is not limited to competitive allocation. It may be shown that, when there are three or more claimants, *any* allocation criterion that is efficient and transparently equitable is nonmonotonic. In other words, it is not possible to give out more goods so as to preserve efficiency and transparent equity while always improving welfare.[9]

This result shows that there is no concept of equity that meets all criteria of reasonableness. Impossibility theorems like this abound, as we have seen in earlier chapters. What they tell us is not that equity is an impossible goal, but that we must make choices among principles. In the present context, it can be argued that transparent inequity is more objectionable than violations of monotonicity. The reason is that the former can be seen directly in a proposed allocation, while violations of monotonicity only become evident once an allocation has been implemented and a revision is required because more or less property becomes available. The latter seems less likely to arise in practice. Thus we would argue that competitive allocation, while not perfect, is the most satisfactory way of distributing multiple goods both equitably and efficiently when the stakeholders have undisputed claims on the property.

9. An Application: Assigning Students to Dormitories

The preceding discussion was conducted on a largely theoretical plane, but the conclusions have important implications for the solution of real problems. Consider the following example. A group of college students are to be assigned to dormitories. Every student can be housed somewhere (the supply of dormitory rooms exactly equals the number of students), but the dorms have different characteristics, and the students have different preferences for them. What is a fair and efficient way of carrying out the assignment?

This problem is considerably more general than the context implies. For example, we could consider the assignment of staff to offices that differ in size, amount of light, and location. Or we could think of assigning workers to jobs of different desirability. Or we might want to allot indivisible goods (a diamond, a boat, a painting) fairly among the heirs to an estate. All of these situations admit similar methods of solution, but for the sake of concreteness we shall frame the discussion in terms of assigning students to dormitories.

To fix ideas, let there be n students and m dormitories or "houses."[10] Each house has a certain number of *spaces*, and the total number of spaces equals the total number of students. An *assignment* is an allocation of spaces to the students so that each student gets one and only one space. We shall assume for simplicity that all spaces in the same house are equivalent. We shall also assume that the students do not care how the *other* students are assigned, only how they

---

[9] Moulin and Thomson (1988).
[10] This section is based on a landmark paper by Hylland and Zeckhauser (1979).

themselves are assigned.[11] An assignment is *efficient* if there is no other assignment that everyone likes as well and some like better. The goal is to assign students to houses in an efficient and equitable manner.

To analyze the equity issue, we must begin with a clear conception of how the property should be distributed *ex ante,* and an appropriate mode of division. The approach that we shall adopt here is to give all students equal *chances* at being assigned to any particular space. Initially, then, each student has a $1/n$ chance of getting into each space, and a s_j/n chance of getting into house j, where s_j is the number of spaces in the jth house. However, we are not actually going to allocate lottery tickets to each student and then let them trade. Rather, we shall compute a competitive allocation based on their initial entitlements and on what they *say* their preferences are. The justification for this approach is that competitive allocation is fair *in principle* (as we showed above), but there is no guarantee that such an allocation would result without some market-clearing mechanism.[12] The mechanism works as follows:

1. A *center* is established to process information and compute prices. The center sets up an account for each student containing an initial allotment of divisible lottery tickets.

2. Each student i reports a *utility* for getting into each house (which may or may not be the same as his true utility).

3. The center computes a *price* for each house, that is, the number of tickets needed to buy a certainty of getting into that house. Half this many tickets buys a 50 percent chance of getting into the house, and so forth.

4. For each student, the center determines a distribution of chances that he would most prefer (given his *reported* utilities) within the set of all distributions he can afford at these prices. Since everyone begins with an equal number of tickets, everyone can afford the same distributions. The prices and the distributions are chosen so that the market clears, that is, all tickets are used up and the total number of chances placed on each house equals the number of spaces in it.[13]

[11] This is clearly an oversimplification, since the desirability of a house may depend on who else is in it.

[12] Moreover, there is a technical difficulty caused by the requirement that, after trading, each student must get into *some* house with probability 1. The algorithm described in the text guarantees this, whereas fully decentralized exchange does not.

[13] Define a *lottery* to be a probability distribution over houses: $p = (p_1, \ldots, p_m)$ where $\Sigma p_j = 1$. Let u_{ij} be student i's utility for house j. We assume that student i strictly prefers lottery p to lottery p' if $\Sigma p_j u_{ij} > \Sigma p'_j u_{ij}$, and is indifferent between them if $\Sigma p_j u_{ij} = \Sigma p'_j u_{ij}$. Let t be the number of tickets in each student's account. The lottery p is *affordable* at prices $\pi_1, \ldots, \pi_m$ if $\Sigma \pi_j p_j \leq t$. Let A be the set of all affordable lotteries. The lottery p^i is *optimal* for student i if it is affordable and among all affordable lotteries it maximizes i's utility. (There may be an infinite number of such lotteries.) The lotteries $p^1, p^2, \ldots, p^n$ *clear the market* if $\Sigma_i p^i_j = s_j$ for each house. The lotteries $p^1, p^2, \ldots, p^n$ are *competitive from equal division,* if they are affordable, optimal, and clear the market at some prices π_j.

We illustrate this procedure with a small example. There are three houses H, H' and H'', each with one space available. There are three students with the following utilities:

		House		
		H	H'	H''
	A	100	30	10
Student	B	75	20	50
	C	60	40	10

The first step is to allot tickets to each student's account at the center. Let us give each student 100 tickets. Next we need to find prices that clear the market. Consider the following prices: 200 for H, 100 for H', 0 for H''. This means that 100 tickets buy a certainty of getting into H' but only a 50 percent chance of getting into H. The chances of getting into H'' are free. The constraints are that each student's chances of getting in somewhere must sum to one, and each space must have probability one of being allocated.

Given the prices quoted above, student A would like to buy as many chances on H as possible. Hence his whole budget of tickets goes to buy a .5 chance of getting into H. Because of the requirement that his chances sum to unity, the slack must be taken up by allotting him a .5 chance of getting into H''. Thus we obtain for A the following distribution of chances: .5 for H, 0 for H', and .5 for H''. This is optimal for A given his initial allotment of lottery tickets. The same distribution is optimal for B. Student C's optimal distribution is: 0 for H, 1 for H', and 0 for H''. The final distribution of chances is:

		House		
		H	H'	H''
	A	.5	0	.5
Student	B	.5	0	.5
	C	0	1	0

The market clears: every student has probability one of getting a space (the row sum), and every space has probability one of being assigned to a student (the column sum). It may be checked that these are the only prices, and that this is the only competitive allocation, that clears the market.

The question now arises as to how the lottery will actually be carried out so that the students have the chances they were promised. Clearly, we cannot conduct the lotteries independently, because the resulting allocations might be infeasible. For example, if we toss a coin to decide whether student A will get into H or H'', and independently toss a fair coin to see whether B will get into H or H'', the probability is $1/2$ that both will get into the same house, which is impossible. The difficulty can be resolved by carrying out the lottery over *complete assignments*. In the present case, for example, we could toss a fair coin to decide which of the following two assignments to implement: (I) $A \rightarrow H$, $B \rightarrow H''$, $C \rightarrow H'$; and (II) $A \rightarrow H''$, $B \rightarrow H$, and $C \rightarrow H'$. Before the coin is tossed, A has a fifty-fifty chance of getting into H or H'', B has a fifty chance of getting into H or H'', and C gets into H' for sure. These are exactly the chances that they were promised. This approach generalizes: *any* distribution of chances that meets the constraints can be implemented by a lottery over complete assignments.[14]

This still leaves open a crucial question however. Why would the students submit their true utility functions to the center? As in the games discussed in the preceding chapter, might it not sometimes pay to misrepresent one's preferences? The answer is that it could. However, if the number of claimants (students) is reasonably large and they have diverse preferences, it is unlikely that anyone would in fact be able to gain by misrepresenting his utilities. The reason is that no one person is likely to be influential enough to change the market-clearing prices in a way that works to his advantage. In other words, when the number of students is large and preferences are suitably diverse, each student can reasonably expect to do at least as well (and often better) by reporting his true preferences instead of reporting something else.[15]

This procedure contrasts in an important way with the games of fair division discussed in the preceding chapter. In those games, it was essential that everyone's preferences be common knowledge for the procedure to yield the desired outcome. For Crawford's divide and choose to guarantee an efficient result, for example, the divider must know the chooser's preferences. (Classical divide and choose does not necessarily yield efficient outcomes *even if* the divider knows the chooser's preferences.) By contrast, the competitive allocation mechanism described above produces an efficient allocation even though the others' preferences are not public information. All that is required is that the claimants report their own true preferences, which, as we argued above, they will often have reason to do.

---

[14] This is an application of the Birkhoff–von Neumann theorem, which states that any square nonnegative matrix in which every row sums to 1 and every column sums to 1 can be written as a convex combination of permutation matrices (Birkhoff, 1946; von Neumann, 1953). The result applies to the case where the houses contain different numbers of spaces as follows: Replace the jth column in the matrix by s_j identical columns (one for each *space* in house j), and allot the student's chances to house j equally among all the spaces in that house.

[15] This is an informal argument that the process is difficult to manipulate, not a proof that the process cannot be manipulated (which it sometimes can be). See Hylland and Zeckhauser (1979, pp. 307–8) for further discussion of this point.

10. Restricting the Domain of Exchange

A noteworthy feature of the scheme described in the preceding section is that students are not allowed to bid with money or other private resources. Trade is restricted to the common property itself, that is, to exchanging chances at getting into the various houses. One might wonder whether it would not be better to distribute the chances equitably to begin with and then let the students barter and trade with all the resources at their disposal. By enlarging the sphere of tradeable goods, one would theoretically obtain an allocation that is even more efficient.

One can easily imagine that objections would be raised to this scheme however. Wealthier students would be able to buy their way into the better or more popular houses, which would create resentment among students who are less well off. On closer inspection, in fact, it is not clear that this arrangement would be more efficient. If a student sells his space in a desirable house to someone else, it is true that the parties to the transaction may be better off, but it is also true that the others may feel that they are worse off. This is because who gets into which house defines the character of college life. Students take an interest in how these privileges are distributed in general, not just in the room that they occupy themselves.[16]

This is part of a larger pattern: when possession of a good (or the discharge of a burden) is strongly connected with membership in the community itself, there are often strictures on transferring it. Thus there are bans on selling one's vote, buying one's way out of the army and out of jury service, and selling the privilege of being admitted to a university. Even academic departments do not normally allow their members to buy their way out of committee assignments. What it comes down to is that members of the community take an interest in who possesses these kinds of goods and how they use them. Under these circumstances, allowing unfettered trade in these items does not necessarily increase welfare. This is not to say, however, that all trade should be banned. The virtue of the college housing scheme is that students can take advantage of their differences in tastes without compromising the egalitarian character of college life. The key point is that trading to a competitive outcome is equitable *provided* that the goods are fairly distributed to begin with. Introducing other goods that for various reasons may be inequitably distributed (such as inherited wealth) creates a bias in favor of those with greater endowments and destroys the equity of the initial distribution. By limiting trade to goods that are equitably distributed to begin with, one can preserve equity while still allowing scope for diversity of tastes.

---

[16] It might be said that students should not take an interest in what others have because such preferences are paternalistic and intrusive. This argument is rather flimsy, however, because to claim that people *ought not* to have certain kinds of preferences is just another form of paternalism.

11. Summary

In this chapter we have examined the interplay between equity, envy, and efficiency in the allocation of multiple goods. We began with the premise that individuals are justly entitled to specific shares of the property, but that they have different tastes and are therefore motivated to trade. The question is: what trades are both equitable and efficient?

We suggested six general principles by which the equity of final allocations can be evaluated. The first is *acceptability:* no claimant should be worse off than under his initial entitlement. The second principle is *transparent inequity:* no claimant should receive less of everything than another claimant who has an equal share. More generally, no claimant should receive a smaller percentage of everything than his share warrants, relative to the shares of the other claimants. A substantially stronger version of this principle that applies when the claimants have equal shares is *no envy:* no claimant should strictly prefer another's portion to his own. The drawback of this concept is that it does not generalize naturally to the case of unequal entitlements.

The fourth equity principle is *consistency:* every subgroup of claimants should fairly divide the common property allotted to them as a group. As we have seen from previous chapters, this key idea makes sense in a wide variety of contexts and binds together a remarkably diverse set of allocative methods. A weak converse of the consistency property is *replicability,* which states that every fair allocation for a given subgroup should be fair when imitated by similar subgroups in the population. Finally, we would like the rule to be *monotonic:* when the bundle of common property grows, no one's welfare should decrease.

The main theoretical result of this chapter is that *competitive allocation is the only method that satisfies the first five principles, and there is no method that satisfies all of them.*

Unlike other methods for dividing common property, such as divide and choose and its elaborations, competitive allocations can be implemented by a straightforward process that puts no demands on the claimants' knowledge of the others' utility functions. Although the outcome can, in theory, be manipulated by claimants who have this information, the likelihood of anyone being able to manipulate it to advantage is small when the number of claimants is large.

Perhaps the most important conclusion to emerge from this chapter is that the supposed trade-off between equity and efficiency is largely chimerical. When the distributive part of the problem is dealt with on its own merits, equity and efficiency complement each other. Competitive markets allocate property both efficiently and equitably *provided* the goods were equitably allocated to begin with.

10

Conclusion

> Justice is the tolerable accommodation of the con-
> flicting interests of society.
>   (*Judge Learned Hand*)

THE TIME HAS COME to tie things together. As stated at the outset, the goal has
not been to put forward a new theory of social justice, that is, a theory about
how society at large should be organized. Rather, we have been concerned with
the specific rules and principles by which societies allocate common property
and collective burdens among qualifying parties. The methods that people use
to solve distributive problems, and the arguments that they have brought forward to justify them, are the building blocks that we have to work with. From
them we have constructed the foundations for a positive theory of equity that
bears some resemblance to how problems like this really are resolved.

As we have seen, the perceived equity of a distribution depends on the
particulars of the case: on the nature of the goods being divided, on the salient
characteristics of the claimants, on their values and beliefs, and on precedent—
on what is normal, customary, and expected in situations of that sort. This is not
to say that equity is an arbitrary concept, or that it exists only in the eye of the
beholder. To assert that arguments based on equity are merely a cover for
arguments based on self-interest is a dubious, perhaps not even a logically
tenable, position. If equity is merely a cover and has no independent validity,
why does anyone bother with it? When a concept is used only as a cover it
ceases to be a cover; it becomes transparent and therefore ineffectual.

The true state of affairs is quite different. Within a given distributive context,
there are relatively few principles that have persuasive power and credibility.
They are the terms in which distributive discussions are conducted and they
shape the outcomes that we can expect. Principles of equity are powerful
precisely because they are *not* arbitrary, but arise from rational arguments and
precedents that create shared expectations among the affected parties. It is true
that the relevant equity principles vary from one situation to another and from
one culture to another. Hence discussions of equity must be grounded in a
specific context. This does not mean, however, that conceptions of equity are
purely parochial. The cases examined in previous chapters reveal general patterns that cut across disparate domains. Let us now recapitulate what these
patterns are.

First, every distributive rule begins with some conception of equality, that is, a conception of when two claimants look the same for the purposes of the distribution. Of course, since two claimants never really do look the same, we must decide which characteristics are "salient" to the problem at hand. One way to determine salience is to look at precedent, to see what counts in similar situations. Another is to survey public opinion and the views of the parties concerned. Once the salient characteristics have been identified, fairness requires that claimants who look alike should be treated alike. This is the *impartiality* principle.

How should claimants be treated when they do not look alike? Here generalizations are more difficult. The case studies clearly show, for example, that purportedly universal formulas like proportionality, utilitarianism, and the difference principle do not capture the richness of actual solutions. Shades of these principles are sometimes discernible, but they are parts of a larger, more complicated picture. These principles do, however, have a key element in common with the more nuanced notions of equity that we see in practice. Namely, almost all equity judgments are based on a standard for comparing pairs of individuals. A distribution is equitable when every two individuals (and every subgroup of individuals) divide the goods equitably among themselves. This is the *consistency principle*.

Consistency can be interpreted in two ways. As a *normative* principle it asserts that a distribution which is fair for society as a whole should also be fair from the standpoint of every subgroup within society. As a procedural principle it asserts that the outcome is *stable*. Suppose, in fact, that society has settled on a criterion for allocating common property among qualifying members of the population, and that an allocation according to this criterion has been carried out. Now suppose that some subgroup of the population finds that the way they divide the amount allotted to them (as a group) does not accord with the agreed-upon criterion. Not only will they feel unfairly treated, they may even try to reallocate the goods among themselves in a more equitable way. But this reallocation may in turn upset the equity of the solution for other subgroups. In this sense the allocation is unstable. Thus there are both procedural and normative arguments in favor of consistency.

These two basic principles—impartiality and consistency—have surprisingly powerful implications when fleshed out with additional assumptions. Let us briefly recall several examples. In sharing a unitary good, like discharges from the army, the two principles imply the existence of a priority list that determines who gets the good and who does not. In the case of a lumpy good, like legislative seats, they imply the existence of a priority list that determines which state gets the first seat, which the second, and so forth until all seats have been distributed. When multiple goods are to be distributed efficiently among claimants with fixed *a priori* shares, the above two principles—together with acceptability, no transparent inequity, and replicability—imply that the goods should be allocated competitively by market clearing prices. Many other characterization theorems of this type have been noted throughout the book. An important point is that almost all of the methods characterized in this way have practical significance. Thus the two principles have positive as well as normative content.

Admittedly this leaves many questions unanswered, perhaps even more than when we began. In the first place we have only considered half a dozen cases, each of which has quite special characteristics. They were selected in part because they illustrate aspects of equity that are not captured by traditional formulas like proportionality, and in part because the details are fascinating in themselves. Clearly, however, this is not enough empirical evidence on which to base a claim that we have constructed an explanatory theory of equity. Much remains to be done along these lines. For example, I have touched only briefly on the experimental literature on equity and its relationship to the ideas presented here. This topic is developing rapidly and promises to offer important new insights into how people think about equity when a distributive problem is framed in a particular way. I do not think that experimental work can *replace* empirical case studies, where the environment is inevitably much richer than can be re-created in the laboratory, but the two clearly complement each other.

While the cases discussed above are rather special, the framework of analysis is general and can be applied to other distributive situations. Moreover, as we have seen, distributive problems are arising all the time through the creation of new property rights and the reassignment of existing ones. How would we approach such a problem given the lessons of the preceding chapters? Suppose, for example, that we are advising an agency in charge of allocating scarce public housing. Or imagine that we are involved in a decision about how to distribute shares of state enterprises among the populace in a formerly socialist regime. Or suppose that we are asked to mediate among a group of countries who are bargaining over how to divide the costs of providing for common defense. How would we proceed?

The framework developed in preceding chapters suggests the kinds of information that we would want to gather, and the ways in which we would use it to construct a solution. Among other things we would want to consider the following questions.

1. What form should the allocation take? As we have seen in previous chapters, common property can often be distributed in a variety of forms. State enterprises, for example, could be sold and the money distributed in the form of a tax rebate or a partial repayment of the public debt. Alternatively, the government could issue shares in the new corporation and distribute them directly to the public. Yet a third solution would be to bundle the shares together into mutual funds run by professional managers, and then distribute the shares in the mutual funds directly to the public. (All of these methods have recently been used to privatize state enterprises in Eastern Europe.) In providing for common defense there are also alternative ways to distribute the burden. Weapons and troops could be provided jointly and the costs divided among the partners, for example, or responsibility for providing various inputs could be allocated directly to the partners, who would then pay the costs out of their own pockets.

II. What are the eligibility criteria? In some cases eligibility is settled by mutual consent among the parties, like the countries who have decided to provide for common defense. In other cases determining eligibility is a key part of the problem. To be eligible for public housing, for example, should family income be below a certain threshold? How should income be adjusted for family size? Does it matter what kind of accommodation the family has now? Similar issues surface in the privatization of a state-run enterprise. Who is entitled to receive a share: all citizens? all adult citizens? the employees?

III. What counts in the distribution? Two people can be eligible for a good or burden, yet differ in the degree to which they are entitled to it. In privatization programs, for example, one could make a case that the employees of the privatized firm are entitled to a larger share than the average citizen. Similarly, a family that has been waiting ten years for public housing would probably take precedence over a similar family that has been waiting for one year, and so forth. Behind these choices lie larger issues. What is the normative basis for the distribution: Need? Ability to pay? Contribution? How can these abstract categories be translated into concrete measures based on available data?

IV. What are the relevant principles? To say that family *A* is more entitled to public housing than family *B* because it has been waiting twice as long is not to say that it is twice as entitled. Comparisons like these have an ordinal but not necessarily a cardinal meaning. Under these circumstances it makes more sense to use the priority principle than, for example, the proportionality principle. On the other hand, just because a cardinal standard is available does not imply that proportionality is appropriate either. If countries are assessed for common defense according to their ability to pay (as measured by their economic product, for example), there would be arguments for using a progressive standard instead. And if there are ways of measuring benefits one might be tempted to base the allocation on a weighted combination of ability to pay and benefit received.

V. What are the relevant precedents? The appropriateness of a distributive rule depends in part on how customary it is in similar or analogous situations. If other international organizations rely on the proportionality principle to allocate costs among their members, for example, this lends additional legitimacy to assessing common defense costs proportionally. On the other hand, if similar organizations use progressive schemes, special arguments may have to be summoned to explain why proportionality is more appropriate in this particular case. Similarly, in distributing state assets, policies adopted by countries that move first may affect the choices of those that decide later. Priority for public housing is very strongly affected by past practice, because it establishes a sense of entitlement in the status quo arrangement. Precedent, in short, is one of the most important sources of shared expectations and must be included in any analysis of how the claimants will perceive the fairness of the distribution.

VI. How should competing principles and criteria be reconciled? When no single distributive criterion is dominant, a compromise or trade-off may be appropriate. In public housing, for example, family income is one relevant factor but number of children is another. Contributions to common defense might plausibly be based on ability to pay (income), but they could also be based on some measure of benefit, like the number of people protected (population). One way to handle this issue is to apply a meta-principle to compromise between two competing principles. For example, one might take the average between the cost shares based on population and the cost shares based on gross domestic product. An alternative approach would be to have the claimants vote on the relative weight to give the two principles. Similarly, to decide the appropriate trade-off between economic income and family size in allocating public housing, one might conduct a public opinion survey much as the army did to determine the point system.

VII. What incentives does a rule create? Distributive rules do not operate in a vacuum; they have important impacts on claimants' behavior. We must look beyond nominal outcomes to the effective consequences of a rule when claimants adjust their actions in response to it. The object of a cost-sharing scheme, for example, is to capture the potential gains from cooperation. This will not occur, however, if the cost-sharing principle causes some of the members to back out. Similarly, the object of public housing is to provide for needy families, but the rule is self-defeating if it encourages families to become "needy" in order to qualify for housing. These incentive considerations seldom *determine* the solution, but they limit the extent to which a perfectly equitable outcome can be achieved. The way to approach the problem is to aim for equity *as near as may be* while distorting individual choices as little as possible.

This list of seven steps provides a framework for analyzing equity in concrete situations. It contains both normative and procedural elements. Normative issues arise in determining the form of the distribution, in articulating plausible criteria of eligibility and entitlement, and in identifying the relevant distributive principles. The main procedural element is to seek the opinions of concerned parties when the answers to these questions are fuzzy or indeterminate from a normative point of view.

One may still ask, however, why all of this is worth doing. Why does it *matter* whether allocations are equitable? The answer should be clear by now. A public agency that undertakes this type of analysis protects itself from charges of favoritism and capriciousness. Even for groups that theoretically could negotiate any solution they please, equity plays a critical role. On the one hand, these groups are frequently composed of representatives that are answerable to constituents, who will no doubt demand to know on what basis the decision was made. On the other hand, the bargainers themselves may need to have such a justification. The reason is that distributive bargains are difficult to achieve without a framework that focuses the bargainers' attention on particular outcomes. Equity principles play this role by defining which outcomes are more appropriate than others.

The reason that equity is important, therefore, is that it *coordinates* and *legitimates* distributive choices. Equity principles are the language in which we discuss and justify such choices. When there is wide agreement in the community about what the appropriate distributive principles are, solutions that contradict them will be seen as illegitimate and untenable. Even when there is substantial disagreement about the relevant principles, however, it may still be possible to fashion outcomes that command broad support by explicitly following a process that takes differences of opinion into account, and strikes a balance between competing points of view.

Appendix _____

The Mathematical Theory of Equity

A.1 Two Fundamental Principles

Basic Definitions

This appendix treats in greater detail the theory that was developed informally in the text. It is not meant to be a complete review of the theoretical literature on fair division. Rather, we shall develop a particular point of view that is motivated by two fundamental conditions—impartiality and consistency—and draw out their implications in various contexts. Proofs are sketched when they are relatively brief. Otherwise the reader is referred to the technical literature.

An allocative situation has two ingredients: the goods to be distributed, and the claimants among whom they are to be distributed. We shall denote the *initial bundle* by $a_0 = (a_{01}, a_{02}, \ldots, a_{0m})$, where $a_{0k} \geq 0$ is the available amount of good k, $1 \leq k \leq m$. The claimants will be indexed by positive integers $i = 1, 2, 3 \ldots$

Given a finite subset of claimants I and an initial bundle a_0, an *allocation of* a_0 is a matrix $\boldsymbol{a} = (a_{ik})$, where $a_{ik} \geq 0$ is the amount of good k allotted to each claimant $i \in I$, and for every k, $\Sigma_{i \in I} a_{ik} = a_{0k}$. If $\Sigma_{i \in I} a_{ik} \leq a_{0k}$ for all k, we shall say that $\boldsymbol{a}$ is a *partial allocation* of a_0. The vector of goods allotted to claimant i will be denoted by a_i and referred to as i's *portion*. Note that a portion is in plain type and an allocation is in boldface type.

The equity or inequity of an allocation is judged in relation to certain characteristics or *attributes* of the claimants. Let there be r relevant attributes. The *type* of a claimant is a vector $\tau = (x_1, x_2, \ldots, x_r) \in R^r$ where x_s is the *level* the individual attains in attribute s, $1 \leq s \leq r$. Some attributes are continuous (height), others are discrete (number of dependents), and some are discrete and binary (gender). The set of relevant attributes and the values they assume depend on the context and define the set of *feasible types T*.

Let us now fix a specific class of situations, that is, we fix the set of m goods to be distributed and the set T of feasible types. An *allocation problem* is a pair (τ, a_0) where $\tau \in T^I$, τ_i is the type of claimant $i \in I$, and a_0 is the bundle to be distributed. An *allocation rule* is a function F that assigns a unique allocation $\boldsymbol{a} = F(\tau, a_0)$ to each given problem $(\tau, a_0) \in T^I \times R^m$. An *allocation criterion* is a multiple-valued function (i.e., a correspondence) F such that, for every problem $(\tau, a_0) \in T^I \times R^m$, $F(\tau, a_0)$ is a nonempty *set* of allocations. Note that F is defined for *every* finite nonempty subset of claimants I and *every* assignment of types to the claimants.

Impartiality

Since a claimant's type is presumed to capture all of the information about the claimant that is salient to the allocation, an allocation criterion should not discriminate among the claimants *except* insofar as they differ in type. This idea can be expressed in the following way. Given a set of claimants I, a vector $\tau \in T^I$ can be thought of as a *function* from I to T, where τ_i is the type of claimant i. Similarly, we may think of an allocation a as a function from I to R^m, where a_i is the bundle allotted to i.

Let π be a permutation of I. The *composition* of τ with π will be denoted by $\tau \circ \pi$.

IMPARTIALITY. An allocation criterion F is *impartial* if, for every problem (τ, a_0) on I, and every permutation π of I, $F(\tau \circ \pi, a_0) = F(\tau, a_0) \circ \pi$.

This condition says that F is independent of the indexing of the claimants. In other words, if each claimant i were of type $\tau_{\pi(i)}$ instead of τ_i, then i would receive the portion $a_{\pi(i)}$ instead of a_i, where $a = F(\tau, a_0)$. It follows that, when everyone is of the same type and F is single-valued, then everyone must receive an equal portion. When F is multiple-valued and everyone is of the same type, it says that *if* some allocation a is equitable, *then* any way of reassigning the portions among the claimants is also equitable.

Consistency

The second fundamental principle of equity states that an allocation is equitable only when every subgroup of claimants believes it to be equitable. In other words, every subgroup should be satisfied that they share the goods allotted to them (as a group) in an equitable way. This condition can be formulated as follows.

WEAK CONSISTENCY. An allocation criterion F is *weakly consistent* if, for every problem (τ, a_0) on I, and every proper subset $J \subset I$,

$$a \in F(\tau, a_0) \text{ implies } a_J \in F(\tau_J, \Sigma_{j \in J} a_j). \tag{1}$$

Here a_J and τ_J mean a and τ restricted to J. If (1) holds for all subsets J of cardinality two, then F is *weakly pairwise consistent*.

This definition is satisfactory when F is single-valued, but not necessarily when F is multiple-valued. To see why, consider an allocation $a = F(\tau, a_0)$ and a subset $J \subset I$. The members of J are collectively allocated the subbundle $b_0 = \Sigma_{j \in J} a_j$. Weak consistency says that the allocation a_J is an equitable way of allocating b_0. There may, however, be other allocations of b_0 among the members of the subgroup that are *also* equitable according to the criterion F. We would like the subgroup to be able to choose any of these alternative distributions without upsetting the equity of the overall allocation. This leads to the following strengthening of (1).

CONSISTENCY. An allocation criterion F is *consistent* if, for every I, every problem (τ, a_0) on I, and every nonempty subset $J \subset I$,

$$a \in F(\tau, a_0) \text{ implies } a_J \in F(\tau_J, \Sigma_{j \in J} a_j),$$

and

$$a \in F(\tau, a_0) \text{ and } b_J \in F(\tau_J, \Sigma_{j \in J} a_j) \text{ implies } (b_J, a_{I-J}) \in F(\tau, a_0). \quad (2)$$

If this definition holds for every subset J of cardinality two, F is said to be *pairwise consistent*. In many contexts, pairwise consistency implies consistency, as we shall see in due course.

Several variations of the consistency condition have been proposed in the literature. In particular, Peleg (1986) has proposed the notion of *converse consistency*, which requires that *if* the restriction of an allocation a to every subset of claimants is an F-allocation, *then* a itself is an F-allocation. In other words, for every I, every problem (τ, a_0) on I, and every allocation a of a_0,

$$a_J \in F(\tau_J, \Sigma_{j \in J} a_j) \text{ for all } J \subset I, |J| \geq 2, \text{ implies } a \in F(\tau, a_0). \quad (3)$$

This condition makes inferences about solutions to *larger* problems from solutions to *smaller* problems, whereas weak consistency makes inferences about *smaller* problems from *larger* problems. Consistency, as defined by (2), makes both kinds of inferences. When F is a single-valued allocation rule, consistency and weak consistency amount to the same thing.[1]

Constraints

Consistency and impartiality extend naturally to situations where the allocation is constrained in some fashion. Let I be a subset of claimants and $a_0 \in R^m$ the initial bundle. Let C be a nonempty *subset* of the allocations of a_0 among I. C is called the *feasible set* for the pair (I, a_0). Often C is convex, though this is not necessary. Given $\tau \in T^I$, the pair (τ, C) defines a *constrained allocation*

---

[1] For other variations of consistency see Thomson (1990a).

problem. A *feasible solution* is an allocation $a \in C$. An *allocation rule* associates a unique feasible solution $F(\tau, C)$ to each constrained problem, and an *allocation criterion* associates one or more feasible solutions to each problem.

In this setting, impartiality says that, for any permutation π of I,

$$F(\tau \; o \; \pi, \; C \; o \; \pi) = F(\tau, C) \; o \; \pi,$$

where we think of τ as a function from I to T and $a \in C$ as a function from I to R^m.

Consistency generalizes in the following way. Let (τ, C) be a constrained allocation problem. For each nonempty subset $J \subset I$, and each $a \in C$, define the *reduced feasible set* $C(a, J)$ as follows:

$$C(a, J) = \{a'_J: a' \in C \text{ and } a'_i = a_i \text{ for all } i \in I - J\}.$$

In other words, the reduced feasible set is obtained from a given allocation a by *projecting* the original feasible set onto the subset of coordinates J, and giving every claimant $i \notin J$ the portion a_i. We assume that the reduced feasible set is feasible whenever the original allocation a is feasible.

An allocation criterion F is *consistent* if, for every finite set of claimants I, every $\tau \in T^I$, every constrained problem (τ, C), and every $J \subset I$,

$$a \in F(\tau, C) \text{ implies } a_J \in F(\tau_J, C(a, J)),$$
$$a \in F(\tau, C) \text{ and } b_J \in F(\tau_J, C(a, J)) \text{ implies } (b_J, a_{I-J}) \in F(\tau, C). \quad (4)$$

In other words, restricting an allocation a to a subset of claimants is a solution to the corresponding reduced problem; moreover, any solution to the reduced problem can be substituted into a to obtain an alternate solution of the original problem.

In the sequel we shall usually consider impartiality and consistency in tandem. This allows us to consider *generic* subgroups of claimants of a given size, which simplifies the notation. To be specific, consider two unconstrained allocation problems $(\tau, a_0) \in T^I \times R^m$ and $(\tau', a'_0) \in T^{I'} \times R^m$. These problems are *isomorphic* if there exists a one-to-one mapping $\pi: I \rightarrow I'$ such that $\tau' \; o \; \pi = \tau$ and $a_0 = a'_0$. Assume for the moment that I and I' are disjoint, and consider the problem $((\tau, \tau'), 2a_0) \in T^{I \cup I'} \times R^m$. Impartiality implies that $(a, a') \in F((\tau, \tau'), 2a_0)$ if and only if $(a', a) \in F((\tau, \tau'), 2a_0)$. From this and consistency it follows that there is a one-to-one correspondence between the allocations in $F(\tau, a_0)$ and the allocations in $F(\tau', a_0)$. If I and I' are not disjoint, we can reach the same conclusion by considering a third subgroup I'' that is disjoint from I and I', and isomorphic to both. This fact allows us to drop references to specific subgroups of claimants and to consider problems defined on *generic* subgroups of agents. A *generic n-agent allocation problem* is a pair $(\tau, a_0) \in T^n \times R^m$ such that the *i*th agent is of type τ_i, and a *solution* is an allocation $a \in R^n$, where a_i is the allotment to the *i*th claimant.

Origins of the Consistency Principle

Variations of the consistency principle were formulated independently by authors working on different allocative problems. A primitive version of the idea was implicit in E. V. Huntington's axiomatic work on apportionment (Huntington, 1921, 1928). Given a measure of inequality in representation between two states, Huntington asked when there exists an apportionment among n states that is consistent with this measure for every pair of states (see chapter 3). This is a rather pale form of consistency because it only asks whether a *given* criterion for solving two-state problems can be consistently extended to n-state solutions; it does not say what class of criteria are *consistent with themselves*.

A similar tack was taken by Harsanyi (1959) in connection with the bargaining problem. He noted that the Nash solution for an n-person bargaining problem remains the Nash solution when restricted to every pair of bargainers. Lensberg (1988) showed conversely that it is the *only* n-person bargaining rule that is continuous and pairwise consistent with the Nash solution.

The idea of an allocation criterion being *consistent with itself,* as opposed to *consistent with a given two-claimant criterion,* was first formulated in the context of apportionment by Balinski and Young (1978). (We used the term "uniformity" instead of consistency, but gave it precisely the same formulation as in (2)). We showed that (subject to an additional regularity condition) an apportionment method is impartial and pairwise consistent if and only if it is based on a priority list (see section A.4).

Thomson (1984) employed the consistency concept to characterize egalitarian solutions of bargaining problems. He also showed that, in exchange economies, consistency is a key property of competitive allocations from equal division (Thomson, 1988). (See section A.8.) Lensberg (1987) axiomatized the set of all efficient, continuous, and weakly consistent bargaining rules, and showed that the Nash solution is the only such bargaining rule that is impartial and scale-invariant (see section A.7).

Aumann and Maschler (1985) showed that allocation criteria from the Talmud can be extended consistently to n-claimant situations, and demonstrated that one of them (the contested garment rule) is the nucleolus of a suitably defined cooperative game. Young (1987) showed that a claims allocation rule is continuous, impartial, and consistent if and only if it maximizes an additively separable objective function (see section A.5). Peleg (1986) showed that weak consistency and converse consistency can be used to characterize the core and the prekernel of cooperative games. Hart and Mas-Colell (1987) showed that consistency can be used to axiomatize the Shapley value (see section A.6). Moulin (1985) used a variation of consistency plus several other axioms to characterize surplus-sharing rules. For an excellent survey of these and other results see Thomson (1991).

In all of these versions the underlying idea is the same, namely, a criterion is consistent if it is invariant when restricted to subgroups of claimants. The differences arise from the way in which the "restricted" problem is defined.

In the remainder of the appendix, we shall explore the ramifications of consistency and impartiality in various applications. The object is not to prove an omnibus theorem that characterizes all allocative criteria with these two properties. Indeed, we do not believe that this approach would be very fruitful. The power and versatility of the two conditions arises from the specific implications they yield when conjoined with other properties that are natural in particular settings.

A.2 Zero-One Allocations

Definitions

We begin by considering a simple case: there is a single scarce good to distribute, it comes in indivisible units, and every claimant receives either zero or one unit. Such an allocation is said to be *zero-one*. An allocation criterion F is *zero-one* if it consists only of zero-one allocations. In the language of section A.1, the feasible set takes the form $C = \{(a_1, a_2, \ldots, a_n): a_i = 0 \text{ or } 1, \text{ and } \Sigma a_i = a_0\}$, where a_0 is any nonnegative integer and n is any positive number of claimants. In this section we shall further assume that the set of distinct types T is either finite or countably infinite. In other words, each claimant is evaluated in a finite number of attributes, where each attribute takes on a countable number of discrete values.

A *standard of comparison* P is a weak ordering of T. In other words, P is a binary relation that is *connected* ($\tau P \tau'$ or $\tau' P \tau$ or both) and *transitive* ($\tau P \tau'$ and $\tau' P \tau''$ implies $\tau P \tau''$) for all τ, τ', τ'' in T. When $\tau P \tau'$ we shall say that τ *has priority over* τ'. If $\tau P \tau'$ and not $\tau' P \tau$ then τ has *strict* priority over τ', written $\tau P^+ \tau'$.

PRIORITY METHOD. Given a standard of comparison P, the *priority method* based on P is the correspondence F defined as follows: given a problem (τ, a_0) on I, $F(\tau, a_0)$ is the set of all zero-one solutions a such that

$$a_i = 1 \text{ and } a_j = 0 \text{ implies } \tau_i P \tau_j.$$

Consistency and Priority

The basic theorem of this section is the following.

THEOREM 1. *A zero-one allocation criterion is impartial and pairwise consistent if and only if it is a priority method.*

PROOF: We leave it to the reader to verify that a priority method is impartial and pairwise consistent. Conversely, suppose that the method F has these two properties. Define a binary relation P as follows:

$$\tau \, P \, \tau' \Leftrightarrow (1, 0) \in F(\tau, \tau'; 1). \tag{5}$$

We shall show that P is a weak ordering of T, and that F is the priority criterion based on P. The relation P defined by (5) is connected, because every problem $(\tau, \tau'; 1)$ has at least one solution, and the only possible solutions are $(1, 0)$ and $(0, 1)$. Hence either $\tau \, P \, \tau'$ or $\tau' \, P \, \tau$ or both.

Next we must verify that P is transitive. Suppose, by way of contradiction, that $\tau \, P \, \tau'$ and that $\tau' \, P \, \tau''$, but that $\tau \, P \, \tau''$ is false. This means that the two-claimant problem $(\tau, \tau''; 1)$ has the *unique* solution $(0, 1)$. Consider now the three-claimant problem $(\tau, \tau', \tau''; 1)$, and let a be one of its solutions under F. If $a_1 = 1$, then by pairwise consistency the problem $(\tau, \tau''; 1)$ has the solution $(1, 0)$, which contradicts the assumption that $(0, 1)$ is the unique solution to $(\tau, \tau''; 1)$. Next suppose that $a_2 = 1$. By pairwise consistency $(0, 1)$ is a solution to $(\tau, \tau'; 1)$. By hypothesis, however, $\tau \, P \, \tau'$, so $(1, 0)$ is also a solution to $(\tau, \tau'; 1)$. Therefore, by pairwise consistency the solution $(1, 0)$ may be substituted into a to obtain the alternative solution $(1, 0, 0)$ for $(\tau, \tau', \tau''; 1)$. This possibility was ruled out by the preceding remark however.

It follows that $(0, 0, 1)$ is the only possible solution to $(\tau, \tau', \tau''; 1)$. By pairwise consistency, $(0, 1)$ is a solution to $(\tau', \tau''; 1)$. Since $\tau' \, P \, \tau''$ by hypothesis, it follows that $(1, 0)$ is also a solution to $(\tau', \tau''; 1)$. Therefore, by pairwise consistency, $(1, 0)$ may be substituted for $(0, 1)$ in a to obtain the alternative solution $a' = (0, 1, 0)$ for $(\tau, \tau', \tau''; 1)$. But this solution was ruled out by our earlier remark. This contradiction establishes that P is transitive.

It remains to be shown that F is the priority criterion based on P, in other words, that $F(\tau; a_0)$ is the set of all solutions a such that $a_i = 1$ and $a_j = 0$ implies $\tau_i \, P \, \tau_j$. This follows directly from impartiality and pairwise consistency, as the reader may verify.

Theorem 1 shows that there is an important parallel between consistent allocation rules and rational choice, namely, if a zero-one allocation criterion treats pairs of claimants consistently, then these pairwise decisions can be rationalized by an ordering. An analogous result holds in other settings, as we shall see in subsequent sections.

Point Systems

Let P be a given priority standard on the set of types T. Each type is described by r real numbers, $\tau = (x_1, x_2, \ldots, x_r)$, where x_s denotes the *level* of attribute s.

Consider two types who differ in the first two attributes and are equal in all others: $\tau = (x_1, x_2, y_3, \ldots, y_r)$ and $\tau' = (x_1', x_2', y_3, \ldots, y_r)$. Now consider a type $\sigma = (x_1, x_2, z_3, \ldots, z_r)$ that is the same as τ in the first two attributes, and another type $\sigma' = (x_1', x_2', z_3, \ldots, z_r)$ that is the same as τ' in the first two attributes, where σ and σ' agree on the remaining $r - 2$ attributes.

SEPARABILITY. The relation P is *separable in attributes* 1 and 2 if, for any such types τ, τ', σ, and σ', $\sigma \, P \, \sigma'$ holds if and only if $\tau \, P \, \tau'$ holds. P is *pairwise separable* if it is separable in every pair of attributes.

POINT SYSTEM. A *point system* is an assignment of a real number $p_s(x_s)$ to every attribute level x_s such that type $\tau = (x_1, x_2, \ldots, x_r)$ has priority over $\tau' = (x_1', x_2', \ldots, x_r')$ if and only if $\Sigma_s p_s(x_s) \geq \Sigma_s p_s(x_s')$.

THEOREM 2. *If the set of types T is countable, then the priority standard P can be represented by a point system if and only if it is pairwise separable.*

This theorem follows from results of Debreu (1959) and Gorman (1968). For a discussion see Keeney and Raiffa (1976, chapter 3), who show how to compute the point values explicitly from a given priority relation.

A.3 Opinion Aggregation

Definitions

We turn next to the problem of defining a priority standard when there are differences of opinion about what the appropriate standard is. Let T be a set of possible types of claimants, where we shall assume that T is finite. Let there be v individuals or *voters* indexed by k, where $1 \leq k \leq v$. Each voter has an opinion about how the set T should be ordered, that is, who should have priority over whom. For simplicity we shall suppose that each voter's priority ordering is strict, that is, either $\tau \, P \, \tau'$ or $\tau' \, P \, \tau$ but not both, for every pair of types. A strict ordering is called a *ranking* of the types. Voter k's ranking will be denoted by P_k, and we shall write $\tau P_k \, \tau'$ if and only if voter k assigns higher priority to τ than to τ'. A list $\mathscr{P} = (P_1, P_2, \ldots, P_v)$ of rankings of T is called an *opinion profile* for the group of voters.

AGGREGATION RULE. An *aggregation rule* on the set of voters $V = \{1, 2, \ldots, v\}$ is a function $g(\mathscr{P})$ that maps every opinion profile $\mathscr{P}$ on V into a weak ordering of T, called the *consensus* ordering.

Let us now consider the meaning of impartiality in the present situation. It has two aspects: we want to treat all *voters* impartially, and we want to treat all *types* impartially. The first condition can be expressed as follows.

ANONYMITY. An aggregation rule g on $V = \{1, 2, \ldots, v\}$ is *anonymous* if, for every profile $\mathcal{P}$ on V, $g(\mathcal{P})$ is a symmetric function of its arguments, that is, if for every permutation π of the indices $1, 2, \ldots, v$,

$$g(P_1, P_2, \ldots, P_v) = g(P_{\pi(1)}, P_{\pi(2)}, \ldots, P_{\pi(v)}).$$

To formulate the second condition, index the set of types $T = \{\tau_1, \tau_2, \ldots, \tau_m\}$ and let γ be any permutation of the indices $1, 2, \ldots, m$. For every ordering P of T, let γP denote the ordering such that: $\tau_{\gamma(i)} \, \gamma P \, \tau_{\gamma(j)}$ if and only if $\tau_i \, P \, \tau_j$.

NEUTRALITY. An aggregation rule g on v voters and m types is *neutral* if for every permutation γ of $1, 2, \ldots, m$,

$$\gamma g(P_1, P_2, \ldots, P_v) = g(\gamma P_1, \gamma P_2, \ldots, \gamma P_v).$$

IMPARTIALITY. An aggregation rule g is *impartial* if it is both anonymous and neutral.

Simple Majority Rule

We may think of the consensus ordering $g(\mathcal{P})$ as a set of ordered pairs, where $(\tau, \tau') \in g(\mathcal{P})$ means that τ has equal or greater priority in the consensus ordering than τ'. When there are just two types, the natural solution to the aggregation problem is *simple majority rule*. This is defined as follows: $g(\mathcal{P}) = \{(\tau_1, \tau_2)\}$ if a majority favors τ_1 over τ_2, $g(\mathcal{P}) = \{(\tau_2, \tau_1)\}$ if a majority favors τ_2 over τ_1 and $g(\mathcal{P}) = \{(\tau_1, \tau_2), (\tau_2, \tau_1)\}$ if the voters are equally divided.

Simple majority rule is obviously impartial, but it is not the only impartial rule on two types. Consider, for example, the following rule: rank a type first if it receives less than 40 percent of the votes, or more than 50 percent and less than 60 percent of the votes. (If the vote splits 50-50, 60-40, or 40-60 a tie is declared.) This procedure is clearly impartial—it is not biased toward any person or type. Just as clearly it makes little sense. Suppose, for example, that a type gets just below 40 percent of the votes, so it is ranked first in the consensus order. If several voters switch their opinion in its favor, it will be knocked out of first place. Such absurdities are ruled out by the following condition.

STRICT MONOTONICITY. Let g be an aggregation rule on v voters and two types. Let τ be first or tied for first in $g(\mathcal{P})$, and suppose that some voter ranks τ second. Let this voter change his opinion, so that he now ranks τ first, and call the resulting profile $\mathcal{P}'$. *Strict monotonicity* requires that τ be ranked *strictly first* in $g(\mathcal{P}')$.

THEOREM 3 [May, 1952]. *For two types and any number of voters* v, *simple majority rule is the unique aggregation rule that is impartial and strictly monotonic.*

The proof is straightforward and is left to the reader.

We now consider a second way of characterizing simple majority rule. Let g be an aggregation rule defined for *two fixed* types τ and τ' and any number of voters. Let the voters be composed of two groups, say two constituencies with different interests. Suppose that the first constituency would rank type τ first if they used the rule g, and the second constituency would also rank τ first using the rule g. Then *together* they should surely rank τ first. Furthermore, if one constituency is indifferent between τ and τ', while the other ranks τ strictly first, then it makes sense for the combined body to rank τ strictly first. In other words, each constituency can break a tie on the part of the other.

REINFORCEMENT. Let V and V' be two disjoint groups of voters with opinion profiles $\mathcal{P}$ and $\mathcal{P}'$ on $\{\tau, \tau'\}$, and let $\mathcal{P} \cup \mathcal{P}'$ denote the corresponding opinion profile on $V \cup V'$. The aggregation rule g is *reinforcing* if

$$g(\mathcal{P}) \cap g(\mathcal{P}') \neq \phi \text{ implies } g(\mathcal{P} \cup \mathcal{P}') = g(\mathcal{P}) \cup g(\mathcal{P}').[2]$$

This condition can be interpreted as a Pareto condition on subgroups: if two disjoint subgroups rank τ ahead of, or on a par with, τ', and at least one of these groups ranks τ strictly ahead of τ', then the whole group ranks τ ahead of τ'.

Simple majority rule is reinforcing, because if a majority favors τ in each constituency separately, then obviously τ has a majority in the whole society. However, reinforcement fails for the peculiar voting rule mentioned above. Suppose, for example, that one group ranks τ first because it gets 35 percent of the vote, while the second group ranks τ first because it captures 55 percent of the vote. Assume that the two groups have the same number of members. In the whole group, τ gets 45 percent of the vote, so it would not be ranked first. This is clearly an absurdity.

A second reasonable requirement is that, if everyone has the same opinion about two alternatives, then this opinion should be reflected in the consensus ordering.

UNANIMITY. If every voter ranks one type τ ahead of another type τ', then τ is ranked above τ' in the consensus ordering.

THEOREM 4. *The unique aggregation rule on two types that is impartial, unanimous, and reinforcing is simple majority rule.*

PROOF: Let g be an aggregation rule that satisfies the three properties. Let τ and τ' be the two types. Because g is impartial, and hence anonymous, we may think of g as a function defined on pairs of nonnegative integers (a, b), where a

---

[2] Recall that $g(\mathcal{P})$ is a subset consisting of one or both of the ordered pairs (τ, τ') and (τ', τ). The condition says that the pairs they agree to jointly are precisely the pairs that both agree to separately, *provided* such pairs exist.

is the number of voters that rank τ above τ', b is the number that rank τ' above τ, and $a + b > 0$. We wish to show that $g(a, b) = \{(\tau, \tau')\}$ if $a > b$, $g(a, b) = \{(\tau', \tau)\}$ if $a < b$, and $g(a, b) = \{(\tau, \tau'), (\tau', \tau)\}$ if $a = b$.

Given a pair (a, b) with $a \geq b$ we consider three cases. If $a = b$, impartiality on types implies that τ and τ' are tied in $g(a, b)$. If $b = 0$, unanimity implies that τ is ranked above τ' in $g(a, b)$. Both of these outcomes agree with simple majority rule. The third case is $a > b > 0$. Write $(a, b) = (b, b) + (c, 0)$ where $c = a - b > 0$. Neutrality on types implies that $g(b, b) = \{(\tau, \tau'), (\tau', \tau)\}$. Unanimity implies that $g(c, 0) = \{(\tau, \tau')\}$. Thus $g(b, b) \cap g(c, 0) = \{(\tau, \tau')\}$. Since $(a, b) = (b, b) + (c, 0)$, reinforcement implies that $g(a, b) = \{(\tau, \tau')\}$. Thus g is simple majority rule whenever $a > b$, and of course the same holds when $a < b$. This completes the proof.

Arrow's Theorem

We turn now to the problem of extending simple majority rule to situations with three or more types. One approach would be to rank the types so that one type τ has priority over another type τ' if and only if a majority of voters rank τ ahead of τ'. Clearly this is impossible whenever there is a cyclic majority. Indeed, one of the central results of social choice theory is that there exists *no* reasonable aggregation rule such that the relative rank of every two types depends only on their relative rank in the voters' opinions. This idea was formulated by Arrow (1963) as follows. We say that two profiles $\mathcal{P} = (P_1, P_2, \ldots, P_v)$ and $\mathcal{P}' = (P'_1, P'_2, \ldots, P'_v)$ *agree on the pair* $\{\tau, \tau'\}$ if, for every voter k, $\tau P_k \tau'$ if and only if $\tau P'_k \tau'$.

INDEPENDENCE OF IRRELEVANT ALTERNATIVES (IIA). An aggregation rule g on voters *satisfies IIA* if whenever two profiles agree on a pair $\{\tau, \tau'\}$, then $g(\mathcal{P})$ and $g(\mathcal{P}')$ agree on $\{\tau, \tau'\}$.

THEOREM 5 [Arrow, 1963]. *Fix the set of voters* V *and the set of types* T, *where* $|T| \geq 3$. *An aggregation rule* g *satisfies unanimity and IIA if and only if it confers all power on one voter, that is, for some fixed* k *and for every profile* $\mathcal{P}$, $g(\mathcal{P}) = P_k$.

Pairwise Consistency and Independence of Irrelevant Alternatives

Independence of irrelevant alternatives (IIA) states that the relative rank of each pair of types in the consensus ordering depends only on the opinions of the voters about those two types. This condition is reminiscent of pairwise consistency, which says that the distribution of a good among a pair of claimants should depend only on their types and how much they receive, not on the types of the other claimants. Nevertheless there are important differences between the two concepts. Indeed there must be, because IIA cannot be met with any reasonable generality whereas pairwise consistency can.

We begin with an illustrative example. Table A.1. shows an opinion profile for one hundred voters and four types *A, B, C, D*. *A* has a majority over *B, B* over *C, C* over *D,* and *D* over *A*. Hence in any ranking of the types there will exist at least one type that has a simple majority over some other type that is ranked higher. If we believe that: (i) the relative ranking of every two types should depend only on the voters' opinions about those types (IIA), and (ii) whenever one type has a majority over another the former should be ranked higher than the latter, then clearly we have an impossibility result.

It makes sense, therefore, to seek a less demanding version of these conditions. To motivate the discussion, consider the ranking *B, C, A, D,* which is the one recommended by Borda's rule (see chapter 2, section 6). Notice that *B* is ranked ahead of *A* in spite of the fact that *A* has a majority over *B*. Therefore we might be tempted to switch their relative rank in the consensus order. Unfortunately, this switch would disturb the relative ordering of other pairs such as *A* and *C,* and *B* and *C*. Hence it is *not* clear that the switch should be made.

We shall say that a switch is *local* if it involves two types that are *adjacent* in the group ordering, i.e., if there is no type in between them. (We assume here that the ordering is strict, i.e., a ranking.) If two types are adjacent, then clearly we can interchange them without disturbing the relative ranking of any other pair of types. In the ranking *B, C, A, D,* for example, *A* and *D* are adjacent, so they can be interchanged without disturbing the rest of the ranking. Moreover, there is good reason to interchange them, because *D* has a simple majority over *A*. The resulting ranking *B, C, D, A* represents an *improvement* over the previous ranking in the sense that it accords more closely with majority rule for a particular pair (namely *A, D*), and does not accord any less closely with majority rule for any other pair.

This argument can be extended in the following way. Let $\mathcal{P}$ be an opinion

TABLE A.1
Opinions of One Hundred Persons
about Four Types of Claimants

Number of Persons with the Given Preference Order (Total 100)			
30	*28*	*24*	*18*
A	B	C	D
B	C	D	A
C	D	A	B
D	A	B	C

profile and P a proposed ranking of the types. Let $v_{\tau\tau'}(\mathscr{P})$ be the number of voters that rank τ ahead of τ' in $\mathscr{P}$, The $m \times m$ matrix of numbers $v = v_{\tau\tau'}(\mathscr{P})$ is the *vote matrix* associated with $\mathscr{P}$.

CONCORDANCE. The *concordance* between the opinion profile $\mathscr{P}$ and the ranking P on the pair $\{\tau, \tau'\}$ is the total *number* of voters that rank τ and τ' in the same order that they are ranked in P. The *total concordance* between $\mathscr{P}$ and P, denoted by $\gamma(\mathscr{P}, P)$, is the sum of the concordances over all pairs.
If we let

$$a_{\tau\tau'}(P) = 1 \text{ if } \tau\, P\, \tau' \text{ and } a_{\tau\tau'}(P) = 0 \text{ if } \tau'\, P\, \tau,$$

then

$$\gamma(\mathscr{P}, P) = \Sigma_{\tau,\tau'} a_{\tau\tau'}(P)\, v_{\tau\tau'}(\mathscr{P}).$$

In other words, the concordance between a given ranking P and the profile $\mathscr{P}$ is just the dot product between the vote matrix and the matrix $a_{\tau\tau'}(P)$. The following ranking criterion was suggested in a rudimentary form by Condorcet (1785). (See also Young, 1988.)

CONDORCET'S CRITERION. Given an opinion profile $\mathscr{P}$, choose a ranking P that maximizes the concordance $\Sigma_{\tau,\tau'} a_{\tau\tau'}(P)\, v_{\tau\tau'}(\mathscr{P})$.

The Condorcet criterion occasionally yields ties, that is, several distinct rankings may have maximum concordance with a given profile P. It is worth noting that these ties do not necessarily collapse into a weak ordering of T except when $|T| = 2$. Moreover, there is no reason why they should. To see this, consider the following example. There are three types τ, τ', and τ'' and three voters 1, 2, 3 with the opinions

Voter	1	2	3
	τ	τ'	τ''
Ranking	τ'	τ''	τ
	τ''	τ	τ'

Each of the above three rankings has the same concordance with the vote profile, namely 5, and this is a maximum. Thus Condorcet's criterion declares a tie between these three rankings. Note, however, that it does not declare a tie between *all* rankings. For example, τ, τ'', τ' has a concordance with the profile of only 4, and the same holds for the rankings τ'', τ', τ and τ', τ, τ''. Therefore these three rankings are less plausible than the other three. These observations lead us to make the following definition.

AGGREGATION CRITERION. An *aggregation criterion* is a correspondence $G(\mathscr{P})$ that associates one or more rankings of T to every profile $\mathscr{P}$ on T. G is defined for every finite subset T, every finite, nonempty subset of voters $V \subset N$, and every opinion profile of V on T.

If P is a ranking of T and $S \subset T$, $S \neq \phi$, we let $P(S)$ denote the *restriction* of P to S. Similarly $\mathcal{P}(S)$ denotes the restriction of the profile $\mathcal{P}$ to S.

PAIRWISE CONSISTENCY. G is *pairwise consistent* if, whenever $P \in G(\mathcal{P})$ and τ and τ' are adjacent in P, then:

(i) $(\tau, \tau') \in P$ implies $(\tau, \tau') \in G(\mathcal{P}(\{\tau, \tau'\}))$,   (5)

(ii) $(\tau, \tau') \in P$ & $(\tau', \tau) \in G(\mathcal{P}(\{\tau, \tau'\})$ implies $(P - \{(\tau, \tau')\} \cup \{(\tau', \tau)\}) \in G(\mathcal{P})$.

In other words, G is pairwise consistent if it is invariant when restricted to any two adjacent alternatives in $P \in G(\mathcal{P})$, with substitution in case of ties.

G is *pairwise consistent with majority rule* if it is pairwise consistent and if it is the same as majority rule on every subset of two types. From the preceding discussion it is clear that Condorcet's criterion is pairwise consistent with majority rule. Indeed in the next subsection we are going to argue that it is the *only* plausible aggregation criterion that is pairwise consistent with majority rule. First, however, we need to justify our use of the term "pairwise consistency" in this context. We shall show that, in fact, it is nothing but a disguised form of condition (2) for a suitably defined class of allocation problems.

Ranking as a Zero-One Allocation Problem

To see this, let P be a ranking of T. We shall write $(\tau, \tau') \in P$ if and only if τ is ranked above τ' in P. Let $a_{\tau\tau'} = 1$ if $(\tau, \tau') \in P$ and let $a_{\tau\tau'} = 0$ otherwise. Let T contain t elements. The problem of finding a ranking of T is equivalent to finding a *zero-one* allocation $(a_{\tau\tau'})$ such that, for all distinct τ, τ', τ'',

$$a_{\tau\tau} = 0,$$
$$a_{\tau\tau'} + a_{\tau'\tau} \leq 1$$
$$a_{\tau\tau'} + a_{\tau'\tau''} + a_{\tau''\tau} \leq 2,$$
(6)

and

$$\sum_{(\tau,\tau')\in T\times T} a_{\tau\tau'} = t(t-1)/2.$$
(7)

The first condition in (6) says that the selected pairs (i.e., the binary relation defined by a) is irreflexive. The second condition says that it is asymmetric. The third says that it is transitive. Conditions (6) and (7) together imply that $a_{\tau\tau'} + a_{\tau'\tau} = 1$ for every distinct τ, τ'. Hence any zero-one vector a satisfying (6) and (7) defines a ranking of T.

An aggregation criterion G therefore defines a zero-one allocation criterion F as follows. Given an opinion profile $\mathcal{P}$ for a group of voters V on a subset T, F acts on a set of t^2 "claimants," one for each pair $(\tau, \tau') \in T \times T$. The "type" of claimant (τ, τ') is the set of voters who rank τ above τ' in $\mathcal{P}$. The amount to be allocated is $a_0 = t(t-1)/2$. As shown above, each ordering $P \in G(\mathcal{P})$ defines a zero-one allocation a of the a_0 units among the t^2 claimants satisfying (6) and (7). The *allocation criterion* $F(\mathcal{P}, T)$ is defined to be the set of all such allocations a that are associated in this way with the orderings in $G(\mathcal{P})$.

Let us now apply pairwise consistency in the sense of (2). Let $a \in F(\mathcal{P}, T)$ and let $\{\tau, \tau'\}$ be any pair of distinct elements from T. Let P be the ranking of T generated by a. Consider the restriction of a to the claimants (τ, τ') and (τ', τ). In other words, consider the allocation $(a_{\tau\tau'}, a_{\tau'\tau})$ while holding fixed all values $a_{\sigma\sigma'}$ such that $(\sigma, \sigma') \neq (\tau, \tau'), (\tau', \tau)$. Since $a_{\tau\tau'} + a_{\tau'\tau} = 1$, pairwise consistency means that the distribution of this one unit between (τ, τ') and (τ', τ) depends only on the opinions of the voters concerning τ and τ' *subject* to the constraints inherited from the original constraints (6) and (7) on a.

We claim that these constraints permit only one solution to the restricted problem *except* when τ and τ' are adjacent in P. Since $a_{\tau\tau'} + a_{\tau'\tau} = 1$, we may suppose without loss of generality that $a_{\tau\tau'} = 1$, and hence that $(\tau, \tau') \in P$. Suppose further that τ is not adjacent to τ' in P. Then there exists $\sigma \in T$ such that $(\tau, \sigma) \in P$ and $(\sigma, \tau') \in P$. Thus $a_{\tau\sigma} + a_{\sigma\tau'} = 2$. From the constraint $a_{\tau\sigma} + a_{\sigma\tau'} + a_{\tau'\tau} \leq 2$ it follows that $a_{\tau'\tau} = 0$. Hence the constraints on the original problem imply that there exists only one solution to the restricted problem (namely $a_{\tau\tau'} = 1$, $a_{\tau'\tau} = 0$). On the other hand, when τ is adjacent to τ', the inherited constraints on the restricted problem are simply that $a_{\tau\tau'} + a_{\tau'\tau} = 1$ subject to the variables being zero or one. Hence the alternate solution $a_{\tau\tau'} = 0$, $a_{\tau'\tau} = 1$ is also feasible when τ is adjacent to τ'.

It follows that, when τ is adjacent to τ', pairwise consistency in the sense of (2) implies that the solution(s) $(a_{\tau\tau'}, a_{\tau'\tau})$ of the restricted problem correspond one-to-one with the orderings in $G(\mathcal{P}(\{\tau, \tau'\}))$. This is precisely the definition of pairwise consistency given in (5).

Pairwise Consistency and Condorcet's Criterion

It is easy to see that Condorcet's criterion is pairwise consistent. Indeed this follows immediately from the fact that it maximizes the additively separable objective function $\Sigma_{\tau,\tau'} a_{\tau\tau'}(\mathcal{P}) v_{\tau\tau'}(\mathcal{P})$ subject to the constraints imposed by (6). Moreover it is clear from the definition of concordance that Condorcet's criterion is pairwise consistent with simple majority rule. Thus we see that pairwise consistency can be satisfied by a plausible method whereas independence of irrelevant alternatives cannot. We shall now argue that Condorcet's criterion is the *only* plausible one that is pairwise consistent.

Let G be a given aggregation criterion. We say that G is *unanimous* if whenever every voter in a profile $\mathcal{P}$ ranks τ above τ', then $\tau P \tau'$ for every $P \in G(\mathcal{P})$. G is *impartial* if permuting the names of the voters in a profile P does not change $G(\mathcal{P})$, and if permuting the names of the types permutes the rankings in $G(\mathcal{P})$ in the same way. Finally, G is *reinforcing* if

$$G(\mathcal{P}) \cap G(\mathcal{P}') \neq \phi \text{ implies } G(\mathcal{P} \cup \mathcal{P}') = G(\mathcal{P}) \cap G(\mathcal{P}').$$

Reinforcement says that if two groups agree on some ordering of *all* types then they agree jointly on those orderings that both groups agree on separately. (Note that this generalizes the definition for the case of two types.)

THEOREM 6. [Young and Levenglick, 1978]. *Condorcet's criterion is the unique aggregation criterion that is impartial, unanimous, reinforcing, and pairwise consistent.*

A.4 Integer Allocation

Definitions

In this section we consider the allocation of a good that comes in whole units. Unlike the situation in section A.2, however, the claimants are not restricted in the number of units they can receive. Let T designate the set of possible claimant-types, which in this section we assume to be finite or countably infinite. An *integer allocation problem* is a pair (τ, a_0), where τ is a list of the claimants by type and $a_0 \geq 0$ is the whole number of units of the good to be distributed. An *integer allocation* is a vector $a = (a_1, a_2, \ldots, a_n)$ of nonnegative integers such that $\Sigma_i a_i = a_0$. An *integer allocation criterion* (or *method*) is a correspondence F that associates a nonempty set of integer allocations to any given problem (τ, a_0). In the terminology of section A.1, this is a constrained allocation problem in which the feasible set is of form $C = \{(a_1, \ldots, a_n): \Sigma a_i = a_0$, all a_i integer$\}$.

The classical example of this situation is legislative apportionment. Here the good is the number of seats in the legislature, a claimant is a state, and the type of the state is the size of its population. Or the claimant could be a political party, and the type of the party is the number of votes it receives.

An allocation criterion F is *impartial* if it depends only on the types of the claimants and on the total quantity to be allocated. A consequence is that claimants of the same type are treated symmetrically. This does not mean, however, that they are treated *equally* in any particular allocation. Suppose, for example, that there are five units to distribute among two claimants of the same type. They cannot be treated equally without throwing away some of the good, which would be inefficient. Impartiality means that if one way of allocating the five units is considered equitable, then so is its mirror image. For example, if (2, 3) is equitable then so is (3, 2). This does not exhaust the possibilities however. For example, the criterion consisting of the two solutions (5, 0) and (0, 5) is also impartial *ex ante*. The difficulty is that, when one of these solutions is implemented, the claimants are treated more unequally than they need be. This motivates the following definition (Balinski and Young, 1977).

BALANCED. An integer allocation criterion is *balanced* if, whenever two claimants are of the same type, their allotments differ by at most one unit.

Consistency and Priority

Pairwise consistency is implicit in many classical solutions to the apportionment problem. In particular, it underlies the idea of minimizing the degree of inequality between every pair of states. This idea was first suggested by Joseph Hill (1911) and subsequently elaborated by Edward Huntington (1921) (see chapter 3, sections 9–10). The key property of a pairwise consistent criterion, however, is not that it minimizes a measure of inequality but that it satisfies a conception of priority.

STANDARD OF COMPARISON (PRIORITY STANDARD). A *standard of comparison P* is a weak ordering of the set of all pairs (τ, a), where $\tau \in T$, a is a nonnegative integer, and $(\tau, a) P^+ (\tau, a + 1)$.

If $(\tau, a) P (\tau', a')$ we say that the first claimant has *priority* over the second, and if $(\tau, a) P^+ (\tau', a')$ the first claimant has *strict priority* over the second. The higher the priority, the greater the claim to the next unit of the good.

Given an allocation a, let claimant j have priority over claimant i. We shall say that transferring one unit from claimant i to claimant j is *justified* if the priority of i *after* the transfer is strictly lower than the priority of j *before* the transfer. If no transfer is justified, then

$$\forall i, j, \ (\tau_i, a_i - 1) \ P \ (\tau_j, a_j). \tag{8}$$

This implies that, for every other allocation a', there is an i such that $(\tau_i, a_i') P (\tau_j, a_j)$ for all j.

EQUITY. An allocation is *equitable* relative to the standard of comparison P if no transfer is justified.

PRIORITY METHOD. The *priority method* based on P is the multiple-valued function $F(\tau, a_0)$ consisting of all allocations a satisfying (8).

The set of allocations satisfying (8) may be constructed as follows. Given a problem (τ, a_0), consider the finite subset of pairs $Y = \{(\tau_i, a): 0 \leq a \leq a_0, a$ integer, $1 \leq i \leq n\}$. Choose any a_0 of these pairs that stand *highest* in the priority list, that is, any subset $Y' \subseteq Y$ such that

$$|Y'| = a_0 \ \& \ (\tau_i', a') \in Y' \ \& \ (\tau_i, a) \in Y - Y' \Rightarrow (\tau_i', a') P (\tau_i, a). \tag{9}$$

For each claimant i, let a_i be the *maximum* integer such that $(\tau_i, a_i - 1) \in Y'$. (If there exists no such integer let $a_i = 0$.) Then (8) is satisfied. Moreover, by definition of P we have $(\tau_i, 0) P^+ (\tau_i, 1) P^+ \ldots P^+ (\tau_i, a_i - 1)$ and therefore all of these a_i pairs are in Y'. Since Y' contains a_0 pairs altogether, it follows that $\Sigma_i a_i = a_0$. Thus we have constructed an *allocation* of a_0 that satisifies (8). Conversely, any allocation of a_0 that satisfies (8) can be obtained in this way.

THEOREM 7. *An integer allocation method is impartial, balanced, and pairwise consistent if and only if it is a priority method.*

Given a method with these three properties, the associated standard of comparison P is constructed as follows. Let $X = \{(\tau, a): \tau \in T \text{ and } a \geq 0 \text{ is integer}\}$, and define P such that

$$(\sigma, a) P (\tau, b) \text{ iff there exists } a_0' \text{ and } (a', b') \in F((\sigma, \tau), a_0')$$
$$\text{such that } a' > a \text{ and } b' \leq b.$$

The proof amounts to showing that P is an ordering of X, and that F is the priority method based on P (see Balinski and Young, 1982, pp. 144–46).

MONOTONICITY. An integer allocation criterion F is *monotone* if, for every problem (τ, a_0) and every allocation $\boldsymbol{a} \in F(\tau, a_0)$, there is an allocation $\boldsymbol{b} \in F(\tau, a_0 + 1)$ such that $b_i \geq a_i$ for every i.

COROLLARY 7.1. *Every priority method is monotone.*

This follows directly from (9): Every allocation $\boldsymbol{a} \in F(\tau, a_0)$ is obtained by taking a_0 pairs that stand highest in the priority list P. When there is one more unit to go around, we dip down in the priority list for one more pair. This amounts to giving one more unit to exactly one claimant and no fewer units to any other claimant.

We remark that Theorem 7 is the analog of Theorem 1, but it does not directly imply Theorem 1. The reason is that pairwise consistency is being applied here to a *larger* domain of problems, so it is a *stronger* axiom. A similar remark applies to later characterizations that rely on the consistency condition. When we change the domain of problems to which the axiom is applied, we change the strength of the axiom. Hence a theorem that holds on a larger domain of allocative problems does not necessarily hold on every subdomain.

Rank-Index Methods

A standard result in utility theory states that a weak ordering (preordering) of a countable set can be represented by a real-valued function (Debreu, 1954). The set N of nonnegative integers is countable, and by assumption so is the set of types T. Hence the set of pairs $X = T \times N$ is also countable. Therefore if P is a priority standard on X, there exists a real valued function $r: X \to R$ such that $(\tau, a) \, P(\tau', a')$ if and only if $r(\tau, a) \geq r(\tau', a')$. By (8) the solutions to the problem (τ, a_0) are precisely those allocations of a_0 that satisfy the following *min-max inequality*

$$\min_i r(\tau_i, a_i - 1) \geq \max_j r(\tau_j, a_j). \tag{10}$$

The function r is called a *rank index* and the criterion it defines is a *rank-index method* (Balinski and Young, 1982). From the preceding discussion it follows that *an integer allocation criterion is impartial, balanced, and pairwise consistent if and only if it is a rank-index method.*

Divisor Methods

We shall now specialize these results to the apportionment of seats in a legislature. To be concrete, we shall assume that a given number of seats is to be allocated among several states in proportion to their populations. The set of *types* is therefore the set of positive integers (i.e., the possible populations). An *apportionment problem* is a pair (p, a_0) where $p = (p_1, \ldots, p_n)$ is a list of the state populations and a_0 is the number of seats to be distributed. In practice there may be lower and upper bounds on the number of seats each state can receive, but we shall assume here that the allocation is unconstrained. The results are easily extended to the case where bounds are imposed.

The ideal is to allocate the seats more or less *proportionally* to the populations. In recognition of this objective several further conditions are warranted. First, the allocation should depend only on the *relative* populations of the states, not on their absolute numbers. Second, if the seats *can* be allotted proportionally to the populations, then this should be the unique solution. Third, a smaller state should never receive more seats than a larger state. These three conditions may be stated more formally as follows.

HOMOGENEITY. An apportionment criterion F is *homogeneous* if $F(p, a_0) = F(\lambda p, a_0)$ for every positive integer λ.

EXACTNESS. F is *exact* if $F(p, a_0) = p(a_0/\Sigma p_i)$ whenever the latter vector is all integer.

WEAKLY POPULATION MONOTONICITY. F is *weakly population monotone* if, whenever $a \in F(p, a_0)$ and $p_i > p_j$, then $a_i \geq a_j$.

THEOREM 8. *An apportionment criterion F is impartial, pairwise consistent, homogeneous, exact, and weakly population monotone if and only if it is representable by a rank-index of form* r(p, a) = p/d(a) *where* a ≤ d(a) ≤ a + 1 *and* d(a) *is a strictly increasing, real-valued function defined on the nonnegative integers* a. *Such a criterion is called a divisor method.*

The proof of this result is given in Balinski and Young (1982, pp. 147–48). (Balancedness is not needed as a separate condition, because it follows from exactness and pairwise consistency.) The priority standards for the five historical divisor methods (Adams, Dean, Hill, Webster, and Jefferson) are exhibited in table 3.5. There are, of course, an infinite number of divisor methods, one for each divisor function $d(a)$ that satisfies the conditions of Theorem 8.

Objective Functions

It has long been recognized that many of the classical apportionment methods minimize some measure of inequality or "error." For example, Webster's method minimizes the criterion

$$\Sigma p_i(a_i/p_i - a_0/\Sigma p_j)^2.$$

This objective function has the following interpretation. In state i, each individual's share of a representative is a_i/p_i. This may be compared to the ideal share of a representative nationally, which is $a_0/\Sigma p_j$. The above expression is therefore the squared difference between each individual's share and the ideal share, summed over all *individuals*. This criterion was first suggested by Sainte-Lague (1910).

In the same paper, Sainte-Lague referred cryptically to the objective function

$$\Sigma a_i(p_i/a_i - (\Sigma p_j)/a_0)^2,$$

which is the square of the difference between each district size and the ideal district size, summed over all districts. Although Sainte-Lague did not show it, Hill's method minimizes this objective (Huntington, 1928).

What has not been clearly recognized heretofore is that *every* rank-index method minimizes an additively separable objective function of this general form. To see this, consider again the algorithm that defines a priority method. When a_0 units are to be distributed among n claimants of types $\tau_1, \tau_2, \ldots, \tau_n$, they are given to the claimants that have highest priority according to the ordering P. Let P be representable by the rank-index $r(\tau, a)$. We may choose r so that it is everywhere positive. For every pair $(\tau, a) \in X$ define the function

$$H(\tau, a) = \sum_{b=0}^{a-1} r(\tau, b). \tag{11}$$

The function H is strictly increasing in a. It is also *strictly concave* in the sense that the finite "derivative" $r(\tau, a) = H(\tau, a + 1) - H(\tau, a)$ is a strictly decreasing function of a. (This follows from the definition of P.)

Given an allocation problem (τ, a_0), the priority algorithm selects the a_0 values $r(\tau_i, b)$ that are largest. That is, it distributes a_0 units such that

$$\sum_{1 \le i \le n} \sum_{0 \le b \le a_i - 1} r(\tau_i, b) \text{ is maximized.} \tag{12}$$

Hence it maximizes the additively separable objective function

$$\sum_{i=1}^{n} H(\tau_i, a_i) \text{ subject to } a \ge 0, \sum a_i = a_o. \tag{13}$$

Conversely, given any real-valued function $H(\tau, a)$ that is strictly increasing and strictly concave in a for each τ, the allocations that maximize (13) define the rank-index method based on $r(\tau, a) = H(\tau, a + 1) - H(\tau, a)$. Thus we have

THEOREM 9. *An integer allocation method is impartial, balanced, and pairwise consistent if and only if it maximizes an additively separable, strictly increasing, symmetric, strictly concave objective function of form* (13).

Webster's Method

Merely knowing that an allocation method maximizes an objective function is not enough to justify the use of that method. Indeed, as we have just seen, *every* impartial, balanced, and pairwise consistent method maximizes *some* objective function. Hence the justification must come from the particular *form* that the objective takes. This approach to equity has two difficulties, however. The first is that similar objective functions may lead to quite different methods. Examples are the objective functions defining the methods of Webster and Hill.

The second difficulty is that the *same* method may maximize *different* objective functions. The simplest way to see this is to note that any monotone increasing transformation of a rank-index $r(\tau, a)$ yields an *equivalent* rank-index—one that yields the same priority relation and the same method—but the associated objective function, as defined by (11), is different. This shows why objective functions are not a very fruitful way to discriminate among methods.

A better approach is to look for other properties that are germane to the situation at hand. In the context of apportionment, we would argue that Webster's method is the right choice for two reasons. First, it is unbiased in its treatment of small and large states. This proposition is strongly supported by empirical evidence cited in the text (chapter 2, section 10) and by a variety of theoretical models (Balinski and Young, 118–28). Second, Webster's method yields the most natural solution when there are just two states. Given a problem $((p_1, p_2), a_0)$ compute the quotas $q_1 = a_0 p_1 / (p_1 + p_2)$ and $q_2 = a_0 p_2 / (p_1 + p_2)$, then round them to the nearest whole numbers. (If the fractional parts of q_1 and

q_2 are both $\frac{1}{2}$, there is a tie and both $(q_1 - \frac{1}{2}, q_2 + \frac{1}{2})$ and $(q_1 + \frac{1}{2}, q_2 - \frac{1}{2})$ are Webster solutions.) This is called the *standard two-state solution*.

THEOREM 10. *Webster's method is the unique apportionment criterion that is pairwise consistent with the standard two-state solution.*

PROOF: We already know that Webster's method is pairwise consistent with the standard two-state solution (see pp. 49–50). Suppose there exists another criterion F that is also pairwise consistent with the standard two-state solution but differs from Webster's method W. Let $(\boldsymbol{p}, a_0)$ be a problem with an F-solution $\boldsymbol{a}$ that is not a Webster solution. Let $\boldsymbol{a}'$ be a Webster solution of $(\boldsymbol{p}, a_0)$ that differs from $\boldsymbol{a}$ in a *minimal* number of components. Choose states i and j such that $a_i' < a_i$ and $a_j' > a_j$. Without loss of generality $a_i' + a_j' \geq a_i + a_j$. By assumption, a_i' is an ordinary rounding of the quota $q_i' = (a_i' + a_j')p_i/(p_i + p_j)$ and a_i is an ordinary rounding of the quota $q_i = (a_i + a_j)p_i/(p_i + p_j)$. Thus $q_i' \geq q_i$, but $a_i' < a_i$. This is clearly impossible unless $q_i' = q_i$, and both fractional remainders equal $\frac{1}{2}$. But then *both* a_i', a_j' and a_i, a_j are Webster allocations for the subproblem. Substituting a_i, a_j into components i and j of $\boldsymbol{a}'$ yields a Webster solution $\boldsymbol{a}''$ that differs from $\boldsymbol{a}$ in fewer components. This contradiction shows that every F-solution is a Webster solution. The converse is established similarly.

A.5 Claims and Liabilities

Definitions

In this section we shall consider criteria for allocating a homogeneous, divisible good equitably among a group of claimants. A variety of examples fall under this heading, perhaps the most important being the division of money. In this case the good is not perfectly divisible (few goods are); nevertheless, perfect divisibility is a convenient idealization. We shall focus on the situation where each individual has a numerical claim (or liability) against a common property resource, and the sum of the claims equals or exceeds the amount available. This seemingly special case covers a variety of important applications, including conflicting property claims, taxation, and other forms of assessments. The situation where there are minimum or maximum constraints on how much various *coalitions* of players can receive is considered in section A.6.

The *type* of a claimant is a positive real number c that represents the extent of his claim against the common resource, or, in the case of a burden, the extent of his liability. A *claims problem* $(\boldsymbol{c}, a_0)$ consists of a list of claims $\boldsymbol{c} = (c_1, c_2, \ldots, c_n) > \boldsymbol{0}$ against a quantity a_0 of a divisible good, where $0 \leq a_0 \leq \Sigma_i c_i$. Given the problem $(\boldsymbol{c}, a_0)$, a *solution* or *allocation* is a vector $\boldsymbol{a} \in R^n$ such that $\Sigma a_i = a_0$ and $0 \leq a_i \leq c_i$ for $1 \leq i \leq n$. An *allocation rule* is a single-valued function F that associates a unique solution $\boldsymbol{a} = F(\boldsymbol{c}, a_0)$ to every claims problem $(\boldsymbol{c}, a_0)$ where F is defined for every number of claimants.

STANDARD OF COMPARISON. Let $X = \{(c, a): c > 0 \text{ and } 0 \le a \le c\}$. A *standard of comparison* is a weak ordering P of X such that $0 \le a < a' \le c$ implies $(c, a) \, P^+ \, (c, a')$.

Let P be a standard of comparison, and let a be a solution to a claims problem (c, a_0). We shall say that a transfer of ϵ from claimant i to claimant j is *justified* if the priority of i after the transfer is strictly lower than the priority of j before the transfer, that is, if

$$(c_j, a_j) \, P^+ \, (c_i, a_i - \epsilon).$$

If no transfer is justified, then for all sufficiently small ϵ,

$$\forall i, j, \, (c_i, a_i - \epsilon) \, P \, (c_j, a_j).$$

Here "sufficiently small" means that $\epsilon \le \min a_i$ so that no allotment is negative. From this it follows that, for all i, j

$$(c_i, a_i - \epsilon) \, P^+ \, (c_i, a_i - \epsilon/2) \, P \, (c_j, a_j).$$

Hence, for all sufficiently small $\epsilon > 0$,

$$\forall i, j, \, (c_i, a_i - \epsilon) \, P^+ \, (c_j, a_j). \tag{14}$$

Conversely, if (14) holds, then no transfer is justified.

EQUITY. An allocation is *equitable* with respect to P if no transfer is justified.

Note that (14) implies that, for every other feasible allocation a' of a_0,

$$\text{there exists } i \text{ such that } (c_i, a_i') \, P^+ \, (c_j, a_j) \text{ for all } j. \tag{15}$$

In other words, for every allocation $a' \ne a$, $\max_i (c_i, a_i')$ is greater than $\max_i (c_i, a_i)$, where the maximum is taken with respect to the ordering P. From this it follows that there is at most one allocation a that satisfies (14).

Existence of Equitable Allocations

The question now arises as to whether equitable allocations exist. Suppose that the standard P can be represented by a real-valued function $r: X \to R$, that is, $r(c, a) \ge r(c', a')$ if and only if $(c, a) \, P \, (c', a')$. From the above remarks it follows that a is the unique equitable solution of (c, a_0) if and only if

a minimizes $\max_i r(c_i, a_i)$ over all a such that $0 \le a \le c$, $\Sigma a_i = a_0$.

A sufficient condition for P to be representable is that it be *closed*, that is,

$$\forall (c^*, a^*) \in X, \, \{(c, a) \in X: (c, a) \, P \, (c^*, a^*)\} \text{ is closed in } R^2 \tag{16}$$

and

$$\forall (c^*, a^*) \in X, \, \{(c, a) \in X: (c^*, a^*) \, P \, (c, a)\} \text{ is closed in } R^2. \tag{17}$$

If (16) holds then P is *closed above,* while if (17) holds P is *closed below.* Together these conditions are sufficient for P to be representable (Debreu, 1954), but they are not necessary. In particular, we want to consider situations in which P is closed below (the set of situations with lower or equal priority to a given situation is closed), but not necessarily closed above. This is enough to guarantee that the minimax problem (14) has a unique solution, as the following theorem shows.

THEOREM 11. *If* P *is representable and closed below, then for every problem* $(\mathbf{c}, a_0)$ *there exists a unique allocation* $F(\mathbf{c}, a_0)$ *that is equitable relative to* P.

PROOF: Let $r(c, a)$ be a representation of P. Since P is closed below, $r(c, a)$ is lower semicontinuous in a for each c. Given a problem $(\mathbf{c}, a_0)$, let A be the set of all solutions $\mathbf{a}$ to $(\mathbf{c}, a_0)$. Define the function $G: A \to R$ such that $G(\mathbf{a}) = \max_i r(c_i, a_i)$. $G(\mathbf{a})$ is lower semicontinuous and bounded below on A. Let $b = \inf \{G(\mathbf{a}): \mathbf{a} \in A\}$ and let $\mathbf{a}^k$ be a sequence in A such that $G(\mathbf{a}^k) \to b$. Since A is closed and bounded, $\{\mathbf{a}^k\}$ has a limit point $\mathbf{a} \in A$. Lower semicontinuity implies that $G(\mathbf{a}) \le \lim G(\mathbf{a}^k) = b$. Hence G achieves its minimum at $\mathbf{a}$, that is, $G(\mathbf{a}) = b$.

It remains to be shown that $\mathbf{a}$ satisfies (14). Given a small $\epsilon > 0$, suppose that $r(c_j, a_j) > r(c_i, a_i - \epsilon)$ for some i and j. Let M be the set of indices k that maximize $r(c_k, a_k)$. Define a new allocation $\mathbf{a}'$ such that $a_k' = a_k + \epsilon/|M|$ for every $k \in M$, $a_i' = a_i - \epsilon$, and $a_k' = a_k$ for every $k \ne i$, $k \notin M$. By construction, $\max_h r(c_h, a_h') < \max_h r(c_h, a_h)$, which contradicts the fact that $\mathbf{a}$ minimizes G. From this we conclude that $r(c_i, a_i - \epsilon) \ge r(c_j, a_j)$ for all i and j and all small $\epsilon > 0$. As in the derivation of (14), it follows that $r(c_i, a_i - \epsilon) > r(c_j, a_j)$ for all i and j, hence $\mathbf{a}$ is equitable.

Equity, Consistency, and Monotonicity

It is clear that an equitable rule is impartial and pairwise consistent. We shall now show that the converse holds provided that F is continuous. First we need some definitions.

MONOTONICITY. A claims allocation rule is *monotonic* if for every vector of claims $\mathbf{c} > 0$, and every two amounts $0 \le a_0 < a_0'$, $F_i(\mathbf{c}, a_0) \le F_i(\mathbf{c}, a_0')$ for every claimant i. It is *strictly monotonic* if $F_i(\mathbf{c}, a_0) < F_i(\mathbf{c}, a_0')$ for every i.

Let $\sim$ be the indifference part of the relation P, that is, $(c, a) \sim (c', a')$ if and only if both $(c, a) P (c', a')$ and $(c', a') P (c, a)$ hold. In this case (c, a) and (c', a') are *on a par.*

PERFECT EQUITY. An allocation rule F is *perfectly equitable* relative to the standard of comparison P if every solution $\mathbf{a} = F(\mathbf{c}, a_0)$ satisfies $(c_i, a_i) \sim (c_j, a_j)$ for all i and j, that is, all claimants are on a par.

CONTINUITY. F is *continuous* if, whenever a sequence of claims problems (c^k, a_0^k) converges to a claims problem (c, a_0), then $F(c^k, a_0^k)$ converges to $F(c, a_0)$.

THEOREM 12. *If a claims allocation rule is impartial, pairwise consistent, and continuous, then it is equitable relative to a representable standard and it is monotonic. If in addition it is strictly monotonic, then it is perfectly equitable.*

We shall establish the second statement, namely, if an allocation rule is impartial, pairwise consistent, continuous, and strictly monotonic, then it is perfectly equitable. Fix a particular level of claim $c^* > 0$ and call it the *reference claim*. Given any claim $c > 0$, consider the solutions to the family of problems $((c^*, c), a_0)$ as a_0 varies between 0 and $c^* + c$. Specifically, define the functions $f(a_0)$ and $g(a_0)$ such that

$$(f(a_0), g(a_0)) = F((c^*, c), a_0) \text{ for } 0 \le a_0 \le c^* + c.$$

We know that $f(0) = 0$ and $f(c^* + c) = c^*$. Similarly, $g(0) = 0$ and $g(c^* + c) = c$. Both f and g are continuous because F is continuous in a_0. Given $0 \le a \le c$, there exists a value of a_0 for which $g(a_0) = a$, and by strict monotonicity this value is unique. Let

$$r(c, a) = \text{unique } x \text{ such that } (x, a) = F((c^*, c), a_0) \text{ for some } a_0. \quad (18)$$

We assert that F is perfectly equitable with respect to the standard of comparison $-r(c, a)$. (We take the negative because a standard of comparison is required to be *decreasing* in a.)

To prove this assertion, fix an arbitrary claims problem (c, a_0) and let $a = F(c, a_0)$. We need to show that $r(c_i, a_i)$ is a constant for all i. Given the fixed vector of claims c and the reference claim c^*, construct an $(n + 1)$-person claims problem of the form $((c^*, c), b_0)$. Let the solution be (a, b), that is, a is the first coordinate of the solution and $b = (b_1, b_2, \ldots, b_n)$ is the remaining part of the solution. Both a and b are continuous functions of b_0, so we shall write $a(b_0)$ and $b(b_0)$. The value of $b_1(b_0) + b_2(b_0)$ increases continuously from 0 (when $b_0 = 0$) to $c_1 + c_2$ (when $b_0 = \Sigma c_i$). Since $0 \le a_1 + a_2 \le c_1 + c_2$, there exists a value of b_0, say b_0', such that $b_1(b_0') + b_2(b_0') = a_1 + a_2$. (Recall that a is the fixed solution to the original problem (c, a_0), and a_1, a_2 are its first two coordinates.) By pairwise consistency,

$$(b_1, b_2) = F((c_1, c_2), a_1 + a_2).$$

On the other hand, pairwise consistency applied to the solution $a = F(c, a_0)$ shows that

$$(a_1, a_2) = F((c_1, c_2), a_1 + a_2).$$

It follows from these two statements that $b_1 = a_1$ and $b_2 = a_2$.

Similarly, there exists a value of b_0, say b_0'', such that $b_1(b_0'') + b_3(b_0'') = a_1 + a_3$. As above, conclude that $b_1 = a_1$ and $b_3 = a_3$. By strict monotonicity, however, there is only one value of b_0 such that $b_1(b_0) = a_1$. Therefore $b_0' = b_0''$. Continuing in this fashion, we deduce that there is a single value of b_0, say b_0^*, such that $b_i(b_0^*) = a_i$ for *every* i, $1 \leq i \leq n$. Therefore the problem $((c^*, c), b_0^*)$ has a solution of form (a^*, a) for some a^*. By pairwise consistency, $(a^*, a_i) = F((c^*, c_i), a^* + a_i)$ for every i, $1 \leq i \leq n$. It follows from the definition of r that $r(c_i, a_i) = a^*$ for all i. Therefore $r(c_i, a_i)$ is a constant, which shows that F is perfectly equitable. This establishes the second statement of the theorem.

The proof of the first statement is more involved and will only be outlined here. The first step is to show that, *if F is pairwise consistent, impartial, and continuous, then F is monotone increasing in a_0*, though it need not be *strictly* monotone increasing (see Young, 1987, Lemma 1). The proof then proceeds as follows. For every $c^* > 0$ define

$$\rho(c^*, c, a) = \max x: (x, a) = F((c^*, c), a_0) \text{ for some } a_0. \tag{19}$$

Then let

$$r(c,a) = \int_0^\infty \rho(c^*, c, a)e^{-c^*}dc^*. \tag{20}$$

Note that $\rho(c^*, c, a) \leq c^*$ by definition, so

$$r(c,a) = \int_0^\infty \rho(c^*, c, a)e^{-c^*}dc^* \leq \int_0^\infty c^* e^{-c^*}dc^* = 1.$$

This construction is similar to (18), except that the reference claim c^* is a variable and we take the exponentially weighted average of the functions $\rho(c^*, c, a)$ as the definition of $r(c, a)$. It may then be shown that F is equitable relative to the standard $-r(c, a)$, which is lower semicontinuous (see Young, 1987, Theorem 1).

As an example, consider the contested garment rule that was discussed in chapter 4. Two individuals have positive claims c_1 and c_2 against an amount a_0, where $a_0 \leq c_1 + c_2$. Without loss of generality we may assume that $c_1 > c_2$. The rule is as follows:

$$
\begin{array}{ll}
a_1 = a_2 = a_0/2 & \text{if } 0 \leq a_0 \leq c_2, \\
a_1 = a_0 - c_2/2,\ a_2 = c_2/2 & \text{if } c_2 < a_0 < c_1, \\
a_1 = (a_0 + (c_1 - c_2))/2,\ a_2 = (a_0 - (c_1 - c_2))/2 & \text{if } c_1 \leq a_0 \leq c_1 + c_2.
\end{array}
$$

In particular, the claimants have equal gains when $a_0 \leq c_2$ and equal losses when $a_0 \geq c_1$. It may be verified that these solutions are equitable (satisfy (14)) with respect to the following standard of comparison:

$$
\begin{array}{ll}
r(c, a) = c - a & \text{if } 0 \leq a < c/2, \\
r(c, a) = -a & \text{if } c/2 \leq a \leq c.
\end{array}
$$

The level curves of this standard are shown in figure 19. The function $r(c, a)$ is strictly decreasing in a for each c, and it is lower semicontinuous (but not

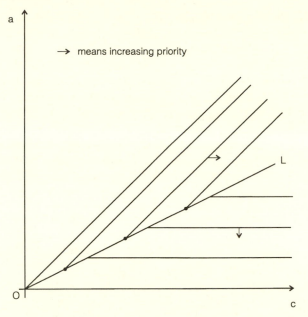

Fig. 19. The level curves of the priority standard for the contested garment rule. The level curves above L meet L; the level curves below L approach but do not meet L. All points strictly below L have strictly higher priority than all points on and above L.

continuous) at points of form $(c, c/2)$. Nevertheless this standard defines an allocation method $F((c_1, c_2), a_0)$ that is jointly continuous in (c_1, c_2, a_0). It is not strictly monotonic, however, and the solutions are not perfectly equitable.

Objective Functions

In section A.4 we showed that every integer allocation criterion that is pairwise consistent, impartial, and balanced maximizes an additively separable objective function (Theorem 9). An analogous result holds here. Let the claims allocation rule F be pairwise consistent, impartial, and continuous. (Balancedness is a weak sort of continuity condition in the integer case.) Then F is equitable relative to the numerical standard of comparison $-r(c, a)$ defined as in (20). Of course, any strictly monotone decreasing transformation of r yields the same method. In particular, since $0 \le r(c, a) \le 1$ for every (c, a), $r^*(c, a) = 1/(1 + r(c, a))$ represents the same method, and r^* is *strictly positive* and *bounded*. Define

$$\phi(c,a) = \int_0^a r^*(c,a')da'. \tag{21}$$

The right derivative of $\phi(c, a)$ with respect to a exists and equals $r^*(c, a)$, which is strictly decreasing. Hence ϕ is strictly concave in a. It is also strictly increasing in a because r^* is strictly positive.

Given an allocation problem (c, a_0), we claim that $F(c, a_0)$ is the unique solution of the optimization problem

$$\max_a \Sigma \; \phi_i(c_i, a_i) \text{ subject to } 0 \leq a_i \leq c_i \text{ and } \Sigma a_i = a_0. \tag{22}$$

THEOREM 13. *If a claims allocation rule is pairwise consistent, impartial, and continuous, then it maximizes an additively separable, strictly increasing, strictly concave objective function.*

We shall outline the proof under the additional assumption that F is perfectly equitable. In this case, F is representable by the standard of comparison $r^*(c, a)$ defined in (18), and $\partial\phi(c, a)/\partial a$ exists and equals $r^*(c, a)$. Suppose that $a = F(c, a_0)$. We shall show that a is the unique maximum of the function $H(c, a) = \Sigma \; \phi_i(c_i, a_i)$ subject to the constraints.

Consider first the case where $0 < a_0 < \Sigma c_i$. Then $0 < a_i < c_i$ for every i because F is strictly monotonic in a_0. Since F is perfectly equitable, $r^*(c_i, a_i) = x$ for some common value x. Therefore $\partial\phi(c_i, a_i)/\partial a_i = r^*(c_i, a_i) = x$ for all i. Since a is an interior solution, this is a necessary and sufficient condition that a maximize $H(c, a)$ subject to $\Sigma a_i = a_0$.

The other cases to consider are $a_0 = 0$ and $a_0 = \Sigma c_i$. In the former case the unique allocation that satisfies the constraints is $a = 0$. In the latter case the unique allocation that satisfies the constraints is $a = c$. It follows that in all cases F maximizes the objective function $H(c, a)$ subject to the constraints $0 \leq a_i \leq c_i$ and $\Sigma a_i = a_0$.

Finally, we must show that *if* a^* maximizes $H(c, a)$ subject to the constraints, *then* it is an F-solution. Suppose it is not. We just showed that the F-solution maximizes $H(c, a)$ subject to the constraints. This implies that $H(c, a)$ has two distinct maxima, which is impossible because H is strictly concave in a for each c. This completes the proof when F is strictly monotonic. The argument proceeds along similar lines in the general case. For details see Young (1987, Theorem 2).

In chapter 4 we discussed various criteria for solving claims allocation problems. Among the simplest are *equal loss* and *equal gain* subject to the constraints $0 \leq a_i \leq c_i$. These may be construed as utilitarian rules in the following sense. Let $u(a)$ be any strictly increasing, strictly concave utility function. Then

Constrained equal gain maximizes $\Sigma u(a_i)$ subject to $0 \leq a_i \leq c_i$.
Constrained equal loss minimizes $\Sigma u(c_i - a_i)$ subject to $0 \leq a_i \leq c_i$.

Another simple rule is proportional allocation. This has a variety of representations, including the following:

$\min \Sigma a_i^2/c_i$ subject to $0 \leq a_i \leq c_i$ and $\Sigma a_i = a_0$.

$\min \Sigma c_i(1 - a_i/c_i)^2$ subject to $0 \leq a_i \leq c_i$ and $\Sigma a_i = a_0$.

$\max \Pi \, a_i{}^{c_i}$ subject to $0 \leq a_i \leq c_i$ and $\Sigma a_i = a_0$.

The latter objective is particularly interesting because in the context of bargaining theory it defines one of the most prominent rules, the Nash bargaining solution (see section A.7).

This list reveals a drawback to objective functions as a way of evaluating equity, however, because the same allocation rule may optimize many different objective functions. Hence the choice of objective is largely a matter of taste. A more fruitful way to narrow down the field is to look for further allocative properties that make sense within a specific context. In the concluding subsections we shall consider two such properties.

The Proportional Rule

A desirable feature of an allocation rule is that it does not create incentives for claimants to pool their claims or to split them up. This property may be stated as follows.

COLLUSION-PROOF. An impartial allocation rule F is *collusion-proof* if for any claims problem $(\boldsymbol{c}, a_0)$:

$$F_1((c_1 + c_2, c_3, \ldots, c_n), a_0) = F_1((c_1, c_2, \ldots, c_n), a_0) + F_2((c_1, c_2, \ldots, c_n), a_0).$$

Since F is impartial, a similar statement holds for every pair of agents.

THEOREM 14 [O'Neill, 1982]. *The proportional rule is the unique claims allocation rule that is impartial and collusion-proof.*

PROOF: The following proof is due to Moulin (1988). It is clear that the proportional rule is both impartial and collusion-proof. Conversely, let F have these two properties. Fix two real numbers $c^* > 0$ and $a_0^* > 0$. For every c in the interval $[0, c^*]$, let $g(c)$ be the amount that a single claimant would receive under F when the total amount to be distributed is a_0^* and the amounts claimed by the other parties total $c^* - c$. Collusion-proofness implies that $g(c)$ is well defined.

Given any c and c' in the interval $[0, c^*]$ such that $c + c' \leq c^*$, construct the following three-person claims problem: $(c, c', c^* - c - c', a_0^*)$. The first claimant receives $g(c)$ and the second receives $g(c')$. Now consider the two-person claims problem $(c + c', c^* - c - c', a_0^*)$. The first claimant in this problem receives $g(c + c')$, and collusion-proofness implies that this equals the sum of what the first two claimants received in the earlier problem. Thus

$g(c + c') = g(c) + g(c')$ whenever $c, c' \geq 0$ and $c + c' \leq c^*$.

By assumption, g is nonnegative and not identically equal to zero. Therefore, by Cauchy's theorem, g must be of the form $g(c) = kc$ for some positive constant k (Aczel, 1966, section 2.1.4, Theorem 3).

Now let $((c_1, c_2, \ldots, c_n), a_0^*)$ be a claims problem on n agents such that $n \geq 2$ and $\Sigma c_i = c^*$. With g defined as above it follows that $F_i(c, a_0^*) = g(c_i) = kc_i$ for every claimant i. Since c^* and a_0^* were chosen arbitrarily, we conclude that F is the proportional method.

Equal Sacrifice

We now consider a principle that is particularly natural in the context of taxation. Let the claims $c_1, c_2, \ldots, c_n$ represent taxable incomes, and let $F(c, a_0)$ be a claims allocation rule, which we shall refer to here as a *taxation rule*. Suppose that there are two different taxing agencies. Agency A gets to tax the incomes first, then agency B gets to levy a tax on whatever income remains after A has taken its cut. Assume that agency A needs to raise a total amount a_0, while B needs to raise a total amount b_0. Assume further that the taxation rule F determines an equitable distribution in any taxing situation, so both agencies plan to use the rule F. The net result is as follows. Given an initial distribution of taxable incomes $c = (c_1, c_2, \ldots, c_n)$, agency A levies the tax $a = F(c, a_0)$. Then agency B levies the tax $b = F(c - a, b_0)$, where $c_i - a_i$ is the amount of income that individual i has after the first tax has been assessed. Thus the sum of the two taxes is $a + b$, and we may ask whether this is fairly distributed relative to the individuals' *original* taxable incomes.

COMPOSITION-INVARIANCE. A taxation rule F is *composition-invariant* if, for every c, a_0, and b_0 such that $a_0 + b_0 \leq \Sigma c_i$,

if $a = F(c, a_0) < c$ and $b = F(c - a, b_0)$, then $a + b = F(c, a_0 + b_0)$. (23)

ORDER-INVARIANCE. A taxation rule F is *order-invariant* if pre-tax incomes are ordered in the same way as after-tax incomes, that is, for any $a = F(c, a_0)$, $c_i \geq c_j$ if and only if $c_i - a_i \geq c_j - a_j$ for all i and j.

THEOREM 15. *An allocation rule* F *is impartial, pairwise consistent, composition-invariant, and order-invariant if and only if* F *is an equal sacrifice rule, that is, if and only if there exists a utility function* U(c) *that is continuous and strictly increasing for all positive incomes* c, *such that for every problem* (c, a_0),

$$a = F(c, a_0) \Leftrightarrow \forall i, j, \ U(c_i) - U(c_i - a_i) = U(c_j) - U(c_j - a_j).$$

It is straightforward to check that an equal sacrifice rule has the four properties asserted in the theorem. The proof of the converse is given in Young (1988, pp. 327–30).

A.6 Cooperative Games

Definitions

In this section we show how cooperative game theory can be used to analyze the equitable allocation of joint costs and gains among groups. Let N be a set of prospective *projects*, each of which is represented by an *agent*. The cost of doing project i by itself is $c(i)$. Similarly, the cost of undertaking any subset S of projects is $c(S)$, which is called the *stand-alone* cost of S. If no projects are undertaken the cost is zero: $c(\phi) = 0$. The function $c(S)$ from the subsets $S \subseteq N$ to the real numbers is called a *cost function* on N.

The *cost-savings* from carrying out the set S of projects jointly rather than separately is $v(S) = \Sigma_{i \in S} c(i) - c(S)$. The function $v(S)$ is called the *cost-savings game*. If $v(N) \geq v(S)$ for all subsets S, then N is an *efficient* set of projects to undertake. The tacit assumption throughout the following discussion is that N is efficient, and the goal is to allocate the cost $c(N)$ among the projects in an equitable way.

COST ALLOCATION RULE. An *allocation or solution* for a cost allocation problem (c, N) is a vector $a \in R^N$ such that $\Sigma a_i = c(N)$. A *cost allocation rule* is a function $F(c, N)$ that assigns a unique allocation to every problem (c, N).

MARGINAL COST CONTRIBUTION. Given a cost function c on N, the *marginal cost contribution* of i with respect to the subset S is

$$c_i(S) = c(S + i) - c(S) \text{ if } i \notin S,$$
$$c_i(S) = c(S) - c(S - i) \text{ if } i \in S.$$

The Shapley Value

Shapley (1953) proposed several properties of cooperative game solutions that translate naturally into the cost allocation context. The first says that a project which contributes zero cost to every subset S should be charged nothing. (Such a project is called a *dummy*.) The second says that the rule should be *impartial*, that is, the cost allocation should distinguish between projects only insofar as they enter into the cost function differently. The third asserts that if costs decompose into two different categories (say capital and operating costs), then the allocation of total cost should be the sum of the allocations for the two cost categories evaluated separately. This assumption seems particularly natural from an accounting standpoint. We may state these properties more formally as follows.

DUMMY. If $c_i(S) = 0$ for some i and all subsets $S \subseteq N$, then $F_i(c, N) = 0$.

IMPARTIALITY. Given any permutation π of N, let $(c \circ \pi)(S) = c(\pi(S))$ for all $S \subseteq N$. Then $F(c \circ \pi, N) = F(c, N) \circ \pi$, that is, $F_i(c \circ \pi, N) = F_{\pi(i)}(c, N)$.

ADDITIVITY. For every two cost functions c and c' on N, define the cost function $[c + c'](S) = c(S) + c'(S)$. Then $F(c + c', N) = F(c, N) + F(c', N)$.

THEOREM 16 [Shapley, 1953]. *There is a unique cost allocation rule satisfying properties I–III, namely, the Shapley value*

$$F_i(c,N) = \sum_{\substack{S \subseteq N \\ i \in S}} \frac{(|S| - 1)!(|N| - |S|)!\ c_i(S)}{|N|!} \ .$$

Of the three axioms, additivity is perhaps the hardest to swallow, but in fact the Shapley value may be characterized without this assumption. One approach is the following. Suppose that the cost function changes over time. Let c^1 be the cost function in period 1 and c^2 the cost function in period 2. Suppose that the marginal cost of some particular project i goes up (or stays the same) relative to *every* subset S. In other words, $c_i^1(S) \leq c_i^2(S)$ for every S. Then it seems justified to charge i at least as much in the second period as in the first. The latter property is called *strong monotonicity* (Young, 1985). A particular consequence of strong monotonicity is that, if i's marginal contribution to costs are the *same* in both periods, then i's assessment should not change.

MARGINALITY. A cost allocation rule F satisfies the *marginality principle* if the charge to project i depends only on i's marginal cost contributions, that is, for every two cost functions c and c' on the same set N,

$$c_i(S) = c_i'(S) \text{ for all } S \subseteq N \text{ implies } F_i(c, N) = F_i(c', N).$$

The Shapley value clearly satisfies the marginality principle, as well as the more demanding principle of strong monotonicity. Moreover the following result holds.

THEOREM 17 [Young, 1985]. *The Shapley value is the unique cost allocation rule that is impartial and satisfies the marginality principle.*

The Core and the Prenucleolus

CORE. The *core* of a cost function c on N is the set of all allocations $a \in R^N$ such that no subset S is charged *more* than its stand-alone cost, that is,

$$a(S) \leq c(S) \text{ and } a(N) = c(N),$$

where in general $a(S)$ denotes $\Sigma_{i \in S} a_i$. An equivalent formulation is this: the core is the set of all allocations $a \in R^N$ such that no subset S is charged *less* than its marginal contribution to total cost, that is,

$$a(S) \geq c(N) - c(N - S) \text{ and } \mathbf{a}(N) = c(N).$$

It is easy to construct examples for which the core is empty (see chapter 5, section 4, for an example). If a cost allocation rule F yields a solution that is in the core whenever the core is nonempty, we call it a *core* allocation rule. When the cost function decomposes into distinct cost elements (as described in chapter 5, section 6), the Shapley value is in the core. In general, however, it is not a core allocation rule, as the example in table 5.7 shows. In this subsection we shall examine the question of how to choose an equitable core allocation when the core is nonempty.

We begin with a simple case. There are two projects, 1 and 2, and it is at least as efficient to undertake the two projects together as it is to do them separately: $c(1, 2) \leq c(1) + c(2)$. The core is nonempty and consists of the line segment

$$\{(a_1, a_2): a_1 + a_2 = c(1, 2), a_1 \leq c(1), a_2 \leq c(2)\}.$$

The natural solution is to choose the *midpoint* of the line segment, that is, the allocation in which both projects realize equal savings relative to their stand-alone costs. It is straightforward to check that this is the same as the Shapley value.

STANDARD SOLUTION. The *standard solution* of a two-project cost function is to split the cost-savings equally:

$$a_1 = c(1) - s/2 \text{ and } a_2 = c(2) - s/2, \text{ where } s = c(1, 2) - c(1) - c(2).$$

Note that the standard solution is well defined even when the set of both projects is not efficient and the core is empty.

Unfortunately, the standard solution does not extend in any obvious way to three or more projects, because dividing the cost-savings equally is not necessarily in the core, as the example in chapter 5, figure 5 shows. Nevertheless the principle of equal cost savings can be satisfied in an *approximate* sense. The idea is the following. The cost-savings of an individual project is a measure of how well it fares in the allocation. Similarly, the cost-savings of a subset of projects is a measure of how well they fare as a group. While it is clearly impossible to achieve absolute equality of cost-savings among all subsets of projects, we can say that some allocations are *more equitable* than others relative to the cost-savings standard.

To make this idea precise, consider a cost function c on N and an allocation a of $c(N)$. The *saving* of the subset S is the difference between its stand-alone cost $c(S)$ and its allocated cost $a(S)$. The negative of the savings is a measure of disadvantage or priority:

$$r(S, a) = a(S) - c(S).$$

Given an allocation a, compute the $2^n - 2$ numbers $r(S, a)$ for all proper subsets S of N and order them from largest to smallest. (There are repetitions in the list if several sets have equal priority.) Let $R(a)$ be the resulting ordered vector of length $2^n - 2$.

PRENUCLEOLUS. The *prenucleolus* is the unique allocation of $c(N)$ that minimizes $R(a)$ lexicographically, that is, for every allocation b of $c(N)$ such that $b \neq a$, there exists an index k such that $R_j(a) = R_j(b)$ for all $j < k$ and $R_k(a) < R_k(b)$.

NUCLEOLUS. The *nucleolus* is the unique vector a that lexicographically minimizes $R(a)$ subject to the condition that $a_i \leq c(i)$ for every i.

When the cost function is subadditive, that is, when $c(S \cup S') \leq c(S) + c(S')$ for every disjoint subgroups S and S', the nucleolus is the same as the prenucleolus. It is easy to check that the prenucleolus and nucleolus are the same as the standard solution when there are just two projects. Moreover, both the nucleolus and prenucleolus are in the core whenever it is nonempty.

Consistency

We shall now show that the prenucleolus is consistent. To motivate the discussion, imagine that each project is represented by an agent who is responsible for paying the assessed cost. Let a be an allocation that these agents jointly negotiate, and suppose first that a is in the core of the cost function c on N. Consider a particular subset of agents T. Together they divide charges equal to $a(T)$. If these agents were to renegotiate the division of these charges among themselves, what are the constraints they would face given that the cost assessments for everyone outside of T remain fixed? The answer is that they can redivide $a(T)$ in any way so long as the new division, together with the original assessments for everyone else, does not violate the core constraints. Let b be a redivision of $a(T)$ among the members of T. If the core constraints are not violated, then for every $P \subseteq N$,

$$b(P \cap T) + a(P \cap \overline{T}) \leq c(P).$$

Letting $S = P \cap T$ and $S' = P \cap \overline{T}$, we see that this is equivalent to

$$b(S) \leq \min_{S' \subseteq N-T} \{c(S' \cup S) - a(S')\} \text{ for every } S \subseteq T. \tag{24}$$

Devine a cost game $c^{T,a}$ on the set T as follows:

$$\begin{aligned} c^{T,a}(S) &= \min_{S' \subseteq N-T} \{c(S' \cup S) - a(S')\} \text{ for } \varnothing \subset S \subset T \\ c^{T,a}(T) &= a(T) \\ c^{T,a}(\phi) &= 0. \end{aligned} \tag{25}$$

The function $c^{T,a}$ is called the *reduced cost function* (Davis and Maschler, 1965). Its core is the restriction of the core of the original cost function c to the set of solutions in which every agent k who is not in T pays a_k. The definition of $c^{T,a}$ also makes sense, however, when the original allocation a is *not* in the core of c. For every subset $S \subseteq T$, $c^{T,a}(S)$ is an upper bound on what it would be rational for the agents in S to accept, given that the alternative is the allocation a. To see this, suppose that S were assessed an amount $b(S) > c^{T,a}(S)$. As an alternative, the members of S could team up with some subset of partners $S' \subseteq N - T$ and assess them the amounts they previously agreed to (namely a_k for each $k \in S'$), which leaves S with a payment of $c(S' \cup S) - a(S') = c^{T,a}(S)$. This is less than S is charged under b, so S has no reason to accept b.

Using the reduced cost function, we may define consistency as follows (Sobolev, 1975).

CONSISTENCY. A cost allocation rule F is *consistent* if $a = F(c, N)$ implies $F(c^{S,a}, S) = a_S$ for every pair (c, N) and every nonempty $S \subseteq N$.

We shall now consider two additional properties that make sense in the cost allocation context. The first says that if a cost is *directly attributable* to a given project, then the total cost charged to the project should be independent of whether the direct cost is included in the cost function or not. The second states that if all costs are inflated by a constant factor, then all charges should also be inflated by this factor.

SEPARABILITY IN DIRECT COSTS. If a cost function can be written as $c(S) = c'(S) + \sum_{i \in S} d_i$, where d_i is the *direct cost* for project i, then for every i, $F_i(c, N) = d_i + F_i(c', N)$.

HOMOGENEITY. If a cost function c is rescaled by a positive constant λ, then the solution is rescaled by λ, that is, $F(\lambda c, N) = \lambda F(c, N)$.

THEOREM 18 [Sobolev, 1975]. *The prenucleolus is the unique cost allocation rule that is consistent, impartial, homogeneous, and separable in direct costs.*

We remark that pairwise consistency will not suffice here. Suppose, in fact, that a cost allocation rule F is pairwise consistent, impartial, homogeneous, and separable in direct costs. Impartiality and separability readily imply that F is the standard solution for all *two-project* cost functions. When there are more than two projects, however, there may exist more than one allocation that is pairwise consistent with the standard solution. Indeed, any allocation a of $c(N)$ that satisfies the condition

$$\forall i, j \max \{a(S) - c(S): S \text{ contains } i \text{ but not } j\}$$
$$= \max \{a(S) - c(S): S \text{ contains } j \text{ but not } i\}$$

is pairwise consistent with the standard solution (Peleg, 1986). The set of all allocations with this property is known as the *prekernel* of (c, N). It contains the prenucleolus but often contains other solutions too. It may be shown, more-over, that *the prekernel is the unique cost allocation criterion that is impartial, consistent, pairwise converse consistent (see (3)), separable in direct costs, and homogeneous* (Peleg, 1986).

Consistency and the Shapley Value

We conclude this section by noting that there is another way of defining the reduced game which, when combined with consistency, characterizes the Shapley value. Let F be an allocation rule, and consider an allocation $a = F(c, N)$. Fix a subset $T \subseteq N$ and consider any subset $S \subset T$. Imagine that S forms a coalition with *all* the members of $\overline{T} = N - T$, and that they consider the relevant cost function to be c *restricted to* $S + \overline{T}$. (Here we write $+$ instead of $\cup$.) Thus

$$c|_{S+\overline{T}}(Q) = c(Q) \text{ for every } Q \subseteq S + \overline{T}.$$

Imagine further that the members of $S + \overline{T}$ divide the amount $c(S + \overline{T})$ according to the rule F. Then the amount that S is charged as a group equals $\Sigma_{i \in S} F_i(c|_{S+\overline{T}}, S + \overline{T})$. This motivates the following definition of the *reduced cost function* due to Hart and Mas-Colell (1989):

$$c_{T,a}(S) = \Sigma_{i \in S} F_i(c|_{S+\overline{T}}, S + \overline{T}) \text{ for every } S \subset T,$$
$$c_{T,a}(T) = \Sigma_{i \in T} a_i.$$

A cost allocation rule F is *consistent* with respect to the HM reduced cost function if $a = F(c, N)$ implies $a_T = F(c_{T,a}, T)$ for all $T \subseteq N$.

THEOREM 19 [Hart and Mas-Colell, 1989]. *The Shapley value is the unique allocation rule F that is impartial, separable in direct costs, and consistent with respect to the HM reduced cost function.*

Note that there is an important difference between Hart and Mas-Colell's definition of the reduced allocation problem and the one used elsewhere in this book. In the HM-version, some or all of the agents in the given subgroup T think of renegotiating their allocation with *all* of the agents outside of the subgroup. In other words, they consider the amounts that the others are allotted to be renegotiable. In the Davis-Maschler version (25), by contrast, the allotments to everyone outside the subgroup are assumed to be *fixed*. All thought about renegotiation takes place within the given subgroup. What the agents in every subgroup conclude is that no renegotiation is necessary, which *validates* their assumption that the other agents' allocations are fixed. This is the interpretation of the reduced problem that we have adopted in previous sections, and that we shall continue to use in those to follow.

A.7 Bargaining

Definitions

Up to this point we have evaluated the equity of an allocation in terms of the *amount of goods* that each claimant receives in relation to his claim. In this section we adopt a different point of view by framing the discussion in terms of the *welfare* of the claimants, not the physical portions that they are allotted. This *welfarist* approach to distributive justice presumes that the claimants' utility functions are common knowledge, and that the equity of an outcome is judged solely by the claimants' utility for this outcome in relation to the utility of other feasible solutions. As we argued in chapter 7, the assumption of common knowledge is not particularly realistic, and there is considerable evidence that bargainers tend to frame solutions in terms of *visible* standards of comparison, not in terms of welfare *per se*. Nevertheless, the welfarist approach is the dominant one in the economics literature, and one of the most important welfarist solutions—the Nash bargaining solution—fits neatly into the present framework.

Let R^n_+ denote the nonnegative orthant of n-dimensional euclidean space. An *n-person bargaining problem* is a subset B of R^n_+ with the following properties:

  (i) B is convex and compact.
  (ii) If $x \in B$ and $0 \leq y \leq x$ then $y \in B$.
  (iii) There exists $x \in B$ such that $x_i > 0$ for every i.

Each vector $x \in B$ represents the utility payoffs to the various players from a particular agreement. The origin corresponds to *no agreement*. The assumption that B is convex follows if lotteries between agreements are possible and the utility of a lottery equals its expected utility. Compactness follows if the utility functions are bounded and continuous. Condition (ii) says that utility is freely disposable, which follows if goods can be thrown away. Condition (iii) says that there is some agreement that everyone prefers to no agreement, which follows if utility is strictly increasing in the goods and there is a nonempty bundle to distribute.

To take a concrete example, consider a claims problem as defined in section A.5. There is an amount a_0 of a divisible good to allocate among n claimants, $c_i > 0$ is the size of i's claim, and $0 \leq a_0 \leq \Sigma c_i$. A *partial allocation* of a_0 is a vector $\mathbf{a} = (a_1, a_2, \ldots, a_n)$ satisfying $\Sigma a_i \leq a_0$ and $0 \leq a_i \leq c_i$ for all i. Let $u_i(a_i)$ be i's von Neumann–Morgenstern utility function, which we assume is strictly increasing in the portion a_i. The bargaining set B is the convex hull of all payoff vectors $(u_1(a_1), u_2(a_2), \ldots, u_n(a_n))$ such that $\mathbf{a}$ is a partial allocation of a_0. (We take the convex hull because the bargain may involve lotteries among partial allocations, and the utility of a lottery equals its expected utility.)

BARGAINING RULE. A *bargaining rule* is a function $F(B)$ defined for all n-person bargaining problems B, and every number of persons $n \geq 1$, such that $F(B) \in B$.

In the literature a bargaining rule is sometimes called a bargaining "solution." Here we reserve the term "solution" for the outcome of a particular bargaining problem, and a rule is a function that associates a solution to every problem. Note that the rule depends only on the utility payoffs from various agreements, not the *nature* of these agreements. In particular, the solution to a claims problem does not necessarily depend on the size of the claims.[3]

NASH RULE. Given a bargaining problem $B \subset R^n_+$, the *Nash solution* of B is the unique vector x that maximizes Πx_i subject to $x \in B$. The *Nash rule* associates the Nash solution to every bargaining problem.

KALAI-SMORODINSKY RULE. Given a bargaining problem $B \subset R^n_+$, let $x_i^* = \max \{x_i : x \in B\}$ for each i. The *Kalai-Smorodinsky (KS) solution* to B is the unique vector $rx^* \in B$ that maximizes r. The *KS rule* associates the KS solution to every bargaining problem.

We shall now translate the properties considered in preceding sections into the present framework.

EFFICIENCY. A bargaining rule F is *efficient* if, for every bargaining problem B, there exists no $y \in B$ such that $y_i \geq F_i(B)$ for all i and $y_i > F_i(B)$ for some i.

IMPARTIALITY. Given an n-person bargaining problem B, and a permutation π of the indices $1, 2, \ldots, n$, let $B \circ \pi = \{x \circ \pi = (x_{\pi(1)}, x_{\pi(2)}, \ldots, x_{\pi(n)}) : x \in B\}$. F is *impartial* if $F(B \circ \pi) = F(B) \circ \pi$, that is, $F_i(B \circ \pi) = F_{\pi(i)}(B)$ for all i.

---

[3] See, however, Chun and Thomson (1992), who consider solutions that depend on both the bargaining set and on the claims.

Given an *n*-person bargaining problem B, a vector $x \in B$, and a subset of bargainers S, define the *reduced bargaining problem* $B(x, S)$ as follows:

$$B(x, S) = \{y_S : y \in B \text{ and } y_k = x_k \text{ for all } k \notin S.\} \tag{27}$$

In other words, the reduced problem is the bargaining problem in $R_+^{|S|}$ that consists of all payoff distributions in B to the members of S, such that every bargainer $k \notin S$ is fixed at the predetermined level x_k.

WEAK CONSISTENCY. For every bargaining problem B, and every subset of the bargainers S, $x = F(B)$ implies $x_S = F(B(x, S))$.

This is the analog of weak consistency for allocating physical goods, as defined in (1). The idea is illustrated in figure 20.

Under the assumptions of von Neumann–Morgenstern utility theory, the scaling of the claimants' utility functions is arbitrary; only relative magnitudes matter. This leads us to formulate the following condition. Given an *n*-person bargaining problem B, and a vector of n positive scale factors $\lambda = (\lambda_1, \lambda_2, \ldots, \lambda_n)$, let $\lambda(x) = (\lambda_1 x_1, \lambda_2 x_2, \ldots, \lambda_n x_n)$ for every $x \in B$. The image of B under the mapping λ is denoted by $\lambda(B)$.

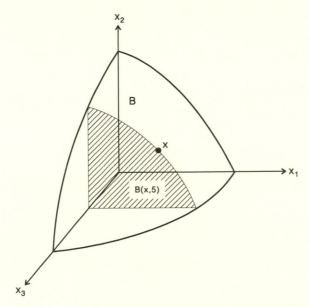

Fig. 20. Consistency illustrated for a three-person bargaining problem. The solution to B is x. If $S = \{1, 2\}$, then the solution to $B(x, S)$ is (x_1, x_2).

SCALE INVARIANCE. $F(\lambda(B)) = \lambda(F(B))$ for every bargaining problem $B \subset R_+^n$ and every vector of scale factors $\lambda \in R_{++}^n$.

Consistency and the Nash Rule

The Nash and KS rules are impartial and scale-invariant. Moreover, the Nash rule is consistent, because it maximizes the additively separable objective function $\Sigma ln\ x_i$. On the other hand, the KS rule is not consistent, as we saw in chapter 7, section 4. An example of a rule that is impartial and consistent but not scale-invariant is the following:

EGALITARIAN RULE. Choose $x \in B$ such that all x_i are equal and as large as possible.

This rule is also efficient provided that B contains no faces that are parallel to the coordinate axes. This will be the case, for example, if B is generated by a claims allocation problem in which the claimants' utility functions are strictly increasing in the good. In this case, the egalitarian rule satisfies all of the above properties except scale-invariance, while the KS rule satisfies all except consistency.

The main result of this section is the following.

THEOREM 20 [Lensberg, 1988]. *The unique bargaining rule that is efficient, impartial, weakly consistent, and scale-invariant is the Nash rule.*

We shall prove this result under the additional assumption that F is *continuous,* that is, if B^k is a sequence of n-person bargaining problems converging to the n-person bargaining problem B in the Hausdorff topology on R_+^n, then $F(B^k)$ converges to $F(B)$.

The first step is to show that efficiency, consistency, and continuity imply the following condition, which Nash adopted as an axiom.

NASH'S INDEPENDENCE OF IRRELEVANT ALTERNATIVES (NIAA). If $B' \subseteq B$ and $F(B) \in B'$ then $F(B') = F(B)$.

LEMMA 1 [Lensberg, 1987]. If a bargaining rule is efficient, weakly consistent, and continuous, then it satisfies Nash's independence of irrelevant alternatives.

PROOF: Let F have the required three properties. Given $B' \subseteq B$ and $x = F(B) \in B'$, we are to show that $x = F(B')$. Since x is efficient in B, it is certainly efficient in the smaller set B'. Therefore the Pareto-efficient boundaries of B and B' intersect. Let δB and $\delta B'$ be the Pareto-efficient boundaries of B and B' respectively. We shall first prove the result under the further assumption that δB and $\delta B'$ intersect nontrivially, that is, $\delta B'$ contains the intersection of δB with an open neighborhood of x. From this and continuity, the result follows in general because one can construct a sequence of problems $B^k \subseteq B$ such that $B^k \to B'$ and the boundaries of B^k and B' intersect nontrivially for every k.

The proof is illustrated in figure 21 for the case where B and B' are two-person bargaining problems. (It will be seen that the argument generalizes readily to the case of more than two persons.) Construct the three-person bargaining problem $C = \{(x_1, x_2, y): (x_1, x_2) \in B \text{ and } 0 \leq y \leq 1\}$. Similarly, let $C' = \{x_1, x_2, y): (x_1, x_2) \in B' \text{ and } 0 \leq y \leq 1\}$.

Given a small $\epsilon > 0$, let D^ϵ be the convex cone spanned by the point $(0, 0, 1 + \epsilon)$ and C'. Let $E^\epsilon = C \cap D^\epsilon$.

First consider the case where $\epsilon = 0$. Efficiency implies that $z^0 = F(E^0)$ lies on the front face of E^0, which is a copy of B. Indeed, z^0 must lie on the Pareto-efficient boundary of the front face of E^0. Consistency implies that the restriction of z^0 to the first two coordinates is $F(B) = x$. In other words, $z^0 = (x, 1)$. For each $\epsilon > 0$, let $z^\epsilon = F(E^\epsilon)$. By continuity, $z^\epsilon \to z^0$ as $\epsilon \to 0$. Since z^ϵ is efficient in E^ϵ, it follows that z^ϵ must lie in $\delta C \cap \delta C'$ for all sufficiently small $\epsilon > 0$, where δC and $\delta C'$ are the Pareto boundaries of C and C'. For every such $\epsilon > 0$, the hyperplane that passes through z^ϵ and is parallel to the 1-2 plane intersects E^ϵ in a copy of B'. Consistency therefore implies that z^ϵ restricted to its first two coordinates is the solution to B' for all sufficiently small ϵ. This means, however, that z^ϵ is *constant* for all sufficiently small ϵ: $z^\epsilon = (w, 1)$, where $w = F(B')$. Since $z^\epsilon \to z^0$, it follows that $z^\epsilon = z^0 = (x, 1)$ for all sufficiently small ϵ. Thus $w = x$, the desired conclusion. The proof of Theorem 20 follows from the lemma and the following classical result of Nash (1950).

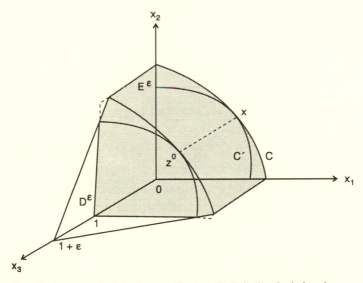

Fig. 21. The proof of the lemma illustrated. E^ϵ is the shaded region.

THEOREM 21 [Nash, 1950]. *The unique bargaining rule that is efficient, impartial, scale-invariant, and satisfies NIIA is the Nash rule.*

PROOF: It is straightforward to verify that the Nash rule satisfies NIIA. Conversely, let F be a bargaining rule with the above four properties. Given a bargaining set $B \subset R_+^n$, there exists a unique $x^* > 0$ that maximizes $\Pi_i x_i$ on B, because $\Pi_i x_i$ is strictly concave. By scale invariance we can scale the utilities so that $x_i^* = 1$ for every i. Define the convex set $C = \{x \geq 0: \Pi_i x_i \geq \Pi_i x_i^* = 1\}$.

By the separating hyperplane theorem there exists a hyperplane H through x^* that separates the convex sets B and C. Since there is a unique tangent hyperplane to C at x^*, the separating hyperplane H takes the form $H = \{x \in R^n: \Sigma_i x_i = n\}$.

Consider the bargaining set $B^* = \{x \in R_+^n: \Sigma_i x_i \leq n\}$. B^* is symmetric, so efficiency and impartiality imply that $F(B^*) = (1, 1, \ldots, 1) = x^*$. Since $x^* \in B \subseteq B^*$, NIIA implies that $F(B) = F(B^*) = x^*$. Therefore F is the Nash rule, as was to be shown.

If we remove the conditions of scale invariance and impartiality, and add continuity, we obtain the following generalization of Theorem 20.

THEOREM 22 [Lensberg, 1987]. *A bargaining rule F is efficient, continuous, and pairwise consistent if and only if it maximizes an additively separable welfare function:*

$$x = F(B) \text{ iff } x \text{ maximizes } \Sigma f_i(x_i) \text{ subject to } x \in B,$$

where each f_i *is strictly increasing and each finite partial sum* $\Sigma f_i(x_i)$ *is strictly quasi-concave. If in addition F is impartial, then all* f_i *are the same function* f, *which is strictly increasing and strictly concave. If also F is scale-invariant, then* $f(x) = \ln x$ *and F is the Nash rule.*

This theorem is analogous to Theorems 9 and 13, which characterize pairwise consistent rules as the solutions of optimization problems.

Standards of Comparison

We know from previous results that impartial and pairwise consistent rules are associated with standards of comparison that determine when a transfer between two claimants is justified. A somewhat analogous result holds here. Suppose that F is efficient, impartial, continuous, and pairwise consistent. By the above theorem, $F(B)$ maximizes an objective function of form $\Sigma f(x_i)$ where f is strictly increasing and strictly concave. We shall show that such a rule defines a standard of comparison on the subclass of bargaining problems that arise from the division of a single homogeneous good.

Let $a_0 > 0$ be the amount to be divided, and let the claimants have utility functions $u_1, u_2, \ldots, u_n$. We shall assume that the utility functions are concave. The associated bargaining problem is

$$B = \{(u_1(a_1), \ldots, u_n(a_n)): \text{all } a_i \geq 0 \text{ and } \Sigma a_i \leq a_0\}.$$

The solution $F(B)$ corresponds to the unique allocation a such that

$$a \text{ maximizes } \Sigma f(u_i(a_i)) \text{ subject to } \Sigma a_i \leq a_0 \text{ and } a \geq 0. \tag{28}$$

Let the *type* of a claimant be his utility function $u(a)$. A *standard of comparison* is a weak ordering P of all pairs (u, a), where $a \geq 0$ and $u: R \to R$ is a concave utility function. We shall show that there exists a standard such that all solutions to (28) are equitable with respect to that standard.

For each utility function u, it is convenient to define the transformed utility function $\bar{u} = f(u)$. Consider a group of claimants with concave utility functions $u_1, u_2, \ldots, u_n$, and an amount $a_0 > 0$ to divide. Assume for the moment that f and all u_i are differentiable, so $\bar{u}_i$ is differentiable for all i. A necessary and sufficient condition for an allocation a to be the solution of (28) is that there exist a Lagrange multiplier λ such that

$$\forall i, \ \bar{u}_i'(a_i) = \lambda.$$

Even if the functions f and u_i are not differentiable, they are concave and hence subdifferentiable. In this case a necessary and sufficient condition for a to be a maximum (Rockafellar, 1970, chapter 28) is that there exist λ such that,

$$\forall i, \ \bar{u}_i^-(a_i) \geq \lambda \geq \bar{u}_i^+(a_i). \tag{29}$$

The function $u_i^+(a_i)$ is strictly *decreasing* in a_i, and

$$\lim_{\epsilon \to 0} u_i^+(a_i - \epsilon) = \bar{u}_i^-(a_i).$$

Hence (29) implies that for all sufficiently small $\epsilon > 0$,

$$\forall i, \ \bar{u}_i^+(a_i - \epsilon) > \lambda \geq \bar{u}_i^+(a_i).$$

From this we can conclude that, for all small $\epsilon > 0$,

$$\forall i, j, \ \bar{u}_i^+(a_i - \epsilon) > \bar{u}_j^+(a_j).$$

This is an instance of the minmax inequality (14), and shows that a is equitable with respect to the standard of comparison P defined by

$$(u, a) \ P \ (v, b) \text{ iff } \bar{u}^+(a) \geq \bar{v}^+(b).$$

A particular instance is the Nash bargaining rule, which corresponds to the transformation function $f(x) = \ln x$. In this case (u, a) has weak priority over

(v, b) if and only if $u^+(a)/u(a) \geq v^+(b)/v(b)$, that is, the claimants are ordered according to their percentage gain in utility from receiving slightly more of the good.

A.8 Multiple Goods

Definitions

Consider a set of m divisible goods that are to be allocated among a group of n claimants. The *initial bundle* is denoted by $a_0 \in R^m_{++}$, which we assume contains a strictly positive quantity of every good k, $1 \leq k \leq m$. The *type* of a claimant consists of two parts: his share and his utility function. The *share* of a claimant is the fraction of the property to which he is entitled. For example, s_i might be the fraction of the "estate" left to claimant i in the "will." We do not need to assume that the shares sum to unity, but we do assume that each share lies strictly between 0 and 1. The *utility function* of claimant i is a real-valued function $u_i(a_i)$, defined for all *portions* $a_i \in R^m_+$. It is an *ordinal* representation of i's preferences and does not necessarily satisfy the von Neumann–Morgenstern expected utility axioms. Throughout this section we shall assume that the utility functions are continuous and strictly increasing in every good, and at times we shall assume they are strictly quasi-concave.

An *allocation problem* (u, s, a_0) consists of a list $u = (u_1, u_2, \ldots, u_n)$ of the claimants' utility functions, a list $s = (s_1, s_2, \ldots, s_n)$ of their respective shares, and the bundle to be divided $a_0 > 0$. An *allocation* is a nonnegative matrix $a = (a_{ik})$ such that $a_{ik} \geq 0$ and for each k, $\Sigma_i a_{ik} = a_{0k}$. An *allocation criterion* is a multiple-valued function $F(u, s, a_0)$ that associates one or more allocations to every problem (u, s, a_0), for *every* finite number of claimants and every positive bundle of the given m goods.

ENTITLEMENT. Given an allocation problem (u, s, a_0), the *entitlement* e_i of claimant i is his proportional share of the initial bundle a_0, that is, $e_i = (s_i/\Sigma s_j)a_0$.

ACCEPTABLE. An allocation a is *acceptable* if for every claimant i, $u_i(a_i) \geq u_i(e_i)$.

EFFICIENT. An allocation a is *efficient* (*Pareto optimal*) if for every allocation a', $u_i(a_i') > u_i(a_i)$ for some i implies $u_j(a_j') < u_j(a_j)$ for some j.

IMPARTIAL. An allocation criterion F is *impartial* if it discriminates among the claimants only insofar as they differ in their utility functions and/or their shares.

Egalitarianism and Equitarianism

EGALITARIAN. An allocation a is *egalitarian* for the problem (u, s, a_0) if there exists a real number $r \geq 0$ such that for every claimant i, $u_i(a_i) = u_i(ra_0)$.

This concept was first proposed by Pazner and Schmeidler (1978). It generalizes in a natural way to the case of unequal shares as follows.

EQUITARIAN. An allocation a is *equitarian* for the problem (u, s, a_0) if there exists a real number $r \geq 0$ such that for every claimant i, $u_i(a_i) = u_i(re_i)$, where e_i is i's entitlement.

The following result generalizes Pazner and Schmeidler (1978).

THEOREM 23. *Given an allocation problem (u, s, a_0) with utility functions that are continuous and strictly increasing, there exists an efficient, equitarian allocation, and every such allocation is acceptable.*

PROOF: Given the problem (u, s, a_0), choose a claimant i and a feasible portion a, where $0 \leq a \leq a_0$. Since a_0 is positive and i's preferences are continuous and strictly increasing, there exists a unique value of r, say r_a, such that i is indifferent between a and $r_a e_i$. If we let $v_i(a) = r_a$ for every a, then v is an ordinal representation of i's preferences that is continuous and strictly increasing.

Let B be the set of utility vectors $v = (v_1(a_1), v_2(a_2), \ldots, v_n(a_n))$ generated by all partial or full allocations a of a_0. By definition, $v_i(e_i) = 1$, so $\mathbf{1} \in B$. Since B is compact, there exists a maximum value of $r \geq 1$ such that $r\mathbf{1} \in B$. Call this maximum value r^*. Any allocation a^* such that $v(a_i^*) = r^*$ for all i is efficient and equitarian. Furthermore, it is acceptable, because each claimant i is indifferent between a_i^* and r^*e_i, and r^*e_i is at least as desirable as e_i because $r^* \geq 1$. This concludes the proof.

No Envy

ENVY-FREE. Given an allocation problem (u, s, a_0), an allocation a is *envy-free* if $u_i(a_i) \geq u_i(a_j)$ of every pair of claimants i and j.

The set of envy-free allocations can be quite complex even for simple problems. Suppose, for example, that there are just two goods and two claimants. The set of allocations $a = (a_1, a_2)$ may be conveniently illustrated using an Edgeworth box, as shown in figure 22. The center of the box is e, which represents equal division. Select one of the claimants, say agent 1. The set of portions a such that 1 is indifferent between a and $a_0 - a$ is 1's *envy boundary*. The portion a is on 1's envy boundary if and only if its reflection a' about e is on the same indifference curve as a (Kolm, 1972). It may be shown that 1's envy boundary is a continuous curve that is downward sloping and passes through e. Claimant 1 envies all allocations to the southwest of his envy boundary. Together, the envy boundaries of the two claimants define the envy-free set, which is the shaded region shown in figure 23.

In general, any competitive allocation from equal division is envy-free, efficient, and acceptable. (In fig. 23 this is point c). Thus, whenever a competitive allocation from equal division exists, so do envy-free, efficient, and acceptable allocations. This will be the case if the utility functions are strictly increasing and strictly quasi-concave, *which we assume from now on*.

Competitive Allocation as a Concept of Equity

The preceding example shows that, when there are just two agents, the set of envy-free and efficient allocations can be rather large. We might imagine that as the number of claimants grows, the envy-free and efficient set shrinks toward the competitive allocation from equal division. Actually this is not true in general. To see why, consider any allocation a for a two-person situation that is envy-free and efficient but is *not* a competitive allocation from equal division. Let n_1 and n_2 be arbitrary positive integers, and consider the following allocation problem with $n_1 + n_2$ agents: agent 1 is replicated n_1 times, agent 2 is replicated n_2 times, and they divide the bundle $a_0' = n_1 a_1 + n_2 a_2$. The allocation in which each agent of type 1 receives a_1 and each agent of type 2 receives a_2 is clearly efficient and envy-free, but it is not competitive from equal division.

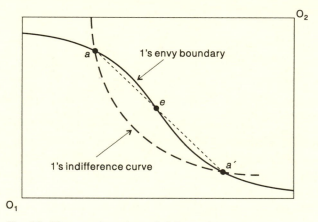

Fig. 22. The envy boundary of claimant 1.

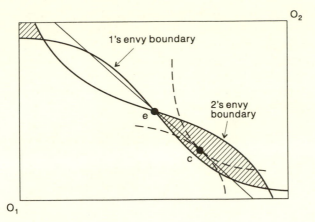

Fig. 23. The envy-free set.

If the preferences of the agents are sufficiently *diverse*, however, then the set of envy-free and efficient allocations *is* approximately the same as the set of competitive allocations from equal division. To make this statement precise, we shall depart momentarily from our assumption of a finite population, and assume a *continuum* of claimants indexed by the real numbers $t \in (0, 1)$. All have equal shares. Let $u(t, a)$ be the utility function of claimant t for the portion $a \in R_+^m$. We shall assume that u is a continuous function of both of its arguments. In other words, agents who lie close together in the interval $(0, 1)$ have similar preferences. We shall also assume that $u(t, a)$ is smooth and strictly concave in a for every fixed t. In this context an *allocation* of $a_0 \in R_{++}^m$ is an integrable function $a(t)$ such that

$$\int_0^1 a(t)dt = a_0. \tag{30}$$

A *competitive allocation from equal division* is an allocation $a(t)$ such that, for every t, $a(t)$ maximizes $u(t, a)$ subject to $p \cdot a(t) \leq p \cdot a_0$ for some price vector p.

THEOREM 24 [Varian, 1976]. *If the allocation* a(t) *is differentiable, efficient, and envy-free, then it is a competitive allocation from equal division.*

The proof proceeds along the following lines. Since by assumption $a(t)$ is efficient, there exists a supporting vector p and nonzero scalars r_t such that $\partial u(t, a(t))/\partial a_k = r_t p_k$ for every $t \in (0, 1)$. Fix $t \in (0, 1)$ and let t' vary over this interval. Since $a(t)$ is envy-free, the function $v(t') = u(t, a(t'))$ attains its maximum when $t' = t$. Therefore $v'(t) = 0$, so, by the chain rule,

$$v'(t) = \Sigma_k\, a_k'(t)\, \partial u(t, a(t))/\partial a_k = 0.$$

Since $\partial u(t, a(t))/\partial a_k = r_t p_k$ for every t, it follows that $\partial(p \cdot a(t))/\partial t = \Sigma_k p_k a_k'(t)$ $= 0$. Therefore $p \cdot a(t)$ is a constant, independent of t. From this it follows that $a(t)$ is a competitive allocation from equal division.

Competitive Allocation and Consistency

This result shows how competitive allocations from equal division can be justified from first principles (envy-freeness and efficiency) in a large economy with a continuum of tastes. But this justification only applies to situations where the claimants have equal shares, since otherwise no envy is not a reasonable requirement. In this section we shall show that competitive allocations can be characterized by consistency rather than envy-freeness. The advantage of this approach is that it works even when the claimants have unequal shares. Moreover, when the claimants have equal shares, we can show that no envy is a *consequence* of consistency, efficiency, and acceptability.

COMPETITIVE ALLOCATION. Given a problem (u, s, a_0), the allocation a is *competitive from proportional division* if there exists a price vector p such that

$$u(a_i) \geq u(b) \text{ for all } b \text{ such that } p \cdot b \leq p \cdot e_i.$$

WEAK CONSISTENCY. The allocation criterion F is *weakly consistent* if for every problem (u, s, a_0), every $a \in F(u, s, a_0)$, and every subset S of claimants, $a_S \in F(u_S, s_S, \Sigma_{i \in S} a_i)$.

Full consistency would further require that, if $a \in F(u, s, a_0)$ and $b_S \in F(u, s, \Sigma_{i \in S} a_i)$, where $b_S \neq a_S$, then b_S is *substitutable* for a_S in a (see (2)). However, this substitution property does not hold for competitive allocation except on domains where the competitive allocation is unique. To see why, suppose that the problem (u, s, a_0) has two distinct competitive allocations from proportional division, say a and a', that are supported by distinct price vectors p and p', respectively. Suppose further that there is no price vector that supports both a and a' simultaneously. Consider the problem $(u, u, s, s, 2a_0)$ in which we duplicate each original claimant and double the original bundle. Substitutability would require that (a, a') be a solution to this new problem, but it is not a competitive allocation because it is not supported by a price vector.

Competitive allocation does satisfy a weaker version of substitutability, however. Let (u, s, a_0) be an allocation problem with n agents, and let k be a positive integer. The *k-fold replication* of (u, s, a_0) is the problem that consists of k replicas of each of the original claimants together with k times the original bundle of goods. We shall denote the k-fold replication by $k(u, s, a_0)$.

REPLICABILITY. An allocation method F is *replicable* if for every problem (u, s, a_0), $a \in F(u, s, a_0)$ implies that $(a, a, \ldots, a) \in F(k(u, s, a_0))$ for every positive integer k.

The following result, which generalizes a theorem of Thomson (1988), shows that competitive allocation is the only satisfactory way of allocating goods both equitably and efficiently. For this result we assume that *the utility functions are differentiable, strictly increasing and strictly quasi-concave, and the marginal utility of every good approaches infinity when the quantity of the good approaches zero.*

THEOREM 25 *Competitive allocation from proportional division is acceptable, efficient, weakly consistent, and replicable. Conversely, every allocation criterion with these four properties consists solely of competitive allocations from proportional division.*

PROOF: The following proof is adapted from Thomson (1988). Let F be acceptable, efficient, weakly consistent, and replicable. (It is straightforward to verify that competitive allocation from proportional division has these properties.) Suppose, by way of contradiction, that $a \in F(u, s, a_0)$ but that a is not competitive from proportional division. Since a is efficient, there is a supporting price vector p at a. The assumptions on preferences imply that a is strictly positive. By assumption, a is not competitive, so there exists some claimant i such that $p \cdot a_i > p \cdot e_i$, where e_i is i's entitlement. Hence there exists another claimant j such that $p \cdot a_j < p \cdot e_j$. Therefore

$$p \cdot a_j < p \cdot e_j = (s_j/s_i)(p \cdot e_i) < (s_j/s_i)(p \cdot a_i). \tag{31}$$

Let $C = \{a \in R_+^m : u_j(a) \geq u_j(a_j)\}$. By the assumption of differentiability, there is a unique hyperplane H that is tangent to C at a_j. The price vector p is normal to H, and $p \cdot a \geq p \cdot a_j$ for all $a \in C$. By (31) and the assumption of differentiability, the line segment connecting $(s_j/s_i)a_i$ and a_j cuts the interior of C. The points on this line segment have the form

$$y(\lambda) = \lambda(s_j/s_i)a_i + (1 - \lambda)a_j,$$

where λ ranges over the interval $[0, 1]$. For all sufficiently small $\lambda > 0$, j strictly prefers $y(\lambda)$ to a_j:

$$u_j(y(\lambda)) > u_j(a_j) \text{ for all sufficiently small } \lambda. \tag{32}$$

Replicability implies that, for each positive integer k,

$$(a, a, \ldots, a) \in F(k(u, s, a_0)). \tag{33}$$

Given a pair of positive integers n_i, n_j, let $k \geq n_i + n_j$ and choose a subset S consisting of n_i claimants of type i and n_j claimants of type j. In the above solution (33), they divide the bundle $a_0' = n_i a_i + n_j a_j$. Denote this restricted problem by (u_S, s_S, a_0'). By weak consistency, the restriction of the above solution, in which each claimant of type i gets a_i and each claimant of type j gets a_j, is in $F(u_S, s_S, a_0')$.

In the restricted problem the *entitlement* of each claimant of type j is

$$e_j' = s_j a_0'/(n_i s_i + n_j s_j) = s_j(n_i a_i + n_j a_j)/(n_i s_i + n_j s_j).$$

If we let $\lambda = n_i s_i/(n_i s_i + n_j s_j)$, then it may be verified that $e_j' = y(\lambda)$. When n_i is sufficiently small relative to n_j, then λ is small, so (32) implies that each j-claimant considers his portion a_j to be inferior to his entitlement in the subproblem, $e_j' = y(\lambda)$. Hence at least one allocation in $F(u_S, s_S, a_0')$ is unacceptable to at least one of the members of S. This contradiction shows that the original allocation a must in fact be competitive from proportional division, and the proof is complete.

Bibliographical Notes ─────────────────────────────

Chapter 1.

The philosophical theories of justice discussed in this chapter include Aristotle's *Ethics* (Book V); John Stuart Mill, *Utilitarianism* (1861); and John Rawls, *A Theory of Justice* (1971). For commentaries on the latter see Daniels (ed.), *Reading Rawls* (1974), and Arrow, "Some Ordinalist-Utilitarian Notes on Rawls's Theory of Justice" (1973). Still other conceptions of social justice are discussed by Nozick (1974) and Ackermann (1980). The distinction between local and global conceptions of justice is a major theme in Walzer's *Spheres of Justice* (1983). Elster's *Local Justice* (1992) develops a taxonomy of local justice criteria and contains a wealth of examples. Theories of distributive justice in which envy-freeness plays a central role include Foley, "Resource Allocation and the Public Sector," (1967); Kolm, *Justice et Equité*, (1972); Baumol, *Superfairness* (1986), and Thomson, "The Theory of Equitable Allocation" (1990). For a wide-ranging treatment of the axiomatic literature on equity see Moulin, *Axioms for Cooperative Decision Making* (1988).

Chapter 2.

The army demobilization case is based on Stouffer et al., *The American Soldier*, (1949, chap. 11). The discussion of the kidney transplant formula is based on United Network for Organ Sharing, *Final Statement of Policy* (April 4, 1989). See also Starzl et al., "A Multifactorial System for Equitable Selection of Cadaver Kidney Recipients" (1987), and Young, "Equitable Selection of Kidney Recipients" (1989). Various methods for rank ordering data based on paired comparisons are discussed in Guttman, "An Approach for Quantifying Paired Comparisons and Rank Order" (1946); Keeney and Raiffa, *Decisions with Multiple Objectives* (1976); and Green and Srinivasan, *Conjoint Analysis in Consumer Research: Issues and Outlook* (1978).

Chapter 3.

Specific apportionment methods were proposed as early as the 1790s, but the first mathematical and statistical papers on apportionment date from this century. Sainte-Lague (1910) proposed minimizing statistical measures of error in apportionment. Willcox (1916) championed the method of major fractions (Webster's method), while Huntington (1921, 1928) argued for the method of equal proportions (Hill's method) based on the idea of minimizing pairwise measures of inequality. The debate between Willcox and Huntington was conducted over more than a decade in *Science* [May 18, 1928, pp. 509–10; June 8, 1928, pp. 581–82; December 14, 1928, pp. 579–82; February 8, 1929, pp. 163–65; March 8, 1929, p. 272; March 29, 1929, pp. 357–58; May 3, 1929, pp. 471–73; May 8, 1942, pp. 477–78; May 15, 1942, pp. 501–3]. For a comprehensive treatment of the history and mathematics of legislative apportionment, see Balinski and Young, *Fair Representation* (1982).

Chapter 4.

The axiomatic analysis of Talmudic sharing rules was pioneered by O'Neill, "A Problem of Rights Arbitration from the Talmud" (1982), and Aumann and Maschler, "Game-Theoretic Analysis of a Bankruptcy Problem from the Talmud" (1985). For various ways of interpreting equality and their relation to justice, see Rae's elegant essay *Equalities* (1981).

Chapter 5.

The traditional approach to distributing joint costs is "Ramsey pricing" which was first proposed by Frank Ramsey in "A Contribution to the Theory of Taxation" (1927). The theoretical literature based on this idea is surveyed by Baumol and Bradford, "Optimal Departures from Marginal Cost Pricing" (1970). For a critique of this approach and a discussion of how prices are regulated in practice see Zajac, "Perceived Economic Justice: The Example of Public Utility Regulation" (1985), and Zajac, *Fairness or Efficiency: An Introduction to Public Utility Economics* (1993). The game-theoretic approach to cost sharing was foreshadowed in Ransmeier's classic study, *The Tennessee Valley Authority* (1942). The connection between game theoretic solutions and modern methods for allocating costs in public works projects is discussed in Straffin and Heaney, "Game Theory and the Tennessee Valley Authority" (1981). Shubik was the first to propose the Shapley value as a method for allocating joint costs in firms ("Incentives, Decentralized Control, the Assignment of Joint Costs and Internal Pricing" [1962]). For applications of these methods to real cost-sharing problems see Littlechild and Thompson, "Aircraft Landing Fees: A Game Theory Approach" (1977); Billera, Heath, and Ranaan, "Internal Telephone Billing Rates: A Novel Application of Non-atomic Game Theory" (1978); and Young, Okada, and Hashimoto, "Cost Allocation in Water Resources Development: A Case Study of Sweden" (1982). The accounting literature on cost sharing is surveyed by Moriarty (ed.), *Joint Cost Allocations* (1981), and by Biddle and Steinberg, "Allocations of Joint and Common Costs" (1984). A comprehensive survey of the theoretical literature on cost sharing, together with public sector applications, may be found in Young, *Cost Allocation: Methods, Principles, Applications* (1985).

Chapter 6.

For a scholarly overview of the history of income taxation see Seligman, "Income Tax" (1932). Shehab, *Progressive Taxation* (1953), gives an engrossing account of progressive tax policy in Great Britain from the seventeenth to the twentieth century. Classical theories of tax justice are discussed in Musgrave, *The Theory of Public Finance* (1959) and in Blum and Kalven, *The Uneasy Case for Progressive Taxation* (1953). For a modern textbook treatment of tax incidence and the incentive effects of taxation see Atkinson and Stiglitz, *Lectures on Public Economics* (1980). Pechman, *Federal Tax Policy* (1987), provides a comprehensive survey of recent income tax policy in the United States. Young, "Progressive Taxation and Equal Sacrifice" (1990) analyzes current income tax schedules and their relationship to equal sacrifice. Aumann and Kurz "Power and Taxes" (1977) suggest a theoretical model of how taxes would be distributed given the bargaining power of various income groups. For an introduction to the litera-ture on income inequality see Sen, *On Economic Inequality* (1973), and Foster, "In-equality Measurement" (1985).

Chapter 7.

The standard game-theoretic form of the bargaining problem was first posed by Nash, "The Bargaining Problem" (1950). For surveys of the modern theoretical literature see Roth, *Axiomatic Models of Bargaining* (1979); Binmore and Dasgupta, *The Economics of Bargaining* (1987); and Thomson and Lensberg, *The Theory of Bargaining with a Variable Number of Agents* (1992). Bargaining theory has been used as a framework for analyzing issues of social justice by Gauthier, "Bargaining and Justice" (1985), and Binmore, *Playing Fair* (1993) There is also a growing number of empirical studies on bargaining behavior and its connections with equity. See in particular Selten, "The Equity Principle in Economic Behavior" (1978); Güth et al., "An Experimental Study of Ultimatum Bargaining" (1982); Roth and Murnighan, "The Role of Information in Bargaining: An Experimental Study" (1982); Roth and Schoumaker, "Expectations and Reputations in Bargaining: An Experimental Study" (1983); Yaari and Bar-Hillel, "On Dividing Justly" (1984); Roth, ed., *Laboratory Experimentation in Economics* (1985); and Isaac, Mathieu, and Zajac, "Institutional Framing and Perceptions of Fairness" (1991).

Chapter 8.

The earliest work on games of fair division was by Banach, Knaster, and Steinhaus. See Steinhaus, "The Problem of Fair Division" (1948), and "La Division Pragmatique" (1949). Another early paper on fair division is by Raiffa, "Arbitration Schemes for Generalized Two-Person Games" (1953). The idea of dividing a heterogeneous good fairly has been studied by (among others): Dubins and Spanier, "How to Cut a Cake Fairly" (1961); Kuhn, "On Games of Fair Division" (1967); Berliant, Dunz, and Thom-son, "On the Fair Division of a Heterogeneous Commodity" (1992); and Brams and Taylor, "An Envy-Free Cake Division Protocol" (1993). The alternating offers model was first analyzed in detail by Rubinstein, "Perfect Equilibrium in a Bargaining Model" (1982). See also Osborne and Rubinstein, *Bargaining and Markets* (1990). The game of bidding to be divider was first proposed by Crawford, "A Procedure for Generating Pareto-Efficient Egalitarian-Equivalent Divisions" (1979a), and subsequently modified by Demange, "Implementing Efficient Egalitarian Equivalent Allocations" (1984).

Chapter 9.

The concept of egalitarian-equivalent allocations is due to Pazner and Schmeidler, "Egalitarian Equivalent Allocations: A New Concept of Economic Equity" (1978). The limitations of this concept were pointed out by Moulin and Thomson, "Can Everyone Benefit from Growth?: Two Difficulties" (1988), which introduced the concept of trans-parent inequality and showed its incompatibility with monotonicity. The idea of allocat-ing indivisible goods both equitably and efficiently by a pseudo-market was first sug-gested by Hylland and Zeckhauser, "The Efficient Allocation of Individuals to

Positions" (1979), who proposed using it to assign students to dormitories. The problem of allocating indivisible goods fairly when compensation is possible is discussed by (among others) Crawford and Heller, "Fair-Division with Indivisible Commodities" (1979); Maskin, "On the Fair Allocation of Indivisible Goods" (1987); Alkan, Demange, and Gale, "Fair Allocation of Indivisible Goods and Money" (1988); and Tadenuma and Thomson, "The Fair Allocation of an Indivisible Good When Monetary Compensations Are Possible" (1993).

Bibliography

Ackerman, B. 1980. *Social Justice in the Liberal State*. New Haven: Yale University Press.

Aczel, J. 1966. *Lectures on Functional Equations and Their Applications*. New York: Academic Press.

Alkan, A., G. Demange, and D. Gale. 1988. "Fair Allocation of Indivisible Goods and Money." Mimeo. École Polytechnique, Paris.

Aristotle, *Ethics*. J.A.K. Thompson, tr. Harmondsworth, UK: Penguin, 1985.

Arrow, K. J. 1963. *Social Choice and Individual Values*. 2d ed. New York: John Wiley.

———. 1973. "Some Ordinalist-Utilitarian Notes on Rawls's Theory of Justice." *Journal of Philosophy* 70:245–63.

Atkinson, A. B., and J. E. Stiglitz. 1980. *Lectures on Public Economics*. Berkshire, U.K.: McGraw-Hill.

Atkinson, T. E. 1953. *Handbook of the Law of Wills and Other Principles of Succession, Including Intestacy and Administration of Decedents' Estates*. 2d ed. St. Paul: West Publishing.

Aumann, R. J., and M. Kurz. 1977. "Power and Taxes." *Econometrica* 45:1137–61.

Aumann, R. J., and M. Maschler. 1985. "Game Theoretic Analysis of a Bankruptcy Problem from the Talmud." *Journal of Economic Theory* 36:195–213.

Balinski, M. L., and H. P. Young. 1974. "A New Method for Congressional Apportionment." *Proceedings of the National Academy of Sciences, USA* 71:4602–6.

———. 1977. "On Huntington Methods of Apportionment." *SIAM Journal on Applied Mathematics—Part C* 33:607–18.

———. 1978. "Stability, Coalitions, and Schisms in Proportional Representation Systems." *American Political Science Review* 72:848–58.

———. 1979. "Criteria for Proportional Representation." *Operations Research* 27:80–95.

———. 1980. "The Webster Method of Apportionment." *Proceedings of the National Academy of Sciences, USA* 77:1–4.

———. 1982. *Fair Representation: Meeting the Ideal of One Man, One Vote*. New Haven, Conn: Yale University Press.

———. 1985. "The Theory of Apportionment." In *Fair Allocation*, edited by H. Peyton Young. *Proceedings of Symposia in Applied Mathematics* 33. Providence, R.I.: The American Mathematical Society.

Bamberg, G., and W. F. Richter. 1984. "The Effects of Progressive Taxation on Risk-Taking." *Zeitschrift für Nationalokonomie* 44:93–102.

Banzhaf, J. F. 1965. "Weighted Voting Doesn't Work: A Mathematical Analysis." *Rutgers Law Review* 19:317–43.

Bardhan, P. 1984. *Land, Labor, and Rural Poverty*. New York: Columbia University Press.

Baumol, W. 1986. *Superfairness*. Cambridge, Mass.: MIT Press.

Baumol, W., and D. Bradford. 1970. "Optimal Departures from Marginal Cost Pricing." *American Economic Review* 60:265–83.

Bell, C., and P. Zusman. 1976. "A Bargaining Theoretic Approach to Cropsharing Contracts." *American Economic Review* 66:578–88.

Berliant, M., K. Dunz, and W. Thomson. 1992. "On the Fair Division of a Heterogeneous Commodity." *Journal of Mathematical Economics* 21:201–16.

Berliant, M., and M. Gouveia. 1993. "Equal Sacrifice and Incentive Compatible Income Taxation." *Journal of Public Economics,* forthcoming.

Biddle, G. C., and R. Steinberg. 1984. "Allocations of Joint and Common Costs." *Journal of Accounting Literature* 3:1–45.

Billera, L. J., D. C. Heath, and J. Ranaan. 1978. "Internal Telephone Billing Rates: A Novel Application of Non-Atomic Game Theory." *Operations Research* 26:956–65.

Binmore, K. G. 1987. "Nash Bargaining Theory II." In K. G. Binmore and P. Dasgupta, *The Economics of Bargaining.* Oxford: Blackwell.

———. 1993. *Playing Fair.* University College, London.

Binmore, K. G., A. Rubinstein, and A. Wolinsky. 1986. "The Nash Bargaining Solution in Economic Modelling." *Rand Journal of Economics* 17:176–88.

Birkhoff, G. 1946. "Three Observations on Linear Algebra." *Rev. Univ. Nac. Tucuman, ser. A* 5:147–51.

Blum, W. J., and H. Kalven. 1953. *The Uneasy Case for Progressive Taxation.* Chicago: University of Chicago Press.

Borda, Jean Charles de. 1784. "Mémoire sur les Elections au Scrutin." Paris: Histoire de l'Academie Royale des Sciences.

Bosworth, B., and G. Burtless. 1992. "Effects of Tax Reform on Labor Supply, Investment, and Saving." *Journal of Economic Perspectives* 6:3–26.

Brams, S. J., D. M. Kilgour, and S. Merrill. 1991. "Arbitration Procedures." In *Negotiation Analysis,* edited by H. P. Young. Ann Arbor: University of Michigan Press.

Brams, S. J., and A. Taylor. 1993. "An Envy-Free Cake Division Protocol." *American Mathematical Monthly.*

Buchholz, W. 1988. "Neutral Taxation of Risky Investment." In *Welfare and Efficiency in Public Economics,* edited by D. Boes et al. Berlin: Springer Verlag.

Calabresi, G., and P. Bobbit. 1978. *Tragic Choices.* New York: Norton.

Chun, Y., and W. Thomson. 1988. "Monotonicity Properties of Bargaining Solutions When Applied to Economics." *Mathematical Social Sciences* 15:11-27.

———. 1992. "Bargaining Problems with Claims." *Mathematical Social Sciences* 24:19–33.

Cohen Stuart, A. J. 1889. "On Progressive Taxation." In *Classics in Public Finance,* edited by R. A. Musgrave and A. T. Peacock. (1958). New York: McGraw-Hill.

Condorcet, M.J.A.N. Caritat, Marquis de. 1785. *Essai sur l'Application de l'Analyse a la Probabilité des Décisions Rendues à la Pluralité des Voix.* Paris: De l'Imprimerie Royale.

Congressional Budget Office. 1988. "The Changing Distribution of Federal Taxes: A Closer Look at 1980." United States Congress: Washington, D.C.

Coon, C. S. 1971. *The Hunting Peoples.* Boston: Little, Brown.

Crawford, V. P. 1977. "A Game of Fair Division." *Review of Economic Studies* 44:235–47.

———. 1979a. "A Procedure for Generating Pareto-Efficient Egalitarian-Equivalent Allocations." *Econometrica* 47:49–60.

————. 1979b. "On Compulsory-Arbitration Schemes." *Journal of Political Economy* 87:131–59.

————. 1980. "A Self-Administered Solution of the Bargaining Problem." *Review of Economic Studies* 47:385–392.

————. 1985. "The Role of Arbitration and the Theory of Incentives." In *Game-Theoretic Models of Bargaining,* edited by A. Roth. New York: Cambridge University Press.

Crawford, V. P., and W. P. Heller. 1979. "Fair Division with Indivisible Commodities." *Journal of Economic Theory* 21:10–27.

Daniels, N. 1974. *Reading Rawls.* New York: Basic Books.

Davis, M., and M. Maschler. 1965. "The Kernel of a Cooperative Game." *Naval Logistics Research Quarterly* 12:223–59.

Debreu, G. 1954. "Representation of a Preference Ordering by a Numerical Function." In *Decision Processes.* R. M. Thrall, C. H. Coombs, and R. L. Davis, eds. New York: Wiley.

————. 1959. "Topological Methods in Cardinal Utility Theory." In *Mathematical Methods in the Social Sciences,* edited by K. J. Arrow, S. Karlin, and P. Suppes. Stanford: Stanford University Press.

————. 1962. New Concepts and Techniques for Equilibrium Analysis." *International Economic Review* 3:257–73.

Demange, G. 1984. "Implementing Efficient Egalitarian Equivalent Allocations." *Econometrica* 52:1167–78.

Domar, E. D., and R. A. Musgrave. 1944. "Proportional Income Taxation and Risk-Taking." *Quarterly Journal of Economics* 58:388–422.

Dubins, L. E., and E. H. Spanier. 1961. "How to Cut a Cake Fairly." *American Mathematical Monthly* 68:1–17.

Edgeworth, F. Y. 1897. "The Pure Theory of Taxation." In *Classics in Public Finance,* edited by R. A. Musgrave and A. T. Peacock. (1958). New York: McGraw-Hill.

Elster, J. 1992. *Local Justice: How Institutions Allocate Scarce Goods and Necessary Burdens.* New York: The Russell Sage Foundation.

Epstein, I., ed. 1935. *The Talmud.* Oxford, UK: Sancino Press.

Fishburn, P. 1973. *The Theory of Social Choice.* Princeton: Princeton University Press.

Foley, D. 1967. "Resource Allocation and the Public Sector." *Yale Economic Essays* 7:45–98.

Foster, J. E. 1985. "Inequality Measurement." In *Fair Allocation,* edited by H. P. Young. *Proceedings of Symposia in Applied Mathematics* 33. Providence, R.I.: The American Mathematical Society.

Friend, I., and M. E. Blume. 1975. "The Demand for Risky Assets." *American Economic Review* 65:900–922.

Gauthier, D. 1985. "Bargaining and Justice." *Social Philosophy & Policy* 2:29–47.

Gibbard, A. 1973. "Manipulation of Voting Schemes: A General Result." *Econometrica* 41:587–601.

Gorman, T. 1968. "Structure of Utility Functions." *Review of Economic Studies,* vol. 53.

Green, P. E., and V. Srinivasan. 1978. "Conjoint Analysis in Consumer Research: Issues and Outlook." *Journal of Consumer Research* 5:103–23.

Güth, W. R. Schmittberger, and B. Schwarze (1982): "An Experimental Study of

Ultimatum Bargaining," *Journal of Economic Behavior and Organization* 3:367–88.

Guttman, L. 1946. "An Approach for Quantifying Paired Comparisons and Rank Order." *Annals of Mathematical Statistics* 17:144–63.

Hammond, P. J. 1976. "Equity, Arrow's Conditions, and Rawls's Difference Principle." *Econometrica* 44:793–804.

Harsanyi, J. C. 1955. "Cardinal Welfare, Individualistic Ethics, and the Interpersonal Comparison of Utility." *Journal of Political Economy* 63:309–21.

———. 1959. "A Bargaining Model for the Cooperative *n*-Person Game." In *Contributions to the Theory of Games IV,* edited by A. W. Tucker and R. D. Luce. *Annals of Mathematical Studies* 40. Princeton: Princeton University Press.

Hart, H.L.A., and A. M. Honore. 1959. *Causation in the Law.* Oxford: The Clarendon Press.

Hart, S., and A. Mas-Colell. 1989. "Potential, Value and Consistency." *Econometrica* 57:589–614.

Hill, J. 1911. Letter to William C. Huston, Chairman, House Committee on the Census, dated April 25, 1911. In U.S. Congress, House, Apportionment of Representatives, House Report 12, 62d Congress, 1st Session.

Hobbes, T. *Leviathan.* C. B. Macpherson, ed. Harmondsworth, UK: Penguin, 1982.

Hoffman, E., and M. Spitzer. 1985. "Entitlements, Rights, and Fairness: An Experimental Examination of Subjects' Concepts of Distributive Justice." *Journal of Legal Studies* 14:

Hofstee, W.K.B. 1983. "The Case for Compromise in Educational Selection and Grading." In *On Educational Testing,* edited by S. B. Anderson and J. S. Helmick. San Francisco: Jossey-Bass.

Huckabee, D. C. 1991. "House Apportionment Following the 1990 Census: Using the Official Counts." Washington, DC: Congressional Research Service of the Library of Congress.

Huntington, E. V. 1921. "The Mathematical Theory of the Apportionment of Representatives." *Proceedings of the National Academy of Sciences, U.S.A.* 7:123–27.

———. 1928. "The Apportionment of Representatives in Congress." *Transactions of the American Mathematical Society* 30:85–110.

Hylland, A., and R. Zeckhauser. 1979. "The Efficient Allocation of Individuals to Positions." *Journal of Political Economy* 87:293–313.

Isaac, R. M., D. Mathieu, and E. E. Zajac. 1991. "Institutional Framing and Perceptions of Fairness." *Constitutional Political Economy* 2:329–70.

Jackson, M., and H. Moulin. 1992. "Implementing a Public Project and Distributing Its Cost." *Journal of Economic Theory* 57:125–40.

Kalai, E., and D. Samet. 1988. "Weighted Shapley Values." In *The Shapley Value,* edited by A. Roth. New York: Cambridge University Press.

Kalai, E., and M. Smorodinsky. 1975. "Other Solutions to Nash's Bargaining Problem." *Econometrica* 43:510–18.

Kastl, L., ed. 1963. *Kartelle in der Wirklichkeit. Festschrift fuer Max Metzner.* Cologne/Berlin/Bonn: Carl-Heymans-Verlag.

Keeney, R., and H. Raiffa. 1976. *Decisions with Multiple Objectives.* New York: John Wiley.

Kolm, S. 1972. *Justice et Equité.* Paris: Editions du Centre National de la Recherche Scientifique.

Kuhn, H. 1967. "On Games of Fair Division." In *Essays in Mathematical Economics*, edited by M. Shubik. Princeton: Princeton University Press.

Lensberg, T. 1987. "Stability and Collective Rationality." *Econometrica* 55:935–62.

———. 1988. "Stability and the Nash Solution." *Journal of Economic Theory* 45:330–41.

Lewis, D. K. 1969. *Convention: A Philosophical Study.* Cambridge, Mass.: Harvard University Press.

Lindahl, E. 1919. *Die Gerechtigkeit der Besteuerung.* Lund: Gleerup.

Littlechild, S. C., and G. F. Thompson. 1977. "Aircraft Landing Fees: A Game Theory Approach." *Bell Journal of Economics* 8:186–204.

Locke, J. 1776. *The Second Treatise of Government.* Edited by C. B. Macpherson. Hackett Publishing, 1980.

Manne, A. 1952. "Multi-Purpose Public Enterprises—Criteria for Pricing." *Economica* N.S.19:322–26.

Maskin, E. 1987. "On the Fair Allocation of Indivisible Goods." In *Arrow and the Foundations of Economic Policy,* edited by G. Feiwell. London: Macmillan.

May, K. O. 1952. "A Set of Independent Necessary and Sufficient Conditions for Simple Majority Decision." *Econometrica* 20:680–84.

Megiddo, N. 1974. "On the Nonmonotonicity of the Bargaining Set, the Kernel, and the Nucleolus of a Game." *SIAM Journal on Applied Mathematics* 27:355–58.

Mill, J. S. 1848. *Principles of Political Economy.* London: Longmans Green, 1917.

———. 1861. *Utilitarianism.* In *Utilitarianism and Other Essays,* edited by A. Ryan. Harmondsworth, U.K.: Penguin, 1987.

Mirrlees, J. A. 1971. "An Exploration in the Theory of Optimum Income Taxation." *Review of Economic Studies* 38:175–208.

Montreal Accord on Substances that Deplete the Ozone Layer, Final Act. 1987. United Nations Environmental Program, Nairobi.

Moriarty, S. 1981. *Joint Cost Allocations.* Norman, Okla.: University of Oklahoma.

Morse, M., J. von Neumann, and L. P. Eisenhart. 1948. *Report to the President of the National Academy of Sciences.* Princeton, N.J.

Moulin, H. 1983a. "Noncooperative Implementation: A Survey of Recent Results." *Mathematical Social Sciences* 3:243–57.

———. 1983b. *The Strategy of Social Choice.* Amsterdam: North-Holland.

———. 1985. "The Separability Axiom and Equal-Sharing Methods." *Journal of Economic Theory* 36:120–48.

———. 1988. *Axioms of Cooperative Decision Making.* New York: Cambridge University Press.

———. 1990a. "Joint Ownership of a Convex Technology: Comparison of Three Solutions." *Review of Economic Studies* 57:439–52.

———. 1990b. "Fair Division under Joint Ownership: Recent Results and Open Problems." *Social Choice and Welfare* 7:149–70.

———. 1990c. "Uniform Externalities: Two Axioms for Fair Allocation." *Journal of Public Economics* 43:305–26.

———. 1991. "Welfare Bounds in the Fair Division Problem." *Journal of Economic Theory* 54:321–37.

———. 1992a. "An Application of the Shapley Value to Fair Division with Money." *Econometrica* 60:1331–49.

Moulin, H. 1992b. "Welfare Bounds in the Cooperative Production Problem." *Games and Economic Behavior* 4:373–401.

Moulin, H., and S. Schenker. "Serial Cost Sharing." *Econometrica* 60:1009–37.

Moulin, H., and W. Thomson. 1988. "Can Everyone Benefit from Growth?: Two Difficulties." *Journal of Mathematical Economics* 17:339–45.

Musgrave, R. A. 1959. *The Theory of Public Finance*. New York: McGraw-Hill.

Nash, J. 1950. "The Bargaining Problem." *Econometrica* 18:155–62.

———. 1953. "Two-Person Cooperative Games," *Econometrica* 21:128–40.

Neumann, J. von. 1953. "A Certain Zero-Sum Two Person Game Equivalent to the Optimal Assignment Problem." In *Contributions to the Theory of Games,* edited by H. W. Kuhn and A. W. Tucker. Princeton: Princeton University Press.

Newbery, D.M.G., and J. Stiglitz. 1979. "Sharecropping, Risk Sharing and the Importance of Imperfect Information." In *Risk, Uncertainty, and Agricultural Development,* edited by J. A. Roumasset, J. M. Broussard, and I. Singh. New York: Agricultural Development Council.

Nozick, R. 1974. *Anarchy, State and Utopia*. New York: Basic Books.

Nydegger, R. V., and G. Owen, "Two-Person Bargaining: An Experimental Test of the Nash Axioms," *International Journal of Game Theory* 3, 1974, 239–49.

O'Neill, B. 1982. "A Problem of Rights Arbitration from the Talmud." *Mathematical Social Sciences* 2:345–71.

Osborne, M. J., and A. Rubinstein. 1990. *Bargaining and Markets*. New York: Academic Press.

Owen, G. 1982. *Game Theory*. 2d ed. New York: Academic Press.

Parker, T. 1927. "Allocation of the Tennessee Valley Authority Projects." *Transactions of the American Society of Civil Engineers* 108:174–87.

Pazner, E., and D. Schmeidler. 1974. "A Difficulty in the Concept of Fairness." *The Review of Economic Studies* 41:441–43.

———. 1978. "Egalitarian Equivalent Allocations: A New Concept of Economic Equity." *Quarterly Journal of Economics* 92:671–87.

Pechman, J. E. 1987. *Federal Tax Policy*. 5th ed. Washington, D.C.: The Brookings Institution.

Peleg, B. 1985. "An Axiomatization of the Core of Cooperative Games without Side Payments." *Journal of Mathematical Economics* 14:203–14.

———. 1986. "On the Reduced Game Property and Its Converse." *International Journal of Game Theory* 15:187–200.

———. 1988. *Introduction to the Theory of Cooperative Games*. Typescript. Jerusalem: The Hebrew University.

Plato. *The Republic*. H. D. Lee, tr. Harmondsworth, UK: Penguin, 1955.

Pratt, J. 1964. "Risk Aversion in the Small and in the Large." *Econometrica* 32:122–36.

Rae, D. 1981. *Equalities*. Cambridge, Mass.: Harvard University Press.

Raiffa, H. 1953. "Arbitration Schemes for Generalized Two-Person Games." In *Annals of Mathematics Studies*. Princeton: Princeton University Press.

———. 1982. *The Art and Science of Negotiation*. Cambridge, Mass.: Harvard University Press.

Ramsey, F. 1927. "A Contribution to the Theory of Taxation." *Economic Journal* 37:47–61.

Ransmeier, J. S. 1942. *The Tennessee Valley Authority: A Case Study in the Economics of Multiple Purpose Stream Planning*. Nashville, Tenn.: Vanderbilt University Press.

Rawls, J. 1971. *A Theory of Justice*. Cambridge, Mass.: Harvard University Press.

Robertson, A. F. 1987. *The Dynamics of Productive Relationships*. Cambridge: Cambridge University Press.

Rockafellar, R. T. 1970. *Convex Analysis*. Princeton: Princeton University Press.

Roemer, J. E. 1986a. "Equality of Resources Implies Equality of Welfare." *Quarterly Journal of Economics* 101:751–84.

————. 1986b. "The Mismarriage of Bargaining Theory and Distributive Justice." *Ethics* 97:88–110.

————. 1988. "Axiomatic Bargaining Theory on Economic Environments." *Journal of Economic Theory* 45:1–31.

Roth, A. 1979. *Axiomatic Models of Bargaining*. Berlin and New York: Springer Verlag.

————, ed. 1987. *Laboratory Experimentation in Economics*. Cambridge: Cambridge University Press.

Roth, A., and M. Malouf. 1979. "Game-Theoretic Models and the Role of Information in Bargaining." *Psychological Review* 86:574–94.

Roth, A., and J. K. Murnighan. 1982. "The Role of Information in Bargaining: An Experimental Study." *Econometrica* 50:1123–42.

Roth, A., and F. Schoumaker, 1983. "Expectations and Reputations in Bargaining: An Experimental Study." *American Economic Review* 73:362–72.

Roth, A., M. Malouf, and J. K. Murnighan. 1981. "Sociological versus Strategic Factors in Bargaining." *Journal of Economic Behavior and Organization* 2:153–77.

Roth, A., V. Prasnikar, M. Okuno-Fujiwara, and S. Zamir. 1991. "Bargaining and Market Behavior in Jerusalem, Ljubljana, Pittsburgh, and Tokyo: An Experimental Study." *American Economic Review* 81:1068–95.

Rousseau, J-J. 1762. *The Social Contract*. Translated by Maurice Cranston. Harmondsworth, UK: Penguin, 1968.

Rubinstein, A. 1982. "Perfect Equilibrium in a Bargaining Model." *Econometrica* 50:97–110.

Sainte-Lagüe, 1910. "La Représentation et la méthode des moindres carrés." *Comptes Rendus de l'Academie des Sciences* 151:377–78.

Samuelson, P. A. 1947. *Foundations of Economic Analysis*. Cambridge, Mass.: Harvard University Press.

Sasaki, H. 1992. "Consistency, Continuity and Monotonicity in Assignment Problems: A Characterization Theorem for the Core." Discussion Paper 144, Faculty of Economics, Nagoya City University.

Satterthwaite, M. 1975. "Strategy-proofness and Arrow's Conditions: Existence and Correspondence Theorems for Voting Procedures and Social Welfare Functions." *Journal of Economic Theory* 10:187–217.

Schelling, T. 1960. *The Strategy of Conflict*. Cambridge, Mass.: Harvard University Press.

Schmeidler, D. 1969. "The Nucleolus of a Characteristic Function Game." *SIAM Journal on Applied Mathematics* 17:1163–70.

Seade, J. K. 1977. "On the Shape of Optimal Tax Schedules." *Journal of Public Economics* 7:203–35.

Sebenius, J. 1984. *Negotiating the Law of the Sea*. Cambridge, Mass.: Harvard University Press.

Seligman, E.R.A. 1932. "Income Tax." In *Encyclopedia of the Social Sciences*. New York: Macmillan.

Selten, R. 1975. "Equity and Coalition Bargaining in Experimental 3-Person Games." Working Paper 154. Institut für Gesellschafts- und Wirtsschaftswissenschaften, University of Bonn.

———. 1978. "The Equity Principle in Economic Behavior." In *Decision Theory and Social Ethics,* edited by H. W. Gottinger and W. Leinfellner. Dordrecht: Reidel.

Sen, A. 1970. *Collective Choice and Social Welfare*. San Francisco: Holden-Day.

———. 1973. *On Economic Inequality.* Oxford: Clarendon Press.

———. 1979. "Utilitarianism and Welfarism." *The Journal of Philosophy* 76:463–89.

Shapley, L. S. 1953. "A Value for *n*-Person Games." In *Contributions to the Theory of Games* II. edited by H. W. Kuhn and A. W. Tucker. *Annals of Mathematics Studies* 28:307–17.

———. 1981. "Comments on R. D. Banker's 'Equity Considerations in Traditional Full Cost Allocation Practices: an Axiomatic Perspective." In *Joint Cost Allocations,* edited by S. Moriarty. Norman, Oklahoma: University of Oklahoma Press.

Shapley, L. S., and M. Shubik. 1954. "A Method for Evaluating the Distribution of Power in a Committee System." *American Political Science Review* 48:787–92.

Shehab, F. 1953. *Progressive Taxation*. Oxford: The Clarendon Press.

Shubik, M. 1962. "Incentives, Decentralized Control, the Assignment of Joint Costs and Internal Pricing." *Management Science* 8:325–43.

Smith, A. 1776. *The Wealth of Nations*. E. Cannan, ed. Chicago: University of Chicago Press, 1976.

Sobolev, A. I. 1975. "Characterization of the Principle of Optimality for Cooperative Games through Functional Equations." In *Mathematical Methods in the Social Sciences,* edited by N. N. Voroby'ev. Vilnius. Vipusk 6:92–151.

Starzl, T. E. et al. 1987. "A Multifactorial System for Equitable Selection of Cadaver Kidney Recipients." *Journal of the American Medical Association* 257:3073–75.

Steinhaus, H. 1948. "The Problem of Fair Division." *Econometrica* 16:101–4.

———. 1949. "Sur la Division Pragmatique." *Econometrica* 17, supplement:315–19.

———. 1960. *Mathematical Snapshots*. 2d ed. New York.

Stern, M. 1982. "Communication Satellites and the Geostationary Orbit: Reconciling Equitable Access with Efficient Use." *Law and Policy in International Business* 14:859–83.

Stouffer, S. S. et al. 1949. *The American Soldier*. Princeton: Princeton University Press.

Straffin, P. D. 1988. "The Shapley-Shubik and Banzhaf Power Indices." In *The Shapley Value: Essays in Honor of Lloyd S. Shapley,* edited by A. Roth. New York: Cambridge University Press.

Straffin, P. D., and J. Heaney. 1981. "Game Theory and the Tennessee Valley Authority." *International Journal of Game Theory* 10:35–43.

Sugden, R. 1986. *The Economics of Rights, Co-operation, and Welfare*. Oxford: Basil Blackwell.

Tadenuma, K. 1992. "Reduced Games, Consistency, and the Core." *International Journal of Game Theory* 20:325–34.

Tadenuma, K., and W. Thomson. 1991. "No-Envy and Consistency in Economies with Indivisibilities." *Econometrica* 59:1755–68.

———. 1993. "The Fair Allocation of an Indivisible Good When Monetary Compensations Are Possible." *Mathematical Social Sciences* 25:117–32.

Tennessee Valley Authority. 1938. *Allocation of Investment in Norris, Wheeler, and Wilson Projects.* U.S. House of Representatives, Document No. 709, Congress Third Session. Washington, D.C.: U.S. Government Printing Office.

Thomson, W. 1980. "Two Characterizations of the Raiffa Solution." *Economics Letters* 6:225–31.

———. 1983a. "The Fair Division of a Fixed Supply Among a Growing Population." *Mathematics of Operations Research* 8:319–26.

———. 1983b. "Problems of Fair Division and the Egalitarian Principle." *Journal of Economic Theory* 31:211–26.

———. 1983c. "Equity in Exchange Economies." *Journal of Economic Theory* 29:217–44.

———. 1984. "Monotonicity, Stability, and Egalitarianism." *Mathematical Social Sciences* 8:15–28.

———. 1986. "Replication Invariance of Bargaining Solutions." *International Journal of Game Theory* 15:59–63.

———. 1987a. "Monotonicity of Bargaining Solutions with Respect to the Disagreement Point." *Journal of Economic Theory* 42:50–58.

———. 1987b. "Individual and Collective Opportunities." *International Journal of Game Theory* 16:245–52.

———. 1987c. "Monotonic Allocation Mechanisms. Working Paper 116. Rochester Center for Economic Research, University of Rochester.

———. 1988. "A Study of Choice Correspondences in Economies with a Variable Number of Agents." *Journal of Economic Theory* 46:237–54.

———. 1990a. "The Consistency Principle." In *Game Theory and Applications,* edited by T. Ichiishi, A. Neyman, and Y. Tauman. New York: Academic Press.

———. 1990b. "Monotonic and Consistent Solutions to the Problem of Fair Division When Preferences Are Single-Peaked." Working Paper 231, Rochester Center for Economic Research, University of Rochester.

———. 1990c. *The Theory of Equitable Allocation.* Manuscript, University of Rochester.

———. 1991a. Population-Monotonic Solutions to the Problem of Fair Division When Preferences Are Single-Peaked." Working Paper 301, Rochester Center for Economic Research, University of Rochester.

———. 1991b. "Resource-Monotonic Solutions to the Problem of Fair Division When Preferences are Single-Peaked." Working Paper 301, Rochester Center for Economic Research, University of Rochester.

Thomson, W., and T. Lensberg. 1983. "Guarantee Structures for Problems of Fair Division." *Mathematical Social Sciences* 4:205–18.

———. 1992. *The Theory of Bargaining with a Variable Number of Agents.* New York: Cambridge University Press.

Thomson, W., and H. R. Varian. 1985. "Theories of Justice Based on Symmetry." In *Social Goods and Social Organizations: Essays in Memory of Elisha Pazner,* edited by L. Hurwicz, D. Schmeidler, and H. Sonnenschein. New York: Cambridge University Press.

Thomson, W., and L. Zhou. 1991. "Consistent Allocation Rules in Atomless Economies." Working Paper 294, Rochester Center for Economic Research, University of Rochester.

Tinbergen, J. 1953. *Redeljke Inkomensverdeling.* Haarlem: N. V. DeGulden Pers.

Tobin, J. 1978. "On Limiting the Domain of Inequality." *Journal of Law and Economics* 6:263–77.

Ullman-Margalit, E. 1977. *The Emergence of Norms*. Oxford: Clarendon Press.

United Network for Organ Sharing. 1989. *UNOS Policy Regarding Utilization of the Point System for Cadaveric Kidney Allocation*. Richmond, Virginia.

United States Congress. 1988. *The Changing Distribution of Federal Taxes: A Closer Look at 1980*. Washington, D.C.: Congressional Budget Office Staff Working Paper.

Varian, H. R. 1974. "Equity, Envy, and Efficiency." *Journal of Economic Theory* 9:63–91.

————. 1975. "Distributive Justice, Welfare Economics, and the Theory of Fairness." *Philosophy and Public Affairs* 4:223–47.

————. 1976. Two Problems in the Theory of Fairness." *Journal of Public Economics* 5:249–60.

Walzer, Michael. 1983. *Spheres of Justice*. New York: Basic Books.

Willcox, W. F. 1916. "The Apportionment of Representatives." *American Economic Review* 6, supplement: 3–16.

Yaari, M., and M. Bar-Hillel. 1984. "On Dividing Justly." *Social Choice and Welfare* 1:1–24.

Young, H. P. 1974. "An Axiomatization of Borda's Rule." *Journal of Economic Theory* 9:43–52.

————. 1985a. "Monotonic Solutions of Cooperative Games." *International Journal of Game Theory* 14:65–72.

————, ed. 1985b. *Cost Allocation: Methods, Principles, Applications*. Amsterdam: North-Holland Publishing.

————. 1987. "Progressive Taxation and the Equal Sacrifice Principle." *Journal of Public Economics* 32:203–14.

————. 1988a. "Distributive Justice in Taxation." *Journal of Economic Theory* 44:321–35.

————. 1988b. "Condorcet's Theory of Voting." *American Political Science Review* 82:1231–44.

————. 1988c. "Individual Contribution and Just Compensation." In *Essays in Honor of Lloyd Shapley,* edited by A. Roth. Cambridge: Cambridge University Press.

————. 1989. "Equitable Selection of Kidney Recipients." *Journal of the American Medical Association* 261:2957.

————. 1990. "Progressive Taxation and Equal Sacrifice." *American Economic Review* 80:253–66.

Young, H. P., and A. Levenglick. 1978. "A Consistent Extension of Condorcet's Election Principle." *SIAM Journal on Applied Mathematics* 35:285–300.

Young, H. P., N. Okada, and T. Hashimoto. 1982. "Cost Allocation in Water Resources Development: A Case Study of Sweden." *Water Resources Research* 18:463–75.

Zajac, E. E. 1978. *Fairness or Efficiency: An Introduction to Public Utility Economics*. Cambridge, Mass.: Ballinger.

————. 1985. "Perceived Economic Justice: The Example of Public Utility Regulation." In *Cost Allocation: Methods, Principles, Applications,* edited by H. P. Young. Amsterdam: North-Holland.

Index